‘It’s the best thing to come out of the Trump Presidency.’

DONALD TRUMP AND ME

Donald Trump and Me

Published by The Conrad Press Ltd. in the United Kingdom 2021

Tel: +44(0)1227 472 874
www.theconradpress.com
info@theconradpress.com

ISBN 978-1-914913-26-6

Printed and bound in Great Britain by Clays Ltd, Elcograf S.p.A

Typesetting and Cover Design by The Book Typesetters,
www.thebooktypesetters.com

The Conrad Press logo was designed by Maria Priestley.

DONALD TRUMP AND ME

My diaries recording the four wild years of an American President

Jim G. Sitch

Donald Trump president of the United States - 2017 to 2021

So, you think you know Donald Trump?

What did Donald J Trump wish to achieve from his time in the White house? It's hard to pin down; the accumulation of power and wealth I think are too simplistic. My feeling is he jumped on the biggest and scariest roller coaster simply for the thrill of the ride; there was never a planned ending.

While many of his supporters will most definitely have increased their own personal wealth and amassed greater fortunes, so very many were left bereft – of life, love and national pride. These diaries simply hold up a mirror to the emperor; unashamedly naked.

Jim G. Sitch, August 2021

Firstly, I would like to sincerely thank my wife Mary for the outstanding patience she has shown during the writing of these diaries, even when I was disrupting our holidays to seek out daily information.

I would also like to praise the very many journalists who courageously took on the President and his team to uncover the truth about the Presidency. I would also like to thank Tim Berners Lee for the invention of the World Wide Web without which I would have only found a fraction of the juicy information.

I'd like to praise my copy-typist Maria who persevered doggedly with the toil of trying to translate my handwriting.

Finally, I'd like to thank James Essinger founder of The Conrad Press for his honesty and professionalism. His belief in me turned my early draft into a real book.

Contents

The Trump Diaries - Any more years?

In the autumn of 2016 Mr Donald J Trump ran as the Republican candidate for the upcoming US presidential election. So far, so yawn. Donald took out the greatest Faustian pact ever to gain the ultimate prize and to my jaw dropping astonishment he was successful. In early 2017 he was inaugurated into the post of POTUS and we sat aghast as he swore his oath of allegiance.

Stunned and just a little flabbergasted by all of this I was curious to see how far he would go, noting that several commentators were seriously suggesting that he might not survive a year, let alone a full term.

Based on this I committed to keeping a diary on the comings and goings of the person who, it turned out, would capture the world's attention and leave everyone continuously wondering whether the button was about to be pushed. By association many other people feature in the diaries including political, religious and national leaders, TV, sports and showbiz personalities; all caught up in the weirdest of gameshows.

Until his victory Donald Trump had seemed like a faux-Kardashian; a TV demi-celeb at best and seemingly failing businessman at worst. After his win, well the sky really was the limit for this monumental vaudeville performance. Oh, my goodness the cast; the characters, the tweets and plot twists, the love interests and the villainy just seemed to go on forever.

It is worth pointing out that as far as the Republicans and Democrats were concerned, I had absolutely no axe to grind with either party and as an impartial Brit I just wanted to record a remarkable time in US political history. As it was, I only had a cursory knowledge of US politics before I started the first diary in 2017 but by the end, well I could tell my Senate from my House of Representatives. Sort of.

Every day for 1404 days I made an entry (every single day…) into a series of 'seven-day view' diaries. Over these days, followed by weeks and months I became more and more obsessed in ensuring that I wouldn't miss an entry, even carrying the books with me when I moved home (twice) and on vacation to New Zealand, Australia, Canada and the USA. The trip to the USA in 2019 left me feeling paranoid that it might be found in my luggage and held up as some form of anti-Trump propaganda but thankfully it remained unnoticed.

Carrying out this arduous, depressing, occasionally hilarious and all-consuming task was no mean feat and 'doing my Donnie' became a thing. 'Have you done Donnie today?' my wife would ask most days before dinner or packing bags for the next trip. On December third 2020 when the Biden/Harris result was announced I was able to (sort of) put down my pen. Due however to the complexities of vote recounts, coupled with the US electoral college system of collating votes, I had to keep up a general reportage for an additional twenty-seven days up until January 21st 2021. Then, after 1462 days I finally realised that thankfully, I didn't need to record any more.

People asked me, 'where did you get your information?' and I'd say my best source was mostly word of mouth; that being mouth of the President himself. From the outset I'd set out to be as impartial as possible, reporting simply what I had seen or heard from online platforms, newspapers and magazines, TV reports, friends in the USA etc. However, it very quickly became apparent that this was nigh on impossible and inevitably, I too became part of the theatre of Trump that was the real life 'West Wing.'

As the bizarre and often painful stories accelerated and built up over the four years (especially in 2020) the daily entries started to affect my own mental health to the point where friends suggested I stop. In Spring 2019, I had nearly given up but I persevered hoping that surely things would change.

As far as the diaries are concerned, there is the distinct possibility that he may run again in 2024 under yet another 'MAGA' or 'KAGA' banner. My diaries, I'm sure, will be of great interest to historians, gossip columnists and people monitoring the crazy world of Trump politics. At the time of writing this introduction he hasn't 'retired' and my diaries will provide a timely reminder to future voters and observers of the reality of another four surreal years of Donald Trump in power. It is especially important to note that every word recorded on these pages, aside from my own personal comments, has previously appeared in the public domain. Very much so!

At the very beginning of what turned out to be my own personal odyssey I scribbled the words *'Welcome to the first of what may be four year-long records – Donnie Tweet and the Tales of Trumpton Towers'* thinking it was all going to be a bit of a comic turn.

How wrong would I be?

Section Intro: 2017 - Year 1

- Buddies
- Bricks
- Bills
- Bombs

On November the 8th 2016 Donald J Trump was successful in the Presidential election and became the 45th President of the United States or POTUS. Between that date and the inauguration on Saturday 21st January 2017, all the political trappings, management and day to day running of the United States was handed over to Donald Trump by the outgoing POTUS Barack Obama.

The Diary begins....

JANUARY 2017

Friday 20th January 2017
Donnie takes a swipe at the CIA. Makes threats about agents and tries to tell jokes. 'The lying Media will pay.' Ho, ho.

Saturday 21st January 2017
Donald Trump takes the oath and pledges allegiance to the flag and the American people… but which ones??

Presidency Day 1
Monday 23rd January 2017
Donald Trump's first statement as President is to accuse the Press of falsehoods re. his inauguration numbers probably 750,000 he says however '1.5 million. Question most people and they'll say this was the biggest inauguration audience ever… *period.'* We may see this word a lot.

Tuesday 24th January 2017
First executive decision is to remove the US from the TPP which sort of benefits most people except NZ and OZ. His hair has gone from campaign tangerine to snow. Big row with Madonna who stupidly talks about 'blowing up the White-house' directly handing DT a propaganda coup.

Wednesday 25th January 2017
Authorised the go-ahead of two oil pipelines through Native American Indian sacred lands. When asked about this, he

says 'I don't care… this means jobs.' Tweets a congrats re. *Fox News* and calls '…*CNN* FAKE NEWS!' Note: his upper case not mine.

Thursday 26th January 2017

Donnie makes a move on Security. It looks like he'll lock 'em up, out, in and over. He says the 2,000-mile wall is going to be built between USA and Mexico and the latter will pay. Executive Order to be signed banning people from seven Muslim countries. DT also says he's going to clamp down on voter fraud although this sounds to me like a set-up for the next presidential election. DT states waterboarding works. He should try it.

Friday 27th January 2017

DT insists that Mexico 'will pay for the wall… one way or another.' The US/Mex border guard chief has resigned – well duh! DT reckons he will put a twenty percent tax on Mexican imports: good luck with that. DT compares himself to Abe Lincoln. They're both human I suppose.

Saturday 28th January 2017

DT meets PM Theresa May. They seek to re-energise the special relationship and they demonstrate this by holding hands. DT says he only wants people in the USA '…who love us!'

Sunday 29th January 2017

DT starts to arrest refugees as they enter the country. PM Theresa 'The New Maggie' May says nothing.

Monday 30th January 2017

DT says his border control plan is 'working excellently.' Clearly, this is evidenced through the daily demonstrations in the US calling for his head. Looks as though he will seek to withdraw the US from the Paris Climate Agreement and coal is back on the agenda. US Acting Attorney General Sally Yates is fired by DT for 'betraying' the Department of Justice.

Tuesday 31st January 2017

DT announces that one of his political supporters has been appointed to the NSC, the first time ever. Still national demos re. immigration blocks both in the US and across UK and Europe. Donald Tusk fears that US policy will undermine Euro security. DT names Neil Gorsuch as the justice in the Supreme Court.

FEBRUARY 2017

Wednesday 1st February 2017

Worldwide demos and bitter condemnation of DT's 'Presidency' so far number in the billions. DT says 'it is nonsense' for people to worry over whether his EO is a 'ban' or a restriction on movement. Meanwhile a white neo-Nazi kills six in a Mosque shooting in Canada. 'I admire Trump' he is reported to have said.

Thursday 2nd February 2017

Apparently, DT cuts off the Aussie PM during a phone call over his 'ridiculous refugee deal.' Arnold Schwarzenegger asks DT if they could maybe switch jobs as he apparently heads up the American Apprentice Show and viewing figures are down. *Twitter* allegedly paid $1m to Trumps campaign. Not surprising as he is their biggest advertiser.

Friday 3rd February 2017

DT sets in motion the first steps to scale back financial regulations that clamp down on irregularities: 'Billionaire wants less control over dodgy dealing,' surely not? 100,000 visas are cancelled as a result of the immigration ban. Nice one DT: who'll serve your food and clean your toilets now?

Saturday 4th February 2017

Apparently, DT is furious that a state judge has reversed his immigration EO; he says it's 'a ridiculous decision.'

Sunday 5th February 2017

DT defends Vladimir Putin saying, 'who are we to say he's bad: we're as bad.' His comments are questioned by US Russia diplomat Michael McFaul.

Monday 6th February 2017

DT speaks to Bill English for twenty-five minutes on Waitangi Day – Bill says the call was civilised and the Whitehouse says there is a good relationship with NZ. Bearing in mind DT allegedly hung up on Malcom Turnbull (Australian PM) he must feel honoured. Putin is apparently upset that he's been referred to as a killer in a TV interview with DT. Big thumbs up to Budweiser for their Superbowl ad – this is America's beer!!

Tuesday 7th February 2017

John Bercow says DT should not be allowed to speak in the House of Commons as 'we don't believe in racism or sexism.' He massively goes up in my estimation. DT tells a load of GIs 'our election went well…' and alludes to 'Unreported terrorism in Europe.' Sean Spicer says he will provide evidence…

Wednesday 8th February 2017

Vice President Mike Pence becomes the first to cast the vote that appoints DT's choice as Educational Secretary. She is Betsy Devos, a billionaire who wants to privatise schools. Several UK Tories say Speaker John Bercow's position is 'at risk.' Democracy and free speech heading down the toilet. Vlad's opposition leader is in hospital after a suspected poisoning: aye Claudius!

Thursday 9th February 2017

DT says that judges are 'not biased and I don't want to say they are.' But they seem, 'so political and hopefully they'll reach the right decision' re. the immigration ban. DT tweets his disappointment at the treatment of his daughter Ivanka by a clothing firm that dropped her range. His appointment for Attorney General Jeff Sessions is approved. A man who seems to have a history of classic Alabama racism.

Friday 10th February 2017

DT's mate Kellyanne Conway has been 'counselled' on her actions in trying to get people to buy Ivanka Trump's products (the fifth to do so). Clearly the boycott has nothing to do with DT's previous comments re. women and their bodies. Wow! The nine Circuit judges tell DT to get stuffed re. his immigration policy. He tweets 'See you in court.' Funny, I thought you had been?

Saturday 11th February 2017

Since DT has failed so miserably in the Courts, he's stated that he'll simply sign another Executive Order for a 'new immigration policy.'

Saturday 12th February 2017

The President has apparently become 'aware of a lot of things since becoming Chief' however evidence of this is now required. DT also says, 'The wall will be much, much cheaper.'

Monday 13th February 2017

DT stands 'right behind' Japan after North Korea launches a missile though he's previously accused the Japanese of stealing American jobs. DT reckons New Hampshire went Democrat due to 'voter fraud.' There is still no evidence of this. Nor, one suspects will there be. DT's team desperately trying to defend Michael Flynn who has allegedly discussed sanctions with Russia before anyone else. Good to have a Communist in the White House.

Tuesday 14th February 2017

Newsflash. Moronic would-be politician Mike Flynn has resigned. Yeah right. Resigned or pushed? It is at this point that many predictions abound re. assassination attempts on the President (probably all pre-planned). DT though may be in for a surprise. Pence in the wings.

Wednesday 15th February 2017

Apparently, DT knew about Mr Flynn's off the record entente cordial viz a vis letting off the Russians over that silly nonsense of the Ukraine sanctions or something. DT goes on his fake news kick again saying the news regarding Mike Flynn was released 'illegally' by the US security forces.

Thursday 16th February 2017

DT's new pick for security chief has opted not to take up the post for 'personal and financial reasons.' As a long-standing military man with an unblemished career, one can see his point. DT's latest press conference goes on for seventy-five minutes and is full of praise for the press, admiration for his critics and oh, sorry different person – DT's speech was utter batshit crazy.

Friday 17th February 2017

Apparently, the US psychiatric community is a little concerned as to DT's mental health and wellbeing. Despite links with energy companies in the US and Democrat objections, Scott Pruitt, a climate change doubter is appointed as the Secretary for Environmental Protection Agency. DT's latest press conference claim, 'we will stop all crime,' seems a little optimistic.

Saturday 18th February 2017

DT's main aim over the weekend seems to focus almost entirely on trying to find various professionals to undertake various governmental roles.

Sunday 19th February 2017

His current crop of picks for top governmental posts are resigning and/or being investigated by the FBI. Pence meanwhile continues with the 'good cop/bad cop' routine to assuage opposition.

Monday 20th February 2017

Demonstrations take place in the UK making it clear that any visit by Donald Trump is going to be less than happily accepted by the jolly old Brits. Russia has apparently compiled a psychological dossier on the President and the Swedish believe that he must be smoking something dodgy after his comments about the 'incident in Sweden.'

Tuesday 21st February 2017

DT finally manages to get a chump, sorry volunteer, to fill the security adviser role following the Mike Flynn debacle. HR McMaster takes up the role declined by Robert Harwood. Plenty of demonstrations form up for 'Not my President Day.'

Wednesday 22nd February 2017

DT scraps the San Francisco Bay area electric railway plans. The system needed a federal grant of $650m and a high-speed link to LA was a train too far apparently for the POTUS. Porn star Jenna Jameson apparently a big fan of DT sticks it to the Muslims and says 'the KKK aren't as bad.'

Thursday 23rd February 2017

Donald Trump claims he's saved $1 billion on the purchase of Airforce One; a claim apparently that is news to the Airforce. He said that he bargained Boeing down from $4.3m. The Airforce says 'This never happened.' Swedish paralegal Max Karlsson and *Twitter* feeder: 'He said what!?' regarding DT's comments.

Friday 24th February 2017

DT goes ape-shit barmy again regarding 'leaks', especially from the FBI. Flies off the handle about 'the Press' although he didn't name them/it and speaking to the 'Conservative Political Action Conference' he states – 'We're building the wall – it's way, way, way ahead of schedule.' Oh, and he's going to totally obliterate Islamic State.

Saturday 25th February 2017

Sean Spicer bans *CNN*, the *BBC* and the *NY Times* from a news 'gaggle.' So much for democracy in the land of the free...

Sunday 26th February 2017

George Clooney reckons DT compares rather aptly to General Macarthur in being able to '...cause alarm with our allies and comfort to our enemies.'

Monday 27th February 2017

DT proposes a defence spending budget hike of – get this – $54 billion! All this while cutting federal and foreign aid and at a time when DT promises to cut tax. Uh oh. On top of this, he thinks his energy bill will drive the US economy – but which way?

Tuesday 28th February 2017

DT claims that all the opposition to his presidency is driven by 'Obama' and if not him directly: 'his team.' He has no evidence of this but hey, that's not stopped him so far. In his first major speech he awards himself on A++ for effort and says he'll make USA great again. He may also draw back on some of his previous ambitions.

MARCH 2017

Wednesday 1st March 2017

DT asks Congress to agree to a $1 trillion infrastructure investment programme. He says he strongly supports NATO. Hmmm. Still, he sticks to his guns to build 'the wall, our great wall' and to get rid of Obama Care. Trump also promises aggressive action on trade. He will probably stand on the beach holding back the tide like Canute to stop the immigration boats arriving.

Thursday 2nd March 2017

Democrats claim his 'Unity' speech failed to reach out to them saying that his 'speech and reality have never been more detached from a President' and 'more rhetoric and no substance.' He even managed to tee off Chicago by saying it was a 'violent place.' The Mayor of Chicago isn't happy, saying 'If the POTUS wants to help, he ought to get on and do his job.'

Friday 3rd March 2017

As a US friend describes DT as the 'Orange Idiot,' Jeff Sessions is under increasing pressure to step aside from an inquiry into Russian/US contact since he is allegedly one of the principle chatty people. Breaking news! Jeff Sessions pleads innocence but withdraws from the Russian inquiry.

Saturday 4th March 2017

Both the Obama administration and the FBI refer to any suggestion that DTs phone was 'hacked' by the former President as 'ridiculous.'

Sunday 5th March 2017

After yesterday's comments, quite frankly if there had been any truth in the hacking rumour, I'd have tapped his phone and played it live on public radio.

Monday 6th March 2017

DT indicates that he will sign a new EO re an immigration ban that affects Muslims from six countries but apparently Iraq (oil producing nation) is ok. Republican senators are still pushing for an inquiry into alleged phone tapping by Obama.

Tuesday 7th March 2017

So now the US President is insisting that Obama almost certainly tapped his phone in order to try to get to the bottom of the Russia 'problem.' The *Independent* mentions that 4 Russian diplomats involved in the scandalous DT 'waterworks' rumours – have died in Russia. Strange that.

Wednesday 8th March 2017

DT says 'a lot of people, a lot of people will be turning up on Friday…' Every time he speaks, he reminds me of Jimmy 'Two times' in Goodfellas. DT also says he's going to bring down the price of drugs. Paracetamol hopefully, as it will be needed by the US citizens to alleviate the pain of his Presidency.

Thursday 9th March 2017

So now Washington, New York and Hawaii register their opposition to DT's 'new' Muslim ban. In addition, the FIFA President suggests that the immigration ban in the US will almost certainly prevent them staging the 2026 World Cup. I don't suppose that DT will understand or care about that.

Friday 10th March 2017

Ben Carson, DT's token black US Department of Housing and Urban Development Secretary says that 'Slaves who 'came' to the US were immigrants in the bottom of ships.' He later suggests on *Twitter* that he was misinterpreted. Perhaps he should chat to Samuel L. Jackson who thinks he's a 'Mutha.' Quite.

Saturday 11th March 2017

DT claims he was unaware that Mike Flynn was a 'foreign agent' despite him appointing Flynn as the National Security Advisor. Poor old DT; he doesn't know much, does he?

Sunday 12th March 2017

The Democratic coalition against Trump is now seeking a case against Steve Bannon for receiving improper payments during the election. And the crooks keep on coming and going.

Monday 13th March 2017

Preet Bharara has been sacked by DT because he didn't bow to a request by the Republicans to support the President. Or he may have been 'sacked to head off a potential corruption investigation.' This comment was made by respected Democrat Elijah Cummings.

Tuesday 14th March 2017

Steve King (Rep) stated that Gert Wilders (Dutch right-wing politician) has the right idea and 'understands that our nation can't be restored with somebody else's babies.' One wonders which babies he thinks will rebuild the US civilisation. Richard Osman suggests on TV show Pointless that DT has 'flyaway hair… Oh, maybe it's flown away hair.' Audience laughs as the world weeps.

Wednesday 15th March 2017

It transpires that, following a 'leaked' tax bill, DT appears to have paid $38m in 2005 as part of a tax payment. It also seems that he is going to abolish the very tax law (Alternative Minimum Tax) that forced him to pay up. Thankfully once he abolishes the law, he'll be safe from those naughty IRS bullies.

Thursday 16th March 2017

Derek Watson – a senior judge in Hawaii has once again blocked DT's new bill banning immigration from mainly Muslim countries. DT says this is 'a judicial over-reach,' and this appears to be a new term from the President. DT also brings about the first step to abolish Obama's 'clean air act' in order to fire up the 'US automotive industry.' Yes, that'll help keep people breathing.

Friday 17th March 2017

Sean Spicer repeats a Fox TV news item stating that DT's phone was wire tapped by GCHQ in the UK in order to keep US 'fingerprints' off the scandal. GCHQ unusually respond to this by saying that this is 'utterly ridiculous' and so nonsensical that 'we will not be responding to this 'news' item again.' Well, who do I trust, GCHQ or Rupert Murdoch?

Saturday 18th March 2017

DT now says he 'did not make an opinion' on the GCHQ claims. He only quoted a 'very talented lawyer' on *Fox News*.

Sunday 19th March 2017

DT met Angela Merkel and seemed reluctant to shake hands. However, Sean 'Icy' Spicer says 'the President did not hear the request.' How about just shaking hands.

Monday 20th March 2017

The FBI is investigating Russian involvement in the US election campaign. In addition, they are looking into claims that there was coordination between DT's team and the Kremlin. Normally the FBI don't make this type of news public but this they said was in the 'public interest.' The FBI also reject emphatically that GCHQ tapped DT's phone.

Tuesday 21st March 2017

Paul Ryan, DT's House Speaker says if the revision of the Affordable Care Act (Obama's) doesn't go through – the Republican Party majority might be lost. It's likely that the American Health Care Act will pass only if DT and his mates put nationalistic pressure on the senators. Next step – repeal of Obama's tax plans; either way this is unlikely to help the poor.

Wednesday 22nd March 2017

Apparently, Paul Manafort who assisted DT for years, is now being accused of taking millions from pro-Russian interests in Ukraine. A former spy reckons the Russian State has 'cultivated, supported and assisted' Trump for years. Mr Manafort says 'it's not true; it's all political propaganda.' Oh well, that's okay then.

Thursday 23rd March 2017

Wow, busy day today – DT is having trouble raising enough support for his 'New Medicare' plans; more on this tomorrow. In the meantime, he proposes axing the clerical safety board and at the same time gets approval for the Keystone XL pipeline through Native American Indian sacred land. Environmental groups have yet to object.

Friday 24th March 2017

News tonight: Paul Ryan and DT have dumped the anti-Obama Care bill principally because not enough people wanted to vote for it. Well, the other key reason is due to the fact that it's all going pear shaped.

Saturday 25th March 2017

DT has pulled (or is about to pull) the investigation into whether the US and Russia had contact prior or during the election.

Sunday 26th March 2017

Following the story re. the investigation being stopped – Republicans are allegedly 'purging' electronic devices of all data…?

Monday 27th March 2017

Jared Kushner, DT's son-in-law and one of the newest of the Presidents associates and senior advisors, is now under close investigation (or not – see previous entry) re. his Russian links. Curiously, his *Twitter* account was wiped. When and if he's questioned, he'll have to delete his own memory. I wonder if being the Presidents son-in-law will make any difference?

Tuesday 28th March 2017

DT signs another EO and this one is cheered to the rafters by the fossil fuel lobby, oil and coal. This order has suspended half a dozen measures brought in by Obama to fight global warming. Businesses love it – environmentalists are not happy. They are enraged and ready to go to court. The US is going to get a whole lot smokier.

Wednesday 29th March 2017

DT is pursuing an early interim payment, as a 'supplemental funding bill' to include money for his wall and the military. It may be however that the Republicans will see this as a 'complication.' The spending bill will be agreed on April 28th. DT will need to put his hands together in prayer.

Thursday 30th March 2017

DT's avoiding of the 'inquiry' may not help him in the long run. Meanwhile in the mad land of this President, his attendance at a women's rally seemed by all accounts to go well? Democrat Mark Warner makes it clear – 'the Russians sought to hijack the democratic process.' Vladimir Putin (President) said he 'flatly denies this.' Yawn again.

Friday 31st March 2017

So, coupled with Christopher '007' Steele and his 'report', Mike Flynn (sacked security guy) is now saying, 'Give me immunity and I'll talk.' It will be interesting to see if he lives that long. In the White House the President gives a stirring speech about an EO, looks pointedly at the camera then scarpers without signing it. Mike Pence dutifully grabs it and follows DT out the door.

APRIL 2017

Saturday 1st April 2017

Hawaiian judge Derrick Watson has extended the ban on DT's immigration plan and the President has subsequently appealed.

Sunday 2nd April 2017

Meanwhile, stories of a possible impeachment abound. It seems the Teflon President may not be as untouchable as he thinks.

Monday 3rd April 2017

So here we are again in court. Only this time DT is taking on the Democrats re. the appointment of Neil Gorsuch to the Supreme Court using filibuster and nuclear option to get him in. While we wait for that, the President has stated to the Financial Times that he will 'sort out Korea on our own,' just as the Chinese Secretary is due to visit the United States.

Tuesday 4th April 2017

Newsflash! DT's ratings are at the lowest ever. This may be to do with Obama Care repeal (failed), immigration ban (failed), clean air repeal (passed but vigorously opposed), oil line from Canada (passed but vigorously opposed – even more so), several appointees being similarly 'de-appointed' and many of his white male supporters, backing off quick.

Wednesday 5th April 2017

As usual, being appointed by DT does not necessarily ensure a decent position. He has removed his senior strategist from the US National Security Council. I'm a bit surprised, he's gone as Steve Bannon was an outspoken right winger and ex-member of Breitbart News.

Thursday 6th April 2017

On the day that DT gets all righteous regarding the alleged gas bombing of Syrian kids and women, the head of the congressional investigation into alleged Russian hacking has stepped down. Devin Nunes is himself under investigation by the Ethics Committee. Poor Devin says 'the charges are motivated by left wing activists.'

Friday 7th April 2017

Hmm – the President decides to act after only a few months of supreme power by bombing Syria. This could be the biggest double bluff of the age since now the Russians are the bad guys and say, 'How dare you!!!!' Or is it simply to put people off the trail of Russian 2016 election involvement?

Saturday 8th April 2017

DT's Deputy National Security adviser, the ex-*Fox News* analyst has been asked to step down after only three months. DT appears to be building a testosterone fuelled War Cabinet.

Sunday 9th April 2017

Today Russian and Iranian military chiefs both threaten to

respond with 'force to any more US' red line attacks on Syria. Bugger.

Monday 10th April 2017

So, DT ultimately got his way regarding Neil Gorsuch. Despite Democrat attempts to filibuster the vote out of time, Republicans did come up with the 'Nuclear option' i.e., ensuring that he got the Supreme Court position, by hook or by crook. Meanwhile, the US Secretary of State Rex Tillerson is waving his fist at the Russians. Why you…!

Tuesday 11th April 2017

Many of the UK right wing newspapers are champing at the bit because of the Syrian bombing by the US. Clearly, they say, this demonstrates that the President has no links with the Russians. Oh yes, clearly. Meanwhile, US lap-cat Boris Johnson has had his G7 request to sanction Russia kicked into touch by his old EU mates.

Wednesday 12th April 2017

Oh dear, oh dear: poor Sean Spicer. Following his car crash of a public statement re. the Nazis and their attitude to laughing gas, Sean has had to make a knuckle crunching apology. Meanwhile, DT says in an interview with *Fox News* that he bombed Syria whilst nibbling on a 'lovely piece of cake.'

Thursday 13th April 2017

As if to stretch the 'we're not buddies' further, DT says 'Right now, we're not getting along with the Russians at all.' This as social media sites are starting to hot up on fragments of news that the FBI have 'certain items of information' that are being described as the 'smoking gun evidence' in order to undertake an impeachment of the new US President.

Friday 14th April 2017

Instead of being concerned about a peachy future, DT instead decides to drop the biggest bomb since Hiroshima onto 'ISIS' terrorists in Afghanistan. North Korea also talks about bombs – slightly more worrying devices if the President oversteps the mark. All this talk of bombs and impeachment makes me wonder exactly what's going on?

Saturday 15th April 2017

North Korea holds a big parade – clowns, balloons, smiling children and IBMs. The US is probably polishing its sabres but who will want a war?

Sunday 16th April 2017

DT reckons that 'China is working with us…' and to demonstrate this, he is out playing golf again. Boy, he's relaxed for a tyrant.

Monday 17th April 2017

DT cavorts with a fluffy bunny. No, I'm just kidding however he really is cavorting with a bunny on the White House parapet. The image is disturbing when it appears on the news and a caption has to explain to the US viewers that the President is on the left. The rabbit looks suspiciously like the one that Sean Spicer appeared dressed as two years ago.

Tuesday 18th April 2017

Back in South Korea, President Elect, sorry VP, takes the nuke rhetoric up a notch before the North Koreans take centre stage by threatening 'first strike.' DT responds by reminding everyone that a despatch of US navy ships was on its way to the area.

Wednesday 19th April 2017

Well, here's a weird situation. DT and Mike Pence have both indicated that 'an armada of fighting ships' was on its way to the China Sea, presumably to be ahead of the nuclear war version of the game of risk. Strangely though, the boats are no-where to be seen...?

Thursday 20th April 2017

After the President suggested he was 'bombing Iraq' (which he didn't) rather than Syria (which he did), he now makes public his world history by stating that 'Korea used to be part of China you know.' Sorry to burst your geography bubble but it's not as simple as that and 'Korea' was not part of 'China.' DT stirs more *Twitter* issues regarding the numbers of football stars standing on stairs...?

Friday 21st April 2017

DT sends his condolences to France after another ISIS shooting in Paris. 'It never ends,' he says. Worth noting that daily American on American killings also never end. DT also suggests that Marie le Pen's chance of winning the French Presidency has halved.

Saturday 22nd April 2017

Today is 'Earth' day and DT makes a speech about climate change. Sorry, he *forgets* to mention climate change in an Earth Day speech.

Sunday 23rd April 2017

DT approaches his one-hundred-day anniversary and he has the worst approval rating of any President at only forty two percent. His supporters say they'd vote for him again. Nuts.

Monday 24th April 2017

DT under pressure from various areas regarding his record so far (Obama's alleged wire-tap, illegal voters, no wall, care packages, women's rights) as he approaches his one-hundred-day marker. His interview with the Associated Press has gone down a storm as well; it is so bizarre that I can't write it down here and give it justice. Apparently 'unintelligible Donald' was trending on *Twitter*.

Tuesday 25th April 2017

Not a good day for the President; i) a SF Judge blocks his 'sanctuary city' financial caps re. immigration rules he can't apply, ii) his climate change appointee turns out to agree that the climate IS a problem and says the 'US should comply with the Paris accord' and iii) as the Democrats can block his application to seek US taxpayer funds to build his wall, DT isn't going to ask for any. Wall, what wall?

Wednesday 26th April 2017

100 Senators are bussed into Congress for a briefing which is

delivered by the President. The US has become far more bellicose and is hell bent on conflict despite the 'if North Korea behaves itself' rhetoric. As Russian and US troops assemble on North Korean borders, the world watches and waits.

Thursday 27th April 2017

During the Election campaign, DT made it clear that the North American Free Trade Agreement (NAFTA) was 'the worst thing for American jobs.' This morning DT indicates that having spoken to Mexico and Canada, he's had a change of mind and he's agreed not to terminate it at this time. Meanwhile, Steve Mnuchin, Treasury Secretary, says they will offer the Middle Class 'the biggest tax cuts ever.'

Friday 28th April 2017

DT's latest advancement in the USA is to sign an Executive Order giving energy companies the go-ahead to drill in the Arctic and offshore of the Alaskan coast. Meanwhile, Ivanka meets up with Angela Merkel and ends up being jeered by the audience as she defends her dad's treatment of women.

Saturday 29th April 2017

The President's one-hundredth day! Well, his main communication today is a tweet saying that the North Koreans are dissing the respectable Chinese President, DT's new mate, Xi Jinping.

Sunday 30th April 2017

DT rounds off his hundredth day line in the sand by moaning yet again about 'fake news.' Tell it often enough and even *he* believes what he says.

MAY 2017

Monday 1st May 2017

DT kicks off the 1st May by suggesting that he might break up the banks, i.e., by splitting the consumer business from the investment operations. 'I'm looking at that right now,' he tells Bloomberg. How on earth this President could possibly comment on the workings of the US financial system is anyone's guess.

Tuesday 2nd May 2017

Just when you think DT can't spout any more tosh, he asks the US public, seriously, 'Why was there a civil war (in the US)? Why couldn't it have been worked out?' A hatful of US historians all say that a fifth Grader in any school would have been able to answer the question – more importantly, it seems to shows yet again the historical ignorance of the POTUS.

Wednesday 3rd May 2017

The head of the FBI has defended the agency's decision to investigate Hilary Clinton's emails. Apparently, he said the idea that there was some sort of bias made him 'nauseous. Meanwhile, some in the US journalistic community are trying to suggest that there might be an as yet unidentified underlying reason for his level of intellect, i.e., that he can't read that well. Wow!

Thursday 4th May 2017

DTs on a roll of moral-testing orders: today he signed an Executive Order that pretty much allows hunters to shoot hibernating bears and track their targets. In doing so, he has repealed a major Obama 'Wildlife Protection Order', one which also applies to wolves. This coupled with his clean air emission Executive Order would suggest that DT has air to sell.

Friday 5th May 2017

So, the President finally gets his way re. Obama Care and (subject to its passage through the final house) his new healthcare package will be available; very much at cost. Polls suggest US people are still supporting him (for now). So subject to a bust-up with North Korea or frankly anyone – he looks like he's got his feet firmly under the table.

Saturday 6th May 2017

Apparently even one of the Trump family has suggested that the golf courses have 'attracted Russian funding.' FORE!

Sunday 7th May 2017

It transpires Obama warned DT about employing Mike Flynn as a security adviser. Sean Spicer says 'Yeah, we know.'

Monday 8th May 2017

Poor old Donald. Former Acting Attorney General Sally Yates testified that 'Mike Flynn could be blackmailed by the Russians.' Since DT and his advisory team did nothing, you could argue that the President placed the US at risk. To address this issue, DT decides to delete all of his previous tweets and press comments. Oops, they're all still on file. The social media have a field day.

Tuesday 9th May 2017

Wow! What a surprise. DT's third sacking since he started – this time the Head of the FBI, James Comey. Woke up and was informed by text that he had been 'terminated.' Thinking this was a joke, he didn't immediately respond. However, this was no joke. The third person undertaking an investigation into the President has been dismissed.

Wednesday 10th May 2017

And just when you think the US couldn't get any more Russian, DT meets the senior Russian envoy the next day and is pictured glad handing him. The photos released by the White House are credited only to TASS the Russian news agency, as no western press representatives were allowed in. Glasnost!

Thursday 11th May 2017

DT comes out all guns blazing; to be fair in the US, that isn't surprising (105 mass shootings this year already). DT tells *NBC* News: 'I was going to fire him (Comey) all along.' This despite continual reports that he was prompted to do so by his Security Council.

Friday 12th May 2017

The President starts the day by tweeting 'Comey had better not have any tapes of our conversations.' In the meantime, the UK is clobbered by a ransomware attack with the NHS being the main victim. The US link here is that it is alleged that the virus was originally created in the US by the NSA. *Wikileaks* is the source of this news though so very much, salt and pinches.

Saturday 13th May 2017

Hmm, Allan Litchman who predicted DT's election victory has claimed his sacking of James Comey may, nay *should* lead to his impeachment. World holds its collective breath... again.

Sunday 14th May 2017

Latest media discussion suggests that DT is in 'the grip of a paranoid delusion.' It also looks like DT has had it with Sean 'make my day' Spicer.

Monday 15th May 2017

Interesting articles appearing in *The Guardian* from journalist Carole Cadwalladr apparently linking UKIP, Trump, Leave .Co.Uk and right-wing polling companies including Cambridge Analytica. The disturbing scent of Steve Barman hangs in the nostrils like the smell left after a wet dog has slept on your carpet. DT is prompting his security team to sue *The Guardian* so lots of laughs will ensue.

Tuesday 16th May 2017

DT apparently had a very chatty meeting with Sergey Kislyak all the way from sunny Moscow. According to the *Washington Post*, DT told his swots a number of 'secrets' re. dealing with

ISIS. The President, instead of crying 'foul', says, 'I'm the President, and I wanted to tell them about the fight against terrorism.' Well, he's the President, he can do what he wants.

Wednesday 17th May 2017

Not sure if I am going to get the chance to fill in this year, let alone all the whole four-year term for the President of the United States. News has leaked that he may have asked the FBI to stop or at least ignore the inquiry into Mike Ryan and his contact with the Russians. In other news, it transpires a law firm suing The *Guardian* over its recent story is Russian.

Thursday 18th May 2017

At last, the Republicans show some moral fibre: they've appointed former FBI Director Robert Weller as Special Counsel. DT goes nuts saying he's the 'victim of a witch hunt.' At the same time a number of US officials have said that DT and his inner circle had eighteen separate calls/ emails with Russian officials during the lead-up to the President of the US election. Meanwhile, the EU says the Paris accord on climate change is 'non-negotiable.'

Friday 19th May 2017

DT is preparing to head off to Saudi Arabia to discuss 'dealing with ISIS.' The key object seems to focus on the fact that the US would like to set up a handy little weapons deal worth many billions of dollars. DT in discussion with the senior Arab intellectuals and I'm minded of Saladin and finger bowls. The President ends the day describing James Comey as a 'nut job.'

Saturday 20th May 2017

DT and his other half Melania arrive in Riyadh to discuss peace and tranquillity... Nah just kidding, it's about arms, lots of them and oil one supposes. Back home the *Washington Post* suggests that there may have been ties between DT's Presidential campaign and the Russians. Soon James Comey will give evidence in open session.

Monday 22nd May 2017

Well, day three of DT's Middle East tour brings him to Israel. Weird really; only yesterday he was curtseying to the Saudi Crown Prince while accepting a medal. For what, God only knows. In Israel he goes to the Wailing Wall, spurns a selfie with a politician and generally behaves himself. It looks suspiciously like Mike Flynn is going to claim the fifth amendment having declined a subpoena request.

Tuesday 23rd May 2017

With this morning's tragic news from Manchester at the Ariana Grande concert, the President's contribution today is his statement offering support. Apart from his very apparent inability to put a sentence together without repetition, he used terms such as 'evil losers', 'I won't call them monsters because they would like that', 'I will call them losers from now on.'

Wednesday 24th May 2017

Today DT sets off to the Vatican to meet the Pope. During the photo shoot line-up, the ladies are veiled and dressed in black, the President of the United States is beaming from ear to ear and the Pontiff has an expression that suggests he has indigestion. 'Great honour,' says DT of meeting the person he once described as 'disgraceful' for his anti-Mexican wall stance.

Thursday 25th May 2017

Tricky as DT the President meets his NATO partners and decides to push past several of the men in a photo shoot, just to get to the front of the queue. Or so it seems: The main guy shoved aside turns out to be the President of Montenegro, a country that the Russians allegedly tried to recently undermine by an assassination plot.

Friday 26th May 2017

DT meets with the European leaders re. a number of issues, not least the Climate Change Commitment. Of the G7 nations leaders, the President sits without translation headphones, presumably because he speaks many languages. Following stirring speeches, six of the seven nations maintain their passion for a system of CO2 reduction that might help the world.

Saturday 27th May 2017

DT has to defend comments regarding his son-in-law, Jared Kushner, who apparently spoke about creating a secret communications channel with Russia!

Sunday 28th May 2017

While the new French President, Emmanuel Macron gets very friendly when he shakes hands with the President,

Angela Merkel states that 'We can no longer rely on the US; we must go it alone.'

Monday 29th May 2017

After Europe pretty much takes the UK and US off their Xmas card list, DT presents his budget message to his adoring citizens. With it comes a clear message, 'Everyone must do more for less.' Hmm? Austerity in the land of the free? Even his fellow Republicans are voicing their discontent with one GOP member saying, 'I don't think he's thought this through.'

Tuesday 30th May 2017

And another one bites the dust! Mike Dubke, a Republican strategist, hired 3 months ago as the President of the United States' Communications Director resigns. As part of another shake-up, Sean 'the lip' Spicer holds onto his position but will be seen on fewer occasions. All of this follows on from reports of 'disarray' in DT's hand-picked comms team. There can't be many remaining.

Wednesday 31st May 2017

Today DT gives the world a new word in a tweet that is proof of his literary prowess; it says 'Despite the constant negative press COVFEFE.' Predictably *Twitter* has gone absolutely nuts which one imagines has stirred up DT's paranoia even more. On top of this, James Comey looks like he will testify that DT asked for the Mike Flynn investigation to be called off.

JUNE 2017

Thursday 1st June 2017

News reaches our shores that the PM Theresa May is trying to water down climate change legislation in Europe. Amazingly, the President is reported today to be considering pulling out of the Paris Accord that was signed up to by Obama. No doubt to please his oily mates. None of this comes as a surprise though. It appears Europe will take a hard stance.

Friday 2nd June 2017

Sure enough, DT makes his big speech about protecting American jobs, focusing on the US but missing the climate change point entirely. Macron uses this to enhance his reputation by saying that 'we should all make the planet great again.' Several governors of US States have made it clear that DT does not represent them and they support the Paris Accord.

Saturday 3rd June 2017

Following DT's withdrawal from the Paris Accord, pretty much everyone else across the world (apart from Theresa May) thinks he's wrong to do so.

Sunday 4th June 2017

Awful stuff on London Bridge last night in what appears to be an ISIS sponsored attack. DT uses this latest terrorist outrage to try to promote his ongoing immigrant travel ban.

Monday 5th June 2017

After the dreadful events of Saturday night, the President decides to go on an anti-London Mayor crusade. Sadiq Khan, the London Mayor, says he 'has no time to respond to tweets.' DT makes more crass remarks as only he can do to which the New York Mayor says 'London is doing a great job and the President of the United States does not represent us in any way.'

Tuesday 6th June 2017

Following his *Twitter* rant regarding London Bridge, it transpires that in conjunction with his support for the Saudis, archives have been released showing DT apparently relaxed, enjoying a fun day out with the then IRA/Sinn Fein leader Gerry Adams; at the height of the troubles.

Wednesday 7th June 2017

Now James Comey presents a written affidavit to the Senate Committee prior to him appearing in front of them. DT makes a weird comment that he's okay with any information (which is a bit worrying). Meanwhile, Lara Trump is apparently proud to be carrying on with the Presidential campaign; the next one in 2020.

Thursday 8th June 2017

So, on the eve of what might be an historic UK General Election vote, James Comey begins his appearance in front of the Senate Judicial Committee. His opening statement states that he 'thought there would be distrust from the outset,' and that he never documented meetings with Obama. He also said, 'I documented meetings with the President of the United States as I felt he might lie,' and said he feels defamed.

Friday 9th June 2017

The President responds to Mr Comey's latest comments re: 'I was told to lay off the investigation into Mike Flynn.' He says 'No obstruction. No lies. He's a leaker.' He also added that he was prepared to swear under oath to respond to any questions put by the Senate Committee. Calls are now increasing for his impeachment but bets are being taken on his departure.

Saturday 10th June 2017

Today, the President is scheduled to spend time at his little family retreat on a national golf course in New Jersey.

Sunday 11th June 2017

Following the uproarious episode of The Last Leg on *Channel 4* Friday saying 'Show your arse to President of the United States' if he visits, DT has called off the State visit. Scared of protests!

Monday 12th June 2017

The former New York Federal prosecutor Preet Baharat says he got sacked because he didn't answer his calls from DT. At the Tony Awards in New York, pretty much everyone including Kevin Spacey took the piss out of DT suggesting that his tenure might end soon.

Tuesday 13th June 2017

Interesting stats both numerical and philosophical, seem to suggest that the fame of the President has set off a resurgence of left-wing political support. References have been made to the recent votes in Austria, Holland, France, and curiously the UK. It would seem inevitable then that the Labour Party are going to win the next Election. Maybe.

Wednesday 14th June 2017

One of DT's Republican Congressmen, Steve Scalise, was gunned down during a baseball game. The gunman, James I Hodgkinson, a member of the 'Terminate the Republican Party Group', was killed. Mr Scalise survived and is recovering. DT in response has cancelled a White House appearance.

Thursday 15th June 2017

US Special Counsel Robert Mueller is investigating DT for possible obstruction of Justice, according to US media. Well, the President will almost certainly cry foul and say that he's being attacked by all and sundry. As the irrational are taking pot shots, the silent are finding their voice and the weak are getting braver.

Friday 16th June 2017

Wow! Melania, that is Mrs Trump, reappears after a hiatus and moves back into the White House, first time since DT was made POTUS. Her immediate reaction doesn't inspire much oomph. In addition, it appears her command of the English language is not so much pigeon as bludgeon when it comes to TV chats.

Saturday 17th June 2017

DT is in trouble with his predecessor's new best friend Cuba. Apparently, he is curtailing some of the previously agreed travel rules, much to the annoyance of the new Cuban regime.

Sunday 18th June 2017

DT's *Twitter* feed goes mad with 'You are witnessing the single greatest WITCH HUNT in American political history.' These are his tweet LETTERS not mine.

Monday 19th June 2017

DT's frustration reaches epic levels as the special counsel Robert Mueller is ever closer to who knows what? A prosecution, maybe an impeached POTUS. DT has decided he's in a 'political fight that I'm going to fight it.' Things are looking tricky for the great orange shark as even John McEnroe says, 'My support of POTUS Trump is fake.' You cannot be serious!

Tuesday 20th June 2017

The name Otto Warmbier may go down in history as the trigger that started a war. After his arrest last year for petty vandalism, he was sentenced by a North Korean court to fifteen years imprisonment but sadly suffered 'a brain injury.' He was repatriated to the US last week and subsequently died. DT blames the brutal regime for his death. Is this enough revenge motive?

Wednesday 21st June 2017

Going slightly off DT piste today to report a couple of news items. 1) A Russian fighter jet flew just one point five metres away from a US aircraft stating that the Americans flew in a 'provocative manner', and 2) today's Queen's speech in the UK following the train wreck of the UK Election didn't feature any news of DT's possible state visit.

Thursday 22nd June 2017

DT has indicated to *Fox News* proprietor Rupert Murdoch that he hasn't in fact 'taped conversations with 'James Comey.' He reckons he only said this to influence his testament before Congress. In environmental news, the American meteorological society has told Rick Perry, the US Energy Secretary that he 'lacks a fundamental understanding of science' after he claimed that CO2 is not a 'primary cause of climate change.'

Friday 23rd June 2017

Johnny Depp kicks off Glastonbury by highlighting the interesting history of Presidents being assassinated by actors. JD goes on to say that he's in the clear as 'I'm just an actor and a guy that lies on a screen for a living.' So far, there's been no formal response from the POTUS.

Saturday 24th June 2017

Australian Prime Minister Malcolm Turnbull was surprised to receive a bright pink tie in the post with the words 'Donald Trump' written on it. The taken aback Prime Minister asks 'Why?'

Sunday 25th June 2017

Against a long-held and widely respected tradition, DT calls off the annual Eid ceremony at the White house marking the end of Ramadan.

Monday 26th June 2017

Sadly, the US Supreme Court has now allowed DT's travel ban to come into force albeit partially. The POTUS says that this will 'enhance our national security and safeguard us from those wishing to do us harm.' The Supreme Court are keeping a close eye on how it works for one month and then who knows?

Tuesday 27th June 2017

DT and his Press (read marketing) team have chosen to take a new approach to blaming others. This time they are saying that the previous President, Barack Obama, is silent on all things pertinent to the US. 'Better to stay silent and let people think you're stupid rather than open one's mouth thereby proving it.' DT should record and note this quote.

Wednesday 28th June 2017

Time Magazine has formally requested that DT takes down a couple of *Time Magazine* front pages from the wall of his golf club. These apparently show DT and his daughter but they're both fakes, mock-ups showing them as equal to previous Presidents, St Mother Theresa and Stalin.

Thursday 29th June 2017

Curious article in the *Washington Post* seemingly indicating again that the POTUS is completely bonkers. Apparently, a show called 'Morning Joe' is his most hated programme and yet he continues to watch it, or claims he never does?! The Republican Party is concerned about his astounding attack on the TV presenter Mika Brzezinski.

Friday 30th June 2017

In another weird incident, DT seems to make an inappropriate and creepy comment to an Irish reporter, 'She has a nice smile so she must treat you well.' He said this to the newly appointed Irish Taoiseach Lea Varadkar while the reporter in question, Caitriona Perry, stood by. This of course is not the first time he has behaved thus.

JULY 2017

Saturday 1st July 2017

DT attacked the retailer Amazon over internet taxes that they've not yet paid. This possibly his quietest Saturday for ages.

Sunday 2nd July 2017

Today Donny appears to be promoting violence against journalists by tweeting an image of himself attacking a *CNN* reporter.

Monday 3rd July 2017

Well, here we go again! New pen and maybe a new DT. Not quite. He's joined in the Charlie Gard (a UK baby with a rare genetic condition) discussion by saying he'll support the family in their hour of need. That won't help his personal profile much in the UK though where a rumour suggests he might visit over the next few days. Trousers down at the ready is the call!

Tuesday 4th July 2017

For his first fourth of July celebration, the President was a bit low profile. He did, however, revert to type in his comments to the group attending. He started with the usual pro-troops gush and his 'blazing economy.' He does make a bit of a glitch by saying, however, that he'd never heard of the term 'Second Lady' re. Karen Pence, despite it being on her website.

Wednesday 5th July 2017

Looks as though North Korean missile test which seems to feature an ICBM missile is likely to trigger some sort of US response, what that might be is yet to be seen. Russia and China initially asked North Korea to calm down but they also say they won't support US military action.

Thursday 6th July 2017

So, DT has arrived in Poland on his way to Germany for the G20 summit. He steps forward to beat Theresa May to their handshake and then makes an impassioned speech, Christian fundamentalists style about upholding the right and asking whether Europe has the courage to maintain its position.

Friday 7th July 2017

So, DT and Vlad the Impaler meet for the first time and apparently, they both say that it is a resounding success. There's a surprise! With this marvellous new right-wing alliance, the world is moving in a very strange direction. I'd love to have been a fly on the wall of the official Russian translators, 'What shall we tell him now comrade?'

Saturday 8th July 2017

DT sums up the G20 Summit by saying it was all a great success. He also reckons a deal with the UK will be arranged 'real soon and be very, very, very etc.'

Sunday 9th July 2017

Europe, however, sees the meeting more like the G19 with the POTUS being set aside like a pariah due to his withdrawal from the Paris Climate Agreement.

Monday 10th July 2017

Turkey appears to be on the verge of withdrawing from the Paris Accord as a result of the President suggesting the US will make it easier for 'friends to access fossil fuels. Although no official announcement has been made, the President's visit to the UK is now apparently taking place 'next year.' In line with DT's love of Mexico, I suspect this might be mañana.

Tuesday 11th July 2017

It would appear that Mike Pence is gearing up to defend his position re. his links with the family of the POTUS because of an apparent link between Donald Trump Jnr and his reported contact with a Russian lawyer asking them to investigate details about Hilary Clinton. He wants to be 'totally transparent.' That will make a change.

Wednesday 12th July 2017

So, today it transpires that Donald Trump Jnr had meetings with Russians who wanted to provide the Republicans with evidence that 'damaged the Clintons.' DT repeats his mantra, 'Attacks on my son are the biggest witch hunt in political history.' When all said and done, I fear the Americans have got him for a while to come yet.

Thursday 13th July 2017

DT meets with the French President this morning but the talk of the town is how he says 'hello' to Brigette Macron by grabbing both her hands, cheek kissing then grabbing her hands again. I wonder what she thought of that. He also tells Mrs Macron that he thought she was in 'great shape,' and was 'very fit.' That's leadership.

Friday 14th July 2017

If you needed evidence that DT is almost completely bonkers, his latest comment re. the wall in Mexico seems to prove this conclusively, 'We need to build the wall of a see-through material like glass. People might be hit by the bags of drugs being thrown over the top.' The Mexican Former Defence Minister says, 'This is the most insane comment I've ever heard.'

Saturday 15th July 2017

Woah! DT steps into the main street of Tweet and draws both forty-fives. He then blasts anyone who's had a pop at Donald Trump Jnr on *Twitter*. Wow, what a dad!

Sunday 16th July 2017

Apparently, the antipathy towards Donald Trump is fuelling a host of Democratic candidates looking to fight in the 2018 mid-term elections. Should be good.

Monday 17th July 2017

Kicking and screaming, DT finally has to concede defeat regarding Obama Healthcare. As he approaches his 6th month marker point, several Republicans were prepared to vote against DT's repeal bill so they wouldn't be tarred with the brush that would have been used to force the poor to pay for healthcare.

Tuesday 18th July 2017

Interesting. The President held a second and undisclosed meeting with Vladimir Putin for an hour with only a Russian translator as the other person present. My goodness, what machinations! Meanwhile, DT threatens the Venezuelan leader with 'Economic actions' if they take the decision to hold an election on the thirtieth of July. Democracy, eh?

Wednesday 19th July 2017

It seems the Trump Administration has held up, or withdrawn completely, support for 469 proposed regulations. These included nineteen that have economic impacts of $100m. This amounts to twenty percent reduction in Federal reform. In other news, DT tells reporters from the *New York Times* that he 'regrets hiring Jeff Sessions as his Attorney General.' He really can't keep it zipped.

Thursday 20th July 2017

More rumblings from the Senate Judiciary with threats to subpoena both DT's former campaign chair and Donald Trump Jnr if they don't appear before the Senate Committee that week. Meanwhile, Mr Sessions has reiterated his commitment to remain as Attorney General so that should stir it up a bit.

Friday 21st July 2017

Only one item for today and that's Sean Spicer. He announces his resignation as White House Press Spokesperson and makes a point of saying that the 'President wanted me to stay.' The fact that DT had appointed another person as Press Administrator didn't help. That and the fact that Sean, to put it bluntly, is fucking unemployable, certainly in terms of public speaking.

Saturday 22nd July 2017

The President now tells people he has the power to pardon amidst reports he's considering Presidential pardons for, well, himself, his family and friends.

Sunday 23rd July 2017

DT has made promises to hold back on his tweets which means he's become almost silent, if that's possible. In this case, less is most definitely less.

Monday 24th July 2017

DT describes the Russian collusion story as a 'nothing burger.' Jared Kushner holds a press conference to say he's completely innocent and that meetings held with Jared Kushner and various Russians before and after the Election were apparently of no consequence. DT standing amidst his young interns in the White House is only too happy to smile for the cameras as the world watches.

Tuesday 25th July 2017

Hold back on *Twitter*? DT opens up yet again on social media, apparently confirming that the US has been funding Syrian rebels via the CIA. These are the same rebels that are now arming themselves on London Bridge etc. DT also promises that a post-Brexit US/UK trade deal is 100% certain. Sean Spicer's replacement is called Anthony Scaramucci.

Wednesday 26th July 2017
DT may have shot himself in the foot as he announces a reversal of allowing transgender people to join the Armed Forces. As many rally-round to condemn him, they are reminding the US that DT was 'unavailable to fight in Vietnam due to educational purposes and a bad foot.'

Thursday 27th July 2017
Subtlety has not been the term that defines the President's rule. Indeed, his new press bloke, Scaramucci, who's just been appointed is now recorded swearing like a New York trooper. Marvellous! In the meantime, DT has finally been kicked into touch viz a viz the Obamacare war. John McCain voted against him.

Friday 28th July 2017
Some comic has suggested that DT could get his face carved into Mount Rushmore. Now that would be a tourist attraction though one can only guess what the selfies would look like. Goodness me, I can't keep up. Reince Priebus, the Chief of Staff, has now gone; an apparent move by DT to move in John F. Kelly, his new best friend and this was pushed by New Yorker Scaramucci.

Saturday 29th July 2017
North Korea launches yet another crap rocket, it's eleventh and this has now stirred up real war values, mainly the value of rockets. Goodness, how rich are the makers of arms!

Sunday 30th July 2017

DT goes stone bonkers angry at China as he thinks they've not done enough to rein in the North Koreans, but he simply doesn't realise it's all a game to both countries.

Monday 31st July 2017

DT's 193rd day in office. Yep! The former Director of US Government Ethics (yes, there is one) Walter Schwab, says he's embarrassed by DT's conflicts of interest and thinks the White House could be seen as a kleptocracy. Walter resigned earlier in July and was concerned that, unlike other Presidents, DT places his business interests and assets central to the office of POTUS.

AUGUST 2017

Tuesday 1st August 2017

This is crazy! Scaramucci is sacked before he's even got to his official start date. It seems that John Kelly said to the President that he'd need to get rid of the New York swearer or he was going. Meanwhile, it turns out Donald Trump Jnr's statement last week was drafted in advance on Airforce One by Donald Trump. This is a guy that not only wipes the arse of his family but flushes too.

Wednesday 2nd August 2017

DT says the reason he spends so much time at any of his golf courses and resorts is due to the fact that the White House is 'such a dump.' DT signs a document that sets sanctions against Russia for various villainous acts, but this is signed without a single camera present. Once he signed them, he called the whole process 'flawed.'

Thursday 3rd August 2017

Just prior to his untimely departure, Mr Scaramucci tried to kick start a personality drive for DT viz a viz a lottery where the winner would win a golf round with the President. Whoops! DT meanwhile is reported to have urged the Mexican President to accept the principle of a border wall. However, when he publicly refuses, DT goes mad saying, 'You can't say that to the Press!'

Friday 4th August 2017

News am US time. A grand jury now being put together. Yep! Although this does not fully guarantee that any form of prosecution will happen, it makes it more likely. As this is happening, the White House is leaking more than Jeff Leak's leaky pants on Planet Leaky and the new head honcho Jeff Sessions is 'demanding an end to leaks!'

Saturday 5th August 2017

Just to put his stamp on his authority and leadership, DT has gone away on a seventeen-day holiday.

Sunday 6th August 2017

There's a suggestion from opponents of the President that Robert Mueller's investigation into Russian election interference might go too far, i.e., make it so big that it will never end.

Monday 7th August 2017

On his 200th day in charge, DT's approval rating is the lowest ever recorded. Only 38% of US voters approve of how he's handling the Presidency. Putting this in context, even Bill Clinton 'I did not have sex with' etc. was at forty four percent at the same time. In astonishing usual news, one of DT's greatest *Twitter* followers appears to be a) not human and b) a Russian bot published to up his *Twitter* rating.

Tuesday 8th August 2017

DT kicks off his villain d'jour game by choosing Canada over Mexico and North Korea. Apparently peeved with their cousins over various reasons, all complaints followed '...very, very, very blah, blah, blah.' DT has also attacked a Democrat senator on *Twitter* re. Vietnam which is a bit rich coming from Mr Heel.

Wednesday 9th August 2017

$1 billion dollar sanctions have been applied to North Korea to which they threaten the US with a fiery response. DT responds by saying he'll use 'fire and fury like the world has never seen.' On the back of his continuing playground name calling, the North Koreans now say they'll bomb Guam and so it goes on.

Thursday 10th August 2017

One more local politician, Alabaman Luther Strange, says 'DT is the greatest President, the greatest thing that has happened to the US. I consider it a biblical miracle that he's here.' DT enraptured, tweets that Senator Strange has done a great job. All this as Mr Strange attempts to win a primary election in Alabama, he's honoured to be supported by the President. With friends like that eh?

Friday 11th August 2017

DT and the North Koreans are still fuelling the fires of war, possibly nuclear. What a strange science fiction time we live in. I'm minded of the many 'Mission Impossible' episodes on TV where the baddie has to be taken down by sleight of hand so the goody can win, but in this instance, who's who? On a domestic front, DT gets the decorators into the White House for a makeover. All that glitters.

Saturday 12th August 2017

In a weirdly ironic gesture, the Venezuelan President says DT's action is a crazy act. This from someone dealing with civil war in his own homeland.

Sunday 13th August 2017

In Charlottesville, Virginia, neo-Nazis clash with protesters, killing 3. The President sends condolences but refuses to lay any blame on white Supremacists.

Monday 14th August 2017

The disgraceful events in Charlottesville have once again seemingly given the green light to American neo-Nazis to conduct serious anti-social upheaval. They are in emboldened with tacit support from the POTUS, simply by his silence when asked by journalists if white Supremacists and neo-Nazis were to blame.

Tuesday 15th August 2017

DT seems to show some humanity by finally saying that 'racists and thugs have no place in America' and this included 'The KKK white supremacists and neo-Nazis.' He does make a statement, however, standing behind a lectern reading robotically from an autocue. John Sopel, the *BBC* US correspondent, says in his TV report that '...in 10 days this will all be forgotten.'

Wednesday 16th August 2017

On the day a tweet from Obama about 'love despite colour' makes history in the number of likes, DT once again true to form says of Charlottesville 'There were good people on both sides.' Again, this type of semi-support for fascism doesn't go down well and even Prime Minister Theresa May disagrees; sort of.

Thursday 17th August 2017

So once again DT decides to step out of line (certainly the official Republican one) by pushing an old fake story about a general in the 1900s who stopped Islamic trouble by soaking bullets in pigs' blood. This was in response to the dreadful events in Barcelona. It does seem odd that the President resorts to petrol when trying to douse flammable situations.

Friday 18th August 2017

DT and Melania have pulled out of the Kennedy Centre so the participants can receive their awards 'without any political interference.' Meanwhile, along with the departure of their Steve Bannon, others are resigning from various advisory boards. Even Arnie Schwarzenegger grabs the headlines re. Charlottesville. He says 'Your heroes are losers. The country that defeated Hitler's armies has no place for Nazi flags.' Leadership.

Saturday 19th August 2017

Seemingly, DT's aides are seeking to revoke the 111-year-old Antiquities Act enabling changes and assaults to take place on national monuments. Republican and democrat opponents not happy.

Sunday 20th August 2017

DT now very happy as his team has been able to provide him with information of those who participated in the Charlottesville act.

Monday 21st August 2017

DT announces that in order to prevent further influences of terrorism from Pakistan, he's going to invest in additional troops being sent to Afghanistan. The UN, the UK and the Afghan President think this is a great idea. However, only last year he absolutely slagged off Obama's policy and wanted troops out. Pakistan is a bit peeved by all of this.

Tuesday 22nd August 2017

DT makes a speech to a group of his favourites and illustrates his love of fake news by pointing out that he spoke immediately after the Charlottesville incident. He fails to mention his bit at the end of his speech saying, 'Good people on both sides.' In wall news, DT claims that the Democrats are 'obstructionists' and that if he has to shut down this government to do it, he will.

Wednesday 23rd August 2017

Apparently sixty two percent of Americans now believe that the President is dividing the nation. DT, meanwhile, has criticised the Senate leader, Mitch McConnell, for his stance or repealing laws presumably what Mitch has done must surely be in the US public interest. Meanwhile, Robert Reich states that the President is a clear and present danger and must be impeached.

Thursday 24th August 2017
James Clapper US Director of National US Intelligence has openly questioned the fitness, physical or mental, of the abilities of the POTUS. He described his recent speech as 'disturbing.' He also added that he questioned his fitness to govern and worries about his access to nuclear codes as 'downright scary.'

Friday 25th August 2017
On the day that Hurricane Harvey is threatening to destroy Texas, DT has hidden news of his ban on transgender troops by saying a lot about how he's on top of the storm. At the same time DT decides to pardon the Senator Joe Arpaio, a man so publicly derided for his racism that it beggar's belief how DT hasn't yet been called out on this.

Saturday 26th August 2017
Yet another Trump aide is 'no longer working' at the White House. Seb Gorka was one of the Steve Bannon sidekicks and resigns. Whoops!

Sunday 27th August 2017
And now the weather. Hurricane Harvey has caused utter devastation in Texas and from above, it looks like a lake.

Monday 28th August 2017
So much to report today. In a meeting with the President of Finland, DT appears to be confused by two blonde female reporters who he thinks are the same person. Jeff Sessions and DT have lifted a ban on military gear (bulletproof helmets,

armoured vehicles etc.) being issued to the Police Mad Max style. North Korea, meanwhile, fires a missile right over Japan.

Tuesday 29th August 2017

DT flew into Corpus Christi to carry on with his 2020 Election campaign, i.e., rallying to flood victims in Texas. DT, however, says, 'Texas can handle anything.' He raises the Lone Star flag and is cheered. Rex Tillerson states on national TV that the President speaks for himself when asked about the impact of the President's comments.

Wednesday 30th August 2017

Following a sparsely attended rally in Phoenix, DT took out his ire on George Gigicos who had organised the event; probably not anymore said Donny. Another person who will almost certainly be spending more time with his family is Duncan Hunter, (Rep) California, who describes DT as, 'an arsehole but he's, our arsehole.'

Thursday 31st August 2017

A poll run by the *Fox News* Agency has found unsurprisingly that approximately a third of US citizens appear to think that the President is an unstable, dishonest and immoral bully. Luckily for him, this is a TV channel that actually supports the POTUS so not all bad then. Mind you, half of the same citizens also said that DT is, 'not at all a moral leader or compassionate.'

SEPTEMBER 2017

Friday 1st September 2017

Mexico is taking a much firmer (read pissed off) position in the forthcoming NAFTA talks with the US and Canada. Usually, they have very much sided with the US. However, threats over the wall have changed their opinion somewhat. Meanwhile, several writers mainly poets using DT's tweets and other communications to put together hilarious verses based on all his crap.

Saturday 2nd September 2017

DT is back in Texas assisting the victims of flooding. He dons some gloves in order to dish out soup. There are no hugs here.

Sunday 3rd September 2017

North Korea launches what transpires to be a new bomb test, only this time a hydrogen bomb. The world watches as this story unfolds.

Monday 4th September 2017

Another step along the DT road viz a viz immigrants. The Republicans have introduced a bill that effectively cancels the DACA, the Deferred Action for Childhood Arrivals. Basically, this means that those citizens previously granted citizenship in the US by Obama having entered the country as children will no longer be given this opportunity. There is clear opposition to this.

Tuesday 5th September 2017

DT urges the specially convened UN group to take action as he claims North Korea is pushing for war. Meanwhile, during a State visit to China, Vladimir Putin says that, 'Donald Trump is not my bride and I am not his groom.' Interesting choice of sexes here. The previous incumbent Mr Obama described the President's decision on DACA as cruel; that seems about right.

Wednesday 6th September 2017

Using his magnificent lexicon of words, DT acknowledges that though Hurricane Harvey was 'Terrible' he says 'Hurricane Irma is bad, very bad.' In other literary news, John LeCarre says that with Donald Trump in charge, 'something very seriously bad is happening,' and he likens his popularity to the rise of fascism in 1930.

Thursday 7th September 2017

DT is cross again. Today about Gary Cohn. Gazza is the White House top economic adviser and comments he made after Charlottesville haven't gone away. DT has a memory like Caligula: anyone who says anything against him is likely to end up unemployed. Meanwhile, as Hurricanes Irma and now Jose head to Florida, DT is doing rallying speeches.

Friday 8th September 2017

Investigative journalism seems to be paying off as news of an apparent change in heart regarding a Trump Tower in Moscow being cancelled, leaks out. As various hurricanes head towards the US, seemingly sent by a vengeful God, shock jocks and other conspiracy theorists are now rethinking their opposition to climate change. Just kidding – of course they're not!

Saturday 9th September 2017

In more weather news, DT warns the citizens of Florida to, 'Prepare for enormous destruction.' He's clearly over-promising and hoping for a meteorological under-delivery.

Sunday 10th September 2017

Sorry DT. Hurricane Irma has hit hard; Florida is now wrecked and Miami is flooded. DT calls the hurricane a 'big monster.' My goodness, leadership in words.

Monday 11th September 2017

A weird one this. Apparently, DT was allegedly recorded in 2001 saying that, 'Now the Twin Towers are down, I've got the tallest building in New York.' This just after 9/11. As always displaying his high level of sensitivity. Hilary Clinton is releasing her memoirs and describes DT's war on truth as Orwellian and that is his associates helped Russia meddle in the 2016 vote.

Tuesday 12th September 2017

DT holds a rally speech to the National Guards' Association in North Carolina and repeats his statement that the riots in Charlottesville had, 'good and bad people on both sides.' DT is also increasing his son's defence profile saying he is completely innocent of accusations of treason re. Russian emails.

Wednesday 13th September 2017

The founder of *Twitter*, Evan Williams, makes a profound statement (yokes are yellow, the sky is up, bears and woods etc.). His quote is that social media platforms are 'dumbing down the world.' He says this because the President has pointed out that he wouldn't be POTUS if it hadn't been for *Twitter*. Yep.

Thursday 14th September 2017

DT makes some weirdly contradictory comments on climate change. At the height of the Hurricane Harvey and Irma storms, he said, 'This is a huge storm system.' Now he's saying, 'Well, they're not that big and if you go back to the 1930s and 40s, there were much bigger storms.'

Friday 15th September 2017

As an amateur IED goes off at Parson's Green tube station on the District Line in London, the President tweets that it is 'yet another bomb left by a loser terrorist.' Scotland Yard says, 'instead of tweeting, you should phone the Met Hotline with information instead.' Martin Amos a Brit now resident in the US compares DT to Mussolini saying, 'he's crazy, deluded and boastful.'

Saturday 16th September 2017

Today's mother of all rallies in Washington DC managed to draw a few hundred Trump supporters but these were heavily outnumbered by anti-Trumpers and Juggalos who I'm led to believe are the followers of the Insane Clan Posse. Neat.

Sunday 17th September 2017

The Californian legislative law makers have now passed measures urging Congress to censor the POTUS, telling him to publicly apologise to the US for his racist and bigoted behaviour.

Monday 18th September 2017

The Associated Press reports that the US Senate has overwhelmingly backed a policy, pumping '$7 billion' (!!) into the military, this at a time when the US government has talked down any policies that might help to pay for its citizens' health. In a speech to the UN, DT states that, 'We will have no choice but to totally destroy North Korea.' Nice.

Tuesday 19th September 2017

French President Emmanuel Macron says he isn't going to give up trying to persuade the POTUS to reverse his decision to exit the Paris Climate Accord. Good luck with that mate! ABC News meanwhile has said DT's comment regarding 'totally destroying North Korea' borders on a threat of committing a war crime. I don't think that serial conflict avoider would care that much.

Wednesday 20th September 2017

At the Grammy Awards even Morgan Freeman gets in on the act. He releases a mini movie-clip explaining how the, 'KGB agent Putin deliberately hacked global IT systems in order to manipulate the US election outcome.' Needless to say, DT has responded with a shrug and commented, 'how poor the awards are this year.' Plus, he thinks he should have been awarded a Grammy.

Thursday 21st September 2017

Once again DT goes on the anti-Iran rampage. He wants to scrap the Nuclear Agreement made in 2015 by Barack Obama. At the UN, he said in his speech that it was, 'an embarrassment to the US.' Meanwhile, DT still attempts to derail Obamacare, this time using several wobbly Republicans.

Friday 22nd September 2017

With the North Korean President saying that DT's comments about total destruction are like that of a dog barking and that there would be severe responses, DT basically shrugs and laughs this off by saying, 'Well look how hard the North Koreans are looking at us right now.' He then goes on to say he may or may not do anything about it?!?

Saturday 23rd September 2017

DT berates a whole raft of National Football League or NFL players and managers, several of whom have protested against the lack of equality by 'taking the knee' and he says that 'they're fired' in his apprentice chief mode.

Sunday 24th September 2017

He may be a President but he can't prevent John McCain and others from setting out their stall against DT's anti-health-care policy.

Monday 25th September 2017

As the 'Take the Knee' row rumbles on, DT now insists that his opposition to it has nothing to do with race. The whole of the NFL is regularly demonstrating whilst NASCAR is saying the exact opposite, but that isn't surprising really. News in brief. Jared Kushner apparently used private emails to do White House business.

Tuesday 26th September 2017

It's reported that Iran had test launched a ballistic missile and DT went bonkers. However, it later turns out that the test was seven months ago and took place as he was getting his size three's under the White House table. DT gets asked about the 'Take the Knee' protest to which he has said again, 'The NFL situation is serious but not a preoccupation.' Regarding the North Korea issue, he responded with, 'They're acting very badly but I'll fix this mess.'

Wednesday 27th September 2017

When questioned about the US response to the terrible damage in Puerto Rico caused by Hurricane Irma, DT says, 'This is a very big storm on an island in a very big ocean.' He also comes up with this gem, 'We got A** for our response to the storms in Texas and Florida.' This stuff seems to work. Forty percent is his rating in the US, up from thirty four percent despite his so-called flood efforts.

Thursday 28th September 2017

DT has announced plans for a tax overhaul (read cut), principally the idea to eliminate the State tax. He reckons it will protect millions of small businesses and farmers. The facts, however, suggest that not many small businesses and farmers will be affected since the tax is paid for primarily by the richest families in America. Now there's a surprise.

Friday 29th September 2017

Ah, another Friday under Donnie's administration and there goes another White House body. This time it's the US Health Secretary Tom Price who has jumped ship before being pushed having allegedly been found using taxpayers' dollars, many of them, to fly jets all over the place. He apparently thought he could do this without asking anyone.

Saturday 30th September 2017

DT sends disparaging tweets about the Mayor of Puerto Rico for complaining about the lack of US support. He's such a gentleman.

OCTOBER 2017

Sunday 1st October 2017

A shooter in Las Vegas has claimed fifty-plus lives at a country music concert; there's no apparent reason and DT sends his 'warmest condolences' via *Twitter*. Odd choice of words.

Monday 2nd October 2017

Playing at the President's Cup golf match, DT dedicates a trophy to all those people in Puerto Rico to which an observer heckles, 'You don't give a shit about Puerto Rico!' This on the back of an increasing row between the POTUS and Carmen Cruz, Puerto Rico's mayor. Mrs Cruz counters with, 'This President is killing us with inefficiency.'

Tuesday 3rd October 2017

DT reckons that the Las Vegas shooter who killed nearly sixty people Steven Paddock, was, 'sick and demented.' The simple fact, though, is that he hasn't been denounced as a terrorist. In the week that more Americans appear to be confident in the news and less so in the POTUS, it will be interesting to see how DT responds to this. Meanwhile, even the Simpsons have dedicated an episode focusing on Puerto Rico.

Wednesday 4th October 2017

While DT throws kitchen towel rolls at the survivors in Puerto Rico, Rex Tillerson, US Secretary of State, says, 'My commitment to the President and the US is still strong.' This is just after he was reported calling Donald Trump a moron. Medical supplies, food and engineering provisions to Puerto Rico have apparently put the US economy 'out of whack' says DT.

Thursday 5th October 2017

As DT visits Las Vegas, an event which left him feeling very, very, very sad, it transpires that almost all of the Republican top jobs are sponsored by the National Rifle Association. Good old Rex for instance, allegedly to the sum of $25,000. Tennessee Republican Senator Bob Corker suggested that 'it is the Secretary of State, James Mattison and John Kelly that have helped separate our country from the chaos.' He's retiring in 2018.

Friday 6th October 2017

It looks like the NRA have taken the hit and are kicking and screaming into a debate about barring attachments that turn high powered rifles into machine guns. Don't hold your breath on this. During a meeting re. the Iran Nuclear Agreement, Donald Trump responds to a journalist question about the possibility of cancelling the policy with, 'Well, this is the calm before the storm.' I think it's hard hat time.

Saturday 7th October 2017

DT's approval rating has taken a bashing as less than a quarter of US citizens think he's honest. He's also now restricting birth control support for women by introducing a ruling that means employers can opt out of a birth control employee scheme.

Sunday 8th October 2017

The President has allegedly had to spend £1.3 million on one of his golf clubs due to the drop in oil prices and the currency dip.

Monday 9th October 2017

So much to note on a Monday. DT praises Columbus but conveniently forgets to mention the atrocities carried out by the Conquistadors. He also claims that he made up the term 'fake' and reckons nobody could have done more for Puerto Rico with so little appreciation. His continued North Korean military threats are unabated and defended Mike Pence who walks out of a Colts v 49r's game due to the players taking the knee.

Tuesday 10th October 2017

Humble? On *CNN* DT gets a rough ride whilst on Fox he declares again that he is 'very humble.' Meanwhile, DT is keeping his cards close to his chest re. Rex Tillerson's alleged 'the President is a fucking moron' comment. DT is also preparing his approach to Iran and the nuclear deal. At the moment he's hedging his bets but who knows?

Wednesday 11th October 2017

There is some debate as to the US economy, mainly the National Debt. DT says, 'When I took over, we owed $20 trillion and we picked up $5.2 trillion in stock. So, in a sense, we are reducing debt.' However, he's getting his US debt mixed up with the value of shares on the US Stock Exchange. On Inauguration Day, the debt was $19 trillion. Well, now it's $20.38 trillion. So, in fact it's actually gone up by $430 billion. Maths not his strong point then.

Thursday 12th October 2017

The US pseudo politicos' fashion yet another coup. This time they've decided to withdraw from UNESCO. Their reason? Apparently, it's a continuing anti-Israeli tone taken by other members of the group. Israel quickly makes moves to withdraw from UNESCO as well. All very peculiar really as at the recent Charlottesville demos, the right-wing masses were shouting 'No to the Jews!'

Friday 13th October 2017

Rather than use democracy, the President signs an Executive Order substantially weaking the Obamacare system stating, 'The citizens of the US will have a great, great, great healthcare and when I say people, I mean millions and millions.' Meanwhile, smarting from comments about US assistance in Puerto Rico, he now threatens to withdraw support entirely yet eighty three percent of the islands still have no power.

Saturday 14th October 2017

As DT delivers a speech to an anti LGBTQ meeting, enemies are circling. Stories abound re. his rapidly descending sanity and ascending temper which will probably do for him in the not-too-distant future.

Sunday 15th October 2017

Larry Flint offers $10 million to anyone who has evidence that would impeach the President. Summer Zervos (an ex-

Apprentice contestant) may well have that evidence.

Monday 16th October 2017

In a moment of jokey humour, DT claims that Mike Pence, the Vice President, wants to 'hang all gay people.' Meanwhile, Republicans are concerned that if DT loses the House next year, he risks a very real chance of impeachment. Donny then says he wants Hilary to run against him in 2020. Hilary says in response that 'DT's *Twitter* use is a risk to global security.'

Tuesday 17th October 2017

DT makes a content-light speech at the homecoming of dead US troops only to top it off with an asinine and probably untrue gesture towards Obama about, 'not calling or comforting the families of dead troops.' Back to news about DT's choices of White House staff with yet another possible drug tzar withdrawing from the appointment as it is alleged Tom Marino had colluded with several drug companies regarding the high levels opiate use in the US.

Wednesday 18th October 2017

DT apparently tells the widow of Sergeant David Johnson killed in the Niger, that he 'knew what he'd signed up to.' A Democrat senator claims she heard him say it although DT now denies this vehemently. His press machine meanwhile has found another widow to back him up with a recorded call, 'He was just a regular guy,' she says.

Thursday 19th October 2017

In weird news, DT apparently claims he has an original Renoir. However, the Art institute of Chicago say that they have the 'authentic version' of the painting adding his is not the original. DT sticks to his guns, insisting his is the original and the right one. Barack Obama is back on the campaign trail for the Democrats saying of DT, 'If you have to win a campaign by division, you can't govern.'

Friday 20th October 2017

The President's tweet trying to align increases in crime with a rise in Islamic terrorism have been described variously as imbecilic and ignorant. Billionaire Democrat donor Tom Steyer has launched a series of acts calling on the US public to drive 'a need to impeach the President.' This looks unlikely, however. The IRS meanwhile may scupper DT's attacks on the Obamacare system.

Saturday 21st October 2017

Calling widows seems to be the flavour of the month. The claims that he called virtually all so-called gold star families who had lost servicemen this year was apparently false. The White House press club going into overdrive on this.

Sunday 22nd October 2017

DT claims this morning that his Administration has been the busiest in US history. A classic example of the price of everything but the value of nothing.

Monday 23rd October 2017

While junior Trump converts Halloween into a money-making scheme (pumpkin hats all for sale etc), DT states that he is the only President in history to stand up to war widows and that he is 'unbelievably brave.' Now that's courage. Correspondents, however, now suggest that this pulpit bullying is a deliberate ploy to rally white supremacists without actually calling them to arms.

Tuesday 24th October 2017

John McCain meanwhile continues to prod the President with a stick labelled 'Vietnam. The poor boys' war.' This war vet Republican makes the point that it was the rich that seemed to avoid the war due to, 'heel bone spurs.' Jeff Flake, a Republican Senator, has had enough. He says he will not seek a new re-election as he 'will not be complicit in this Presidents actions.'

Wednesday 25th October 2017

DT finds himself under-water, i.e., only forty-one percent think he's doing a good job on average, and in Indiana he's down seventeen percent since January. Meanwhile, DT dismissed criticism from Messrs Flake and Bob Corker saying '...they're only retiring because of poor election odds.'

Thursday 26th October 2017

The *Washington Post* runs with an article suggesting that although DT's POTUS victory in 2016 might be seen as a sort of '100-year flood', i.e., never seen again, it may reoccur as many Americans are completely sick and tired of the current state of affairs, certainly when it comes to parity in earnings. The question as we get to the end of this first year is who might be the next President?

Friday 27th October 2017

As promised, DT has released thousands of John Kelly files which in itself is a little surprising. What isn't a shock is that he's held back many of those files saying, 'They need to be checked for risks to our existing security.' In the meantime, DT goes on the attack re. Tom Steyers impeachment ad, calling him 'wacky and totally unhinged.'

Saturday 28th October 2017

Anticipating more Russian info attacks, DT's team muddy the waters again by suggesting the Federal Jury Indictment Approval is a 'Clinton-inspired leak.'

Sunday 29th October 2017

DT makes a move to bolster the US nuclear weapons arsenal with Mike Pence saying that 'the surest path to peace is through American strength.'

Monday 30th October 2017

Following last week's announcement that the first charges were being enacted by Robert Mueller's investigation team, DT goes nuts on *Twitter* saying, 'Do something.' No-one really knows how this is going to pan out, but it's going to be sticky. Stop Press! Paul Manafort, ex-Trump Election Campaign Manager and Rick Gates have now been arrested on conspiracy charges.

Tuesday 31st October 2017

Lots to say! Sarah Sanders, the White House Press Secretary claims that Mueller should be on Hilary Clinton's case for colluding with the Russians. Wow! Fake news doesn't even come close. DT's ratings have dipped below thirty eight percent and allegedly he's losing what little plot he had left. His *Twitter* activists have gone into overdrive to try and save his sorry ass. More news as it happens!

NOVEMBER 2017

Wednesday 1st November 2017

After yesterday's horrific ISIS inspired attack in New York which left eight people dead, DT goes on the immigrant rampage saying he wants to scrap the Green Card lottery etc. It's worth remembering on the first of October an American citizen shot and killed fifty-eight in Las Vegas and DT refused to even discuss the matter as an act of urban terrorism.

Thursday 2nd November 2017

Oh dear, Sam Clovis, DT's nominee for the Department of Agriculture Chief Scientist is already in doubt, even before he's been interviewed due to his links to the Russian scandal. Kim Jong Un North Korean President says that DT is 'incurably and mentally deranged.' Pots and kettles.

Friday 3rd November 2017

DT's *Twitter* account went down. Deactivated apparently by an employee for 10 whole minutes. And breathe! DT and his entourage are visiting Asia for 3 weeks. Ivanka speaks to a half-empty hall in Japan while China says they are the new role model and the POTUS needs to phone. He can be constructive regarding regional issues re. building islands maybe?

Saturday 4th November 2017

As DT arrives in Hawaii, he's met with signs saying 'Welcome to Kenya' and 'Aloha means Goodbye.' Excellent.

Sunday 5th November 2017

Robert Mueller suggests that there is a lot more in the Russian scandal and political issues. Meanwhile, DT has arrived in Japan. He wears a flight jacket. He's never been a pilot.

Monday 6th November 2017

Yet another mass shooting, this time in a church in Sutherland Texas. Once again questions are asked about gun ownership and once again the President and his supporters shout platitudes like 'It's evil versus God and if more people had guns, there would be less shootings.' On top of that, it's interesting that the shooter is a white American, ergo it's only a mental health issue, not terrorism.

Tuesday 7th November 2017

Carter Paige, another DT aide, has admitted that he met with the Russian Deputy PM and several legislators during a campaign-approved trip to Moscow. Meanwhile, with his advisers pondering on how to respond to the news that in Saudi Arabia, several princes had been arrested, DT promptly tweets that he had 'great confidence in Crown Prince Salman.'

Wednesday 8th November 2017

While a transgender Democrat Rachel Levine wins an election in Virginia (amazing!), DT talks to the world from Japan saying that 'North Korea should not test us.' God help him if it's maths. His first year in office is remembered as one that has alienated many, angered fellow citizens and he may well go down in history as the worst President ever and he's not even reached the end of the first year.

Thursday 9th November 2017

On the day that UK PM Boris Johnson made flattering remarks about DT, the President was in China, first of all praising the new Chinese ruler Xi Jinping then refusing to take media questions. This apparently was to show tacit support for China's ruthless control over free journalism. Meanwhile, his party are now saying 'firing Mueller will prevent a coup in the USA.'

Friday 10th November 2017

DT is wined and dined in South Korea with food that angers the Japanese as it's caught on a disputed island. Then just after heaping praise on the Chinese, he launched a tirade on nations he said had 'stripped the US of jobs and trade' which is pretty much aimed at his now best friend. He later said, 'we will not tolerate these abuses.'

Saturday 11th November 2017

Poor old DT. He met with Vladimir Putin again today and says that 'he told me he didn't meddle and he's very insulted that he's been accused of that.' His statement of course has raised many US eyebrows.

Sunday 12th November 2017

And now he possibly, maybe, accepts the US intel findings that Russians did interfere in the election!? And then once again resorting to type, he calls the North Korean President 'short and fat.'

Monday 13th November 2017

Another DT nominee, this time for the post of Federal District Judge for Alabama, turns out to be completely unqualified for the post. Brett Talley also apparently forgot to mention that he's married to a White House lawyer which may have been a tiny bit likely to be a potential conflict of interest. DT meanwhile, met with the President of the Philippines, Rodrigo Duterte.

Tuesday 14th November 2017

The weirdly amusing 'Cards Against Humanity' group have purchased a small plot of land on the Mexican/US border meaning that if DT wants the wall built, he'll have to fight this US body to get this tiny bit of land back. While DT makes up yet another story about Obama 'not going to the Philippines,' (he did so in 2014 & 15) Donald Trump Jr is being investigated yet again, this time about his contacts with *Wikileaks* and Russia.

Wednesday 15th November 2017

Following his name-calling of King Jong-un, the North Koreans have allegedly put a contract on DT. At home after his 10 days in Asia, 6 Democrats in the House of Representatives have started impeachment proceedings. He's also cut and pasting his tweets it seems. He makes a peculiar reference to another shooting which was yesterday in California, but he says, 'May God be with Sutherland,' which seemingly refers to last week's shooting in Texas

Thursday 16th November 2017

It transpires that the Trump organisation may be only worth a tenth of its previously filed value. Publicly DT has claimed sales and assets in all of about $9.5 billion yet his public filings suggest only $600 million. In North Carolina a focus group have described DT variously as 'chaotic, corrupt, dangerous, embarrassing, nightmare and divisive.' There were more negative phrases and it's worth noting that forty percent of these were from Trump supporters.

Friday 17th November 2017

DT has apparently been open to lifting the ban on elephant trophies being imported back to the US from Africa and other countries. This one assumes is as a result of the gun lobby being pressing home their advantage. Most Americans are now blaming the POTUS for the chaos that is the new Medicare system. 1,300 adults interviewed don't trust DT when it comes to American health and why not?

Saturday 18th November 2017

It now seems DT is going to keep Obama's ban on hunting trophies, though for how long? Though Ray Moore is hanging on, his grip is loosening.

Sunday 19th November 2017

The Russian back door communication investigation is stepping up a gear with Jared Kushner now under extreme pressure to disclose what he knows to Mueller.

Monday 20th November 2017

Britain's exported comedian John Oliver takes apart a DT speech and makes it clear that the President is definitely a bit odd and that's saying something. Donald, meanwhile, has dissolved his charitable foundation, principally one supposes because last year there were suggestions, he broke federal rules regarding self-dealing. To be fair to DT, he did make a promise last December to do this.

Tuesday 21st November 2017

Tom Steyer has stepped up his campaign to get DT impeached by buying up to $20 million worth of billboard ads. As if that wasn't a bother a US District Judge, not one of DT's it appears, has permanently blocked the President's Executive Order which sought to cut funding to so-called Sanctuary Cities, in this case San Francisco and Santa Clara, that didn't cooperate with his immigration authorities.

Wednesday 22nd November 2017

Still no official reaction from DT re. the wondrous pipeline across South Dakota which is on Native American Indian land. Did I forget to mention that this pipeline and oil link previously banned by Obama has now spewed 7,000 gallons of crude oil onto pristine soil? Meanwhile DT goes Tweet bonkers again, this time slagging off basketball hero La Varr re. China and their arrest of a basketball players son. 'He's just a poor man's Don King' says the President.

Thursday 23rd November 2017

DT allegedly revealed details of a 'daring top secret mission into Syria by Mossad' to Russian diplomats during a meeting with them in May. Also reported is the technique used by Gary Cohn to cut short a call from the President when he was in Asia. Gary pulled the old 'I'm losing the signal' in order to end the call as he apparently thought DT was talking far too much.

Friday 24th November 2017

DT let slip a claim that he apparently passed on being 'Person of the Year' for *Time Magazine*. They responded by saying, 'The POTUS was incorrect and that *Time Magazine* does not comment on our choice until publication on the sixth of December.' DT mention's Egypt's terrible terrorist atrocity as evidence that he should be allowed to build his wall across the border.

Saturday 25th November 2017

Investigative reporter Jake Bernstein has reported that he's discovered DT's name amongst the Panama Papers selling a condominium.

Sunday 26th November 2017

The POTUS says he will 'end this war on Christmas,' meaning the apparent lack of reference to it in all of the major stores. Important stuff, eh?

Monday 27th November 2017

Ah good old DT. He really knows how to make people relax and friendly. At a celebratory gathering of Navaho 'whisperers' a specialist unit that fought in the Second World War, he decides to praise them by relating all present to a certain Pocahontas. Thoughts of this being seen as insensitive are dismissed by the President.

Tuesday 28th November 2017

A quick DT bullet point list for today. 1) DT claims NFL attendance is down due to the kneelers. The NFL say 'No, it's not.' 2) DT attacks 2 Democrats on *Twitter* and then knocks them because they cancel a meeting with him. 3) DT now goes on full fake news by suggesting that he 'doesn't think that's my voice' on the now infamous Hollywood tape 'Grab Them By The Pussy' etc.

Wednesday 29th November 2017

Following North Korea's new ballistic missile test, DT says, 'It's a situation we will handle. We will take care of it.'

Thursday 30th November 2017

Despite DT's reprehensible forwarding of UK based fascist videos over the last few days and pretty much universal condemnation of him by all, Theresa May says 'An invitation for a State visit to the UK has been offered and accepted.' That will go down well; he'd better be well wrapped up for a frosty reception.

DECEMBER 2017

Friday 1st December 2017

So, Mike Flynn finally puts up both hands and pleads guilty to lying to the Senate. Interestingly, this in itself carried a jail sentence of up to 5 years however, the nub of this conundrum will be whether the US habit of plea bargaining plays any part. I did think that a second-year diary was on the cards but now I'm not so sure.

Saturday 2nd December 2017

Next on the list might be Jared Kushner, a certain son-in-law of the POTUS. So far, DT hasn't spoken on this or the Flynn matter.

Sunday 3rd December 2017

Billy Bush has once again reiterated that 'Sorry Mr President. It was you that said 'Grab 'em by the pussy' on the tape.' DT still continually says 'That might not be me.'

Monday 4th December 2017

Apparently, the White House chief lawyer told DT in January that he believed Mike Flynn had lied to the FBI and Mike Pence. He also said he should be fired. This would seem to suggest that the President knew much more than he's letting on. DT, meanwhile, decides that it is right to shrink a Utah national monument (location of the Bears Ears) by 1 million hectares.

Tuesday 5th December 2017

As DT rearranges the US tax system pretty much to make the mega wealthy much more mega, at the expense of everyone else, the Supreme Court now puts into place the anti-immigration policy preventing seven Islamic nations from entering the US. The Robert Mueller investigation is still ongoing but is being overshadowed by almost everything else.

Wednesday 6th December 2017

DT today formally announces that US now recognises Jerusalem as the capital of Israel. This frankly bizarre statement draws condemnation from much of the world, which includes many of the US allies and of course Palestine. Mr Netanyahu says that the statement is historic. However, we shall see in what context.

Thursday 7th December 2017

Worldwide condemnation gathers pace with most commentators scratching their heads as to why the President chose this moment to support the Israelis in the way he has. Hamas has called for an immediate re-arming. Rumours of Vladimir Putin and DT benefiting from war are clearly greatly exaggerated; something to do with nuclear plants in the desert. It might be soon time to duck.

Friday 8th December 2017

It turns out that in the lead-up to the plan in shrinking the Utah national monument site, DT was lobbied very heavily by a Uranian mining company that currently extracts said mineral in the area. According to the Utah Republicans, this played no part in the decision. Really? DT has already given the green light for exploratory drilling in the Arctic.

Saturday 9th December 2017

DT keeps up his relentless campaign to get Ray Moore' elected as the Republican Senator for Alabama.

Sunday 10th December 2017

The US Ambassador to the UN claims that the sky hasn't fallen in, re. DT's announcement about Israel.

Monday 11th December 2017

Tough start to the week for DT as four of the many women who have accused him of sexual harassment are now formally calling on Congress to investigate these claims. Meanwhile, DT responds to accusations that he 'watches up to 8 hours of TV daily.' The *New York Times* detailed his gogglebox habits, but he tweets that this is another '...false story. Wrong!'

Tuesday 12th December 2017

DT is suddenly all worked up over fake news again. He says that, 'At what point is it appropriate to challenge the network licence for *NBC*?' He appears to be building up a head of steam in his attacks on US media. Meanwhile, he goes all out in asking Alabama voters to get out and vote for Ray Moore despite unseemly allegations against him re. young girls. What next?

Wednesday 13th December 2017

We wake this morning to the astounding news that Ray

Moore has been beaten by a Democrat who actually supports abortion, gay rights and gun law restrictions. This incredible result should be a humiliation for the POTUS. However, he responds by saying, 'I knew he wouldn't win.' Steve Bannon reckons this result is a precursor to the next November 'mid-terms.'

Thursday 14th December 2017

On the day DT's appointed Head of the EPA Office of Chemical Safety withdrew following claims he was knee-deep in the cash given to him by various chemical companies, the President is having to defend himself yet again from allegations of sexual harassment. The main voice is coming from Bernie Sanders who says, 'The guy bragged on tape about his sexual assaults.'

Friday 15th December 2017

In a major step forward for the Mueller case against the POTUS, the special council has asked that the data firm working for DT during the presidential election, Cambridge Analytica, turn over all documents. This of course now means that Jared Kushner is back yet again into the spotlight. At least DT pick Matthew Peterson, can answer questions about law.

Saturday 16th December 2017

Jackie Speier, a Democrat, has suggested that it may be DT is about to fire Robert Mueller. If that happens in the US, I think the country is beyond redemption.

Sunday 17th December 2017

Vladimir Putin makes an impassioned speech thanking the President and the CIA for their efforts in 'holding back the tide of terrorism.'

Monday 18th December 2017

When DT unveils the National Security Strategy, his administration will be dropping climate change as a threat. He also seems to be pretty relaxed as far as the Mueller investigation is concerned. In fact, he's boasting to friends that he thinks 'Bob Mueller will soon clear me of all charges.' Shock, horror! Matthew Peterson withdraws from post!

Tuesday 19th December 2017

A big chunk of US citizens, sixty six percent in fact, in a recent survey have voiced their opposition to the changes to tax laws that DT is trying to bring in. People are finally waking up to the fact that it will benefit mostly those with lots of money already. This comes on the back of the latest approval ratings at just 35 percent which is the lowest for any modern-day President of the USA.

Wednesday 20th December 2017

After all the haggling and devious backstage shenanigans, DT finally gets his super prize tax law changes through. The hyperbole is that all Americans will benefit, but will probably make a much narrower group of rich people richer and a significantly larger group of poor citizens, much poorer.

Thursday 21st December 2017

As Benjamin Netanyahu denounces the UN as a house of lies, the country's already upset over the not-so-subtle threats by the POTUS to financially punish anyone who has the temerity to disagree with his Jerusalem announcement may well vote against the US. If indeed, the UN votes against it, this will be seen as a direct front to the President and his leadership.

Friday 22nd December 2017

The local council in County Clare Ireland have granted DT permission to build a wall (finally a wall for Donald) to protect his golf course in Doonbeg. Although several environmental groups had raised objections to the impact on wildlife, the Hibernian/US links were too strong and the brickies are on standby.

Saturday 23rd December 2017

Ah DT. He has all the finesse of a JCB and claims that '…all Haitians have Aids' and that 'Nigerians own huts.' This President is clearly a worldly guy.

Sunday 24th December 2017

DT tweets that at last he has made it possible for Americans to say 'Happy Christmas' again. Small steps eh.

Monday 25th December 2017

On this day of all days, it turns out that the POTUS has spent at least one-third of his Presidency visiting one of his own properties. This in itself isn't surprising. However, it's always at the cost of others, to the tune of $98 million in fact and still the US people are undecided.

Tuesday 26th December 2017

Following on from the UN vote re. Jerusalem, DT has carried out his threat to cut US funding to the body by $285 million which amounts to about a quarter of that commitment. Bernie Sanders, meanwhile, has attacked the POTUS for the tax-cutting plan that he says will only benefit the wealthiest in America. DT is reported to have told his rich friends, 'You've now all got a lot richer.'

Wednesday 27th December 2017

On the day it transpired Barack Obama had beaten Donald Trump in the 'Most admired Americans', Howard Dean, the former Government of Vermont, says that the President is 'running a criminal enterprise from the White House.' He also went on to say, 'the promotion (of Trump products) is extraordinary. No president in my lifetime has done this.'

Thursday 28th December 2017

DT has been pulled up for falsely claiming that he broke Harry S Truman's record for signing legislation. In the first one hundred days he signed loads, but as he reaches his anniversary as POTUS, he signed the fewest bills since Dwight D Eisenhower. DT has also announced that his latest reduction in the amount of centralised government interference is to reduce or even 'eliminate the monitoring of poor treatment in care homes.'

Friday 29th December 2017

DT has tweeted that he will not prevent children who arrive in the US without long status from being deported unless he gets his wall. He ended DACA in September but still waits for the bricks to be laid. In Puerto Rico, Mayor Carmen Cruz says that 'with half the island without power for 100 days, Donald Trump has been, and is, a disaster in chief.'

Saturday 30th December 2017

DT warns that oppressive regimes cannot last and that the world will be watching the protests in Iran. Apparently, they have the right to express themselves.

Sunday 31st December 2017

On this last day of 2017, the US markets are very happy. Despite many claims of catastrophe, the money-makers are still making money.

Section Intro: 2018 - Year 2

- Tittle tattle
- Tariffs
- Tweets
- Tehran

At this point in time staff turnover into and out of the White House was running at thirty five percent which was some way more than his predecessors in their first year, right back to Ronald Reagan. Amazingly, Donald Trump survives a first year reasonably unscathed. The sharks are circling though…

JANUARY 2018

Monday 1st January 2018

A new year, another round of aggressive tweets from DT, this time taking aim at Pakistan. He says that the US has given them $33 billion over fifteen years and all they've given in return are 'lies and deceit.' It looks like the POTUS is considering withholding $255 million in aid to demonstrate his dissatisfaction. He also tweeted again about the Iranian protests.

Tuesday 2nd January 2018

Leo Varadkar, the Irish Premier, says that as opposed to previous US leaders, 'This President does not have the right skill-set,' in terms of negotiations to bring about a peaceful resolution in Northern Ireland. This of course is based on the situation becoming tense post Article 50 and a possible hard border in Ireland.

Wednesday 3rd January 2018

A relatively unknown author, Michael Wolf, has written a book (Fire and Fury) quoting several people including Tony Blair and Steve Bannon, making all sorts of claims against the President. The juiciest is that Sharon Kushner and two other persons of interest to Robert Mueller met Russian representatives in the White House during the Election and then went on to meet the President.

Thursday 4th January 2018

It transpires that DT has very quietly authorised an expansion in offshore drilling including the Pacific Ocean for the first time in many years. In other news, the President has issued a 'cease and desist' letter to both the writer and publisher of Fire and Fury. Knowing DT's previous legal challenges, this probably won't fare well.

Friday 5th January 2018

Mr Wolf's book is providing tantalising tales re. DT. For instance, it's alleged that the POTUS only eats Mackey Ds to prevent him being poisoned. Following on from Obama's legalisation of marijuana in California which came into force yesterday, DT has now announced a policy that in effect reverses this. The Californians are not happy with this.

Saturday 6th January 2018

While DT assures the world that he is a 'stable genius,' Robert Mueller is now starting investigations into Ivanka Trump's meeting with Russians during the Election.

Sunday 7th January 2018

DT declares that after a year of investigation, there's been absolutely 'no collusion between us and the Russians.' Robert Mueller still investigates.

Monday 8th January 2018

As the President is fast approaching the first anniversary of his Presidency, today's little vignette is the alleged inability of the POTUS to remember the words of the National Anthem.

Tuesday 9th January 2018

Robert De Niro launches a measured attack on DT, calling him a 'Jack Off' and 'fucking fool.' The President, meanwhile, is seething as yet another Judge stalls his DACA changes. As this was happening, the Judiciary also announces that it's keeping an eye closely on the issue of offshore drilling.

Wednesday 10th January 2018

While DT watches *Fox News*, he notices an item on the Foreign Intelligence Surveillance Bill and DT immediately tweets his alarm: 'Will the bill become law!?' thinking it was this process that may be have been used to 'tap his phone.' The only slight issue here is the Bill is one of his own and the GOP actively support it.

Thursday 11th January 2018

Frustrated with US lawmakers when discussing people from Haiti, El Salvador and Africa, but no particular area, DT comments, 'Why do we keep having all these people from shithole countries coming over here?' He certainly redefines the term 'diplomacy.'

Friday 12th January 2018

Oh no! DT has tweeted that he will not now be coming to London to cut the ribbon to the brand-new US Embassy in Battersea. This, no doubt, will be greeted with unrestrained joy by most people including Theresa May because there's a huge saving now in security costs.

Saturday 13th January 2018

On the day that Stephanie Clifford, a porn star, is reported to have been paid off to stay quiet about an encounter with the President and Trump fans tried to arrest Sadiq Khan the Mayor of London, DT faced even more controversy by referring to an intelligence analyst as 'that pretty Korean lady.'

Sunday 14th January 2018

While an irate Democrat insists DT did use the alleged term 'shithole' regarding Africa and other countries, Mahmood Abbas, the Palestinian leader, stressed at a meeting of other leaders that he would 'not accept any peace plan from the US after the President recognised Jerusalem as Israel's capital.'

Monday 15th January 2018

DT very much on the defensive, specifically regarding Shithole Gate. He's very much at pains to say 'I am not a racist.' In fact, he says 'I am the least racist person you've ever met.' He still reckons that he didn't use the 'shithole' term reported.

Tuesday 16th January 2018

On we go with DT's image as porn star Stephanie Clifford who last week listed an affair in 2011, now says in an interview that she did in fact have sexual intercourse with the POTUS. DT's lawyers are on standby but no doubt they'll stall.

Wednesday 17th January 2018

DT today announces the winners of his fake news awards. Unsurprisingly the *New York Times* comes out on top. Not his preferred choice of reading. Some of the items though have yet to be deemed fake, certainly as far as the Russian involvement in the Election.

Thursday 18th January 2018

Mike Pence is apparently the chosen leader out of the Olympic delegation. This in itself is a bit of a surprise however, even more so when you consider some of his ideals. Gay athlete Adam Rippon is concerned re. Mike Pence's previous doctrine of gay conversion therapy.

Friday 19th January 2018

The issue of Senate government funding is once again moving headlong to a position where the US may not be able to govern. Weirdly, Nigel Farage is now coming up on the Mueller radar for links with Julian Assange and the Russians. Well, well.

Saturday 20th January 2018

This is a day to remember. The President's first anniversary. This is one for DT to remember. The funding for the short-term spending bill has not been agreed. In effect, this has resulted in the government technically being out of cash. The only saving grace is that it is the weekend so not so many layoffs at the moment.

Sunday 21st January 2018

After a year with the President in charge of the US, the country is alive with the sound of very upset women. Demonstrations are taking place all over the country, principally raising the profile of the equality, health and women's medical and sexual harassment. So far, the President has been very quiet.

Monday 22nd January 2018

Although started by the previous administration, drone strikes have escalated by some degree under the new President. DT himself claims that he changed the rules of engagement since he took office and there have now been several thousand drone strikes in Syria and Iraq, killing many.

Tuesday 23rd January 2018

DT has hailed the end of the government shutdown as a big win and boasted that the Democrats caved in. The Democrats, however, had a different view. Chuck Schumer says, 'Huh, the great deal-making President sat on the side-lines for most of the time.' The next shutdown looms.

Wednesday 24th January 2018

DT is making conciliatory sounds about the fate of the so-called 'dreamers. These are the children and parents who are undocumented immigrants. The POTUS has said he would support a plan that offered these people a pathway to Citizenship. We will see.

Thursday 25th January 2018

So, the cat is out of the bag. DT is on his way to the UK, allegedly towards the end of 2018. The internet is currently alive with the sound of demo organising. Also, DT had previously suggested that he would meet Mueller's team under oath. However, his lawyers are now saying otherwise.

Friday 26th January 2018

The President is in Davos, Switzerland for the World Economic Forum. He's worked his audience like a slightly worn and rusty PT Barnum with his speech. To add to that, DT apparently was interviewed by who else but Piers Morgan. During their chat, the President has apparently said he will apologise for tweets. What those tweets are we don't yet know.

Saturday 27th January 2018

Apparently, Melania Trump has not headed to Davos in Switzerland to support her husband as had been suggested. She has remained in Washington for 'scheduling reasons.' DT is also being highlighted as undermining the American Constitution by attacking the FBI and trying to sack Robert Mueller.

Sunday 28th January 2018

Oh well, here we are. DT gives an interview on *ITV* to Piers Morgan. The questions are as you'd expect, twee and not really very much in-depth. Though the President does hint that he's willing to apologise for tweeting the stuff about Britain First, this seems to be a bit late. Donald Trump says he's definitely coming to the UK in October.

Monday 29th January 2018

Europe has warned that as the President prepares for his first State of the Union address, they will stand ready to retaliate to any trade restrictions placed upon imports. Apparently, DT has said that he thinks the EU has 'been very unfair on American exporters.' Here we go again!

Tuesday 30th January 2018

DT is going to deliver his first State of the Union address and serious concerns are being raised about his Presidential prowess and mental stability. It hasn't helped that he and the Republicans have declined to impose sanctions on Russia, despite everyone else doing so.

Wednesday 31st January 2018

And so, Donald Trump becomes the first President in history to be booed during the State of the Union speech. His reference to 'increased vigilance and immigration' was met with much derision and cat calls. Meanwhile, DT's infrastructure statement, $1 trillion, is out, but there's no money, there's no detail and certainly no explanation of how this will work.

FEBRUARY 2018

Thursday 1st February 2018

This State of the Union speech just simply won't go away. DT claims that 45.6 million people listened to or watched his speech which was his words, 'the highest number in history.' Oh dear. This has been met with much mirth and micky taking as it's clear that several previous incumbents had much higher numbers: Bill Clinton 66.9 million; George W. Bush 62.1 million etc.

Friday 2nd February 2018

Many commentators are saying that the Speaker of the House, Paul Ryan, has abandoned his duty to defend the authority of the House and the Republic itself. The main driver behind this is the discrediting of the principal US law enforcement agency by releasing the so-called tainted memo.

Saturday 3rd February 2018

The FBI boss, Christopher Wray, has defended his staff by saying he stood by them. This follows DT's approval of the release of an email allegedly saying the FBI abused its power and is biased. All of this is a desperate attempt possibly to rubbish the Christopher Steel document.

Sunday 4th February 2018

Some financial commentators are suggesting that a second '87 could be just around the corner in the US. This was the last time that when a Republican President in charge and with what seemed to be a growing and confident economy, suddenly descended rapidly into recession and US inflation rates are just increasing.

Monday 5th February 2018

Odd that it has taken an attack on the NHS by the POTUS for our own *BBC* News to actually report the huge demo in London yesterday, Saturday. The demonstrators were asking the government for more money while DT used it as an excuse to accuse the NHS of 'failing.'

Tuesday 6th February 2018

Ah, how quickly the US dollar worm can turn. World markets tumble, the Dow Jones by the worst in history it seems as rumours and fears of inflation rates and tax rises affect the money markets. Meanwhile, DT's lawyers have suggested they advised him not to take part in the Mueller-Russian money interviews.

Wednesday 7th February 2018

And up go the markets again! Apparently caused by a 'rethink' in the possibility of rate rises. As some things increase however, some reduce. Meanwhile a video clip of DT boarding Airforce One up a windy staircase reveals large bare patches on the back of the President's head.

Thursday 8th February 2018

And down go the markets again! They plummeted on a second new low bringing all the other world finances with it.

It's reported that Rob Porter, a White House staff secretary, has now resigned after it emerged, he allegedly abused his ex-wives. Main problem here is did anyone know this was going on and why didn't they stop it earlier?

Friday 9th February 2018

It appears that a very smart Russian has conned the US National Security Agency out of $100,000. Shadowy meetings took place meant to work out a plan to hand over stolen cyber weapons and compromising material on DT. A suitcase containing $100,000 in cash was handed over to a Russian as a down payment. And then de nada.

Saturday 10th February 2018

At a time when DT is keen to release lots of information about the White House, on this occasion he sends a memo from the Democrats re-butting the Republican memo alleging FBI abuse. The President has said he is inclined to declassify the tainted memo, but he says due to sensitive passages, on this occasion he's unable to do so.

Sunday 11th February 2018

The President is pushing for cuts to non-defence programmes. Congress broke spending cuts last week and DT is urging austerity for some arms of Federal Government. All this at a time when he is asking for $23 billion for border security, detention centres and $85 billion for vets' healthcare.

Monday 12th February 2018

More momentum on the Stormy Daniels affair. The *Wall Street Journal* reports that DT's lawyer, Michael Cohen, allegedly paid said Stormy $130,000 to keep quiet about their affair. Like John Edwards' 'relationships' in 2008, it is suggested that the President answers questions about his ethical standards.

Tuesday 13th February 2018

DT has gone bill mad. On top of the Constitution busting Religious Bill giving faiths almost political power, now he's keen to sign a bill allowing US citizens nationwide to carry a concealed weapon! This has been met with horror by Police forces across the country but the NRA are very happy.

Wednesday 14th February 2018

The debate about the 'dreamers' goes on but it's becoming clear that it is DT that is holding up the works. On the day that the Republicans and Democrats were in session trying to put words into an empty bill, it still remains to be seen if DT will approve any programme that gives the 'dreamers' citizenship.

Thursday 15th February 2018

The POTUS passes on his most patronising 'My prayers are with you all' tweet button. There's been another mass shooting, eighteen so far this year, in a school in Florida. NRA immediately spouts crap about 'we must arm our teachers.' The second Amendment could ultimately bring about the end of the US freedom.

Friday 16th February 2018

DT apparently can now rest easy. The investigation into Russian collusion seems to suggest that the POTUS is clear of any involvement with the Eastern Block. Robert Mueller, however, has indicated that at least eleven Russian businesses and individuals are subject to legal action.

Saturday 17th February 2018

It appears that DT's new poodle Mrs May has kowtowed to the President by backtracking on a promise to host a session of the Parliamentary inquiry into fake news at the British Embassy in Washington. They fear offending DT and his office has said 'it's unhelpful.'

Sunday 18th February 2018

DT now blames the once fake Russian attempt to disrupt the US election process on the Democrats and Obama. How times change. This is the same day that various US officials are given a message to Europe's policy elite saying 'Ignore tweets from this President.'

Monday 19th February 2018

In Asian news, it appears that Donald Trump Jnr is flogging the family brand. His bribe? Dinner with him for a mere $38,000. US ethics experts are appalled but it seems in the armour-plated world that is Trump, nothing is sacrosanct.

Tuesday 20th February 2018

Following on from comments made by people and students on the ground, DT has started a thing. He describes them as 'crisis actors', i.e., those jumping on the shooting bandwagon. My feeling is that these people would rather see live students.

Wednesday 21st February 2018

On the day that the student uprising starts to get star treatment with $500,000 offered by Oprah Winfrey supporting the 'March for our Lives', DT signs a bill that effectively outlaws semi-automatic rifles being upgraded into machine guns. These are the weapons that have been used in recent shootings.

Thursday 22nd February 2018

DT goes all out patriot by describing the NRA as American heroes. All this as students, politicians and other interested parties talk about the banning of, or at least restricting, semi-automatic weapons. To top this off, DT is proposing bonuses for teachers getting gun training.

Friday 23rd February 2018

Closing this week's references to the very tragic Parkland High School Florida shootings, DT takes his adopted centre stage and berates an armed sheriff who'd been on the scene at the beginning of the violence but hadn't intervened. My guess he was probably just very scared.

Saturday 24th February 2018

Breaking news: Rick Gates, DT's former campaign deputy, has pleaded guilty to conspiracy against the US. On top of that, the FBI's indicted both Paul Manafort and Dana Rohrabacher, each of whom has previous with their associations with Nigel Farage and Julian Assange.

Sunday 25th February 2018

On the day that Samuel L. Jackson calls the President 'a mother-fucker' for suggesting that teachers are armed, DT's approval rating stands at thirty five percent which is down five percent overall since over the last month. DT's legal advisers are still working out a plan of action re. his meeting with Robert Mueller.

Monday 26th February 2018

DT applying his usual and fair impartiality has recommended that his personal pilot becomes Head of the FAA. This is like suggesting his chauffeur should become the Head of the entire car manufacturing industry. This particular President has turned nepotism into an Olympic sport. On the day that DT confirms he will run again for President in 2020, Seth Mayers, a US comedian and commentator has been ripping into the President for his claims that he was 'running into a dangerous situation' and his aims to arm teachers. Seth said the President simply 'blurts out dumb things.'

Wednesday 28th February 2018

After yesterday's row that Jared Kushner's security clearance has been downgraded, Robert Mueller is now asking questions about DT's business dealings with Russians before the Presidential campaign. In Panama, a Trump hotel is under pressure due to a dispute about management.

MARCH 2018

Thursday 1st March 2018

In front of an astonished group of Democrats and Republicans, DT suddenly blurts out that he is behind gun control. Cue the NRA spluttering and congressmen no doubt being tapped up. Meanwhile, just when people think he's gone soft, the President is about to sign off steep tariffs on steel and aluminium imports from China and Canada.

Friday 2nd March 2018

So, the financial week ends with the markets plummeting an average one point two five percent around the world, all because DT has claimed that 'trade wars are a good thing and an easy win.' It seems that most other world trade experts do not agree with him and his ambitious plans.

Saturday 3rd March 2018

Following the Chinese Premier's bid to take China back to an era of one person leadership 'for ever', DT has indicated that US 'might give that a shot.' Other commentators have made the point that history does not work well for those who try to be in charge for ever.

Sunday 4th March 2018

DT's plans to bring in a transatlantic trade war by placing tariffs on steel and aluminium may be held up. How so you say? Well, Theresa May has asked that the President could consider perhaps, possibly not bringing in tariffs? The President is yet to respond.

Monday 5th March 2018

Following global dismay re. the tariff threat, the President has hinted that he may think again, if an improved NAFTA agreement is signed up. Meanwhile, Robert Mueller's team is now reported as treating the whole Presidential campaign group as a 'criminal enterprise.'

Tuesday 6th March 2018

As the rustproof stainless steel letters spelling Trump are ripped from the concourse of a Panama hotel, Sam Nunberg, an early DT adviser, went into a very public meltdown. During a broadcast interview, he said his old boss, '...did wrong during the campaign and that he knew all about it...' referring to the alleged Russian involvement. Will there be legal action soon?

Wednesday 7th March 2018

DT's top economic adviser Gary Cohn has finally had enough and has resigned. It seems he and the President were involved in a heated debate regarding Republican plans to bring in tariffs on steel and aluminium. Mr Cohn gave the usual platitudes 'an honour to serve my country and enact pro-growth economic policies to benefit the American people, in particular the passage of historic tax reform' as did Hope Hicks. He then departed stage left.

Thursday 8th March 2018

With the formal announcement today, that DT has in fact signed off the threatened steel and aluminium tariffs China has called it a 'serious attack on international trade' while the French Economic Minister said, 'there are only losers in a trade war.' Interestingly, Canada and Mexico appear to be exempt from these tariffs.

Friday 9th March 2018

As usual with DT, the unpredictable becomes the norm. Today he announces that he's willing to sit down to a face-to-face meeting with North Korean leader, Kim Jong-un; a meeting that may go down in history as one of the more bizarre leader gatherings that has ever taken place.

Saturday 10th March 2018

British and American Jewish groups are very angry by Mr Putin's comments that groups apparently involved in the US and other elections were probably 'not even Russians but Ukrainian Tartars and Jews.' These comments have been roundly condemned, but so far, nothing from the President.

Sunday 11th March 2018

Well, that didn't take long! DT's previous words regarding a possible increase in the age that young people could buy guns from eighteen to twenty-one have, been dropped from his daily tweets. He states, 'Well, there isn't that much of a political will for changing gun age law.' The murder of children will continue.

Monday 12th March 2018

Stormy Daniels, DT's alleged porn lover, has offered to pay back her $130,000 so she can be free to speak to the Press. If DT stops her in the courts, he will have taken a major step backward. In the UK, the President's comments re. the poisoning of two ex-USSR spies in Salisbury sadly lacks any mention of Russian.

Tuesday 13th March 2018

DT's response to Theresa May's 'it was probably the Russians' has been to respond with a 'We'll condemn whoever is to blame.' Meantime, another one bites the dust in the shape of Rex Tillerson. He is replaced as Secretary of State by Mike Pompeo who is the CIA Director.

Wednesday 14th March 2018

DT named economist Larry Kudlow as his Director of the Economic Council. Efficient, leaderlike and confident? Maybe. But down in sunny south-west Pennsylvania, the Democrats claimed victory in a special election where Tim Murphy had resigned.

Thursday 15th March 2018

DT has held yet another rally, this time in Nashville. He also met Leo Varadkar of Ireland, so it remains to be seen how this will impact on the Brexit process. As DT continues with his diplomacy, his son Donald Trump Jnr was faced with his wife Vanessa requesting a divorce after producing five children with him.

Friday 16th March 2018

As DT and his gang go public in their support of Mrs May and her issues, the New Yorker magazine is placing the President on its next front cover. It's a less than flattering cartoon of a naked President standing behind a lectern suitably covering his modesty. Yuck.

Saturday 17th March 2018

The FBI ex-Deputy, Andy McCabe, has been fired just days before his office retirement. The action carried out by DT's man Jeff Sessions said that 'an internal review found that he'd leaked information and misled the investigators.' DT pleased with this but more to come.

Sunday 18th March 2018

Following the sacking of Andy McCabe twenty-four hours before his retirement, ex-CIA Director John Brennan said of DT, 'When the full extent of your venality, moral turpitude and political corruption becomes known, you'll take your rightful place as a disgraced demagog in a dustbin of history. You made a scapegoat of Andy McCabe but you will not destroy America. America will triumph over you.'

Monday 19th March 2018

As it appears DT Jr slept with a lady from Danity Cane (a girl group apparently) causing his wife to scarper, DT looks at his legal team. He aims to take on an ever-encroaching Rob Mueller and the brilliantly named Ty Cobb one of his lawyers looks to be a likely victim to go.

Tuesday 20th March 2018

Terry Gilliam of Monty Python fame has described the movie Life of Brian as 'redundant satire' with the election of DT as POTUS. 'As somebody who likes turning things upside,' he says, 'I should be enjoying this but Trump is an idiot.' Fran Lebowitz says acerbically, 'You do not know anyone as stupid as Donald Trump.'

Wednesday 21st March 2018

So far, no immediate reaction to the Cambridge Analytica revelations as yet, although Democrats, the UK and Europe are on the war path with *Facebook*. Meanwhile, DT has gone nuts when it went public that he'd been instructed directly by his National Security Agency not to speak to Vladimir Putin after his latest success, but he did it anyway.

Thursday 22nd March 2018

In response to Joe Biden's comments about 'knocking DT down at school if I'd known him then,' DT responds by tweeting, 'He's weak, both mentally and physically. He'd go down fast and hard.' Meanwhile, John Dowd announces his resignation as a DT lawyer amid disagreements on strategy.

Friday 23rd March 2018

And still the replacements keep coming. The President announces that John Bolton will replace HR McMaster as his National Security Adviser. This following a meeting between the POTUS and Mr McMaster where his decision to resign was supposedly with 'mutual agreement.'

Saturday 24th March 2018

The worldwide gun control marches have been well attended and applauded, at least on the face of it by the White House. Only one person, however, has been quiet both on and offline. 'Keeping our children safe is a top priority for the President,' says the White House. The President, however, was unavailable as he was playing golf. Again.

Sunday 25th March 2018

As the Stormy Daniels roadshow continues amidst DT's cries of 'Help! I need allies,' the Grand Old Party frowns are deepening as a $1.3 trillion spending bill gets signed off. The President's squiggle has in effect kept the government going for the moment but it won't go far enough.

Monday 26th March 2018

DT unusually quiet today, probably something to do with the Stormy 60-minutes interview. Meanwhile the White House along with many worldwide nations have expelled sixty Russian diplomats in response to the Salisbury poisoning over who may have done it. How will this all end?

Tuesday 27th March 2018

Uh oh. So now we know why the US military budget has been set so high more recently. DT is keen for part of this particular budget to be spent on building his Mexican wall. It isn't clear how serious he is however, and is likely to face fierce opposition so it's probably a red herring.

Wednesday 28th March 2018

DT still very quiet about Ms Daniels. So much in fact that he's stayed hidden behind the big doors at the Mar-a-Lago club. Meanwhile, DT's attacks on Robert Mueller have led to an increase in attacks by GOP supporting groups like the *Drudge Report* and *Fox News*.

Thursday 29th March 2018

DT scrambling desperately for the moral high ground. He's tweeted that Amazon 'pays little or no tax to State or local governments.' Amazon shares absolutely dive bombed when DT said that he was going after the e-commerce giant. This covers up his dubious 'wall being built' photos.

Friday 30th March 2018

Ted Malloch, a once talented ambassador to the UK and academic with close ties to Nigel Farage (who else) was detained at Boston Logan Airport on Wednesday. He was returning from London and was questioned by the Mueller team about his involvement in the 2016 Trump campaign.

Saturday 31st March 2018

Following DT's hints at the Military paying for his wall, Mark Cancian, an expert in defence spending, has said that 'funding the wall would need Congress to agree. It's never going to happen.' Gordon Adams who served as Associate Director of National Security went further, 'DT doesn't know how to govern.'

APRIL 2018

Sunday 1st April 2018

Well, it looks like the Chinese have retaliated against DT's tariff wheeze. They have in turn introduced their own tariff against 120 different US exports, mainly food, specifically pork. Twenty five percent is the main rate. However, an additional fifteen precent will be added to fruit, nuts and wine. Not so much a trade war as a scuffle.

Monday 2nd April 2018

DT goes all out UKIP today by saying, 'Our country is being stolen due to the influx of illegal immigrants.' He then blames the Democrats for weak border protection. This is probably a wrecking ball for his main issue which is the DACA problem, 'No more DACA deal!' he tweets.

Tuesday 3rd April 2018

Jeff Bezos, founder of Amazon, has some thoughts no doubt about his President. Since DT started tweeting his displeasure of the group and said, 'I'm gunning for them,' the world's richest man has allegedly lost $16 billion. No doubt this will be recovered somehow but $16 billion?

Wednesday 4th April 2018

US comedian Jimmy Kimmel reckons DT's latest humble claim that 'nobody's been tougher on Russia than me' is by far and away the 'most ridiculous claim of his Presidency.

Russia, a country that unquestionably tampered with our election and he's got a very friendly relationship with Vladimir Putin.'

Thursday 5th April 2018

More Stormy Daniels news. DT now claims he 'knew nothing about the $130,000 paid' to the ahem, actress. Meanwhile, the President is considering a further tariff hike, this time $100 billion on Chinese tech and IT. He says, 'this is in light of China's unfair retaliation to previous US tariffs.' People hope that DT is just letting off steam.

Friday 6th April 2018

The White House Chief of Staff who initially was the hard man employed to keep order in the West Wing has effectively been frozen out by DT for pulling him up so many times. DT said, 'I'm tired of being told 'No."' Meanwhile, the President has confirmed he'll be missing the Correspondence Dinner again.

Saturday 7th April 2018

It is reported that Joseph Schmitz approached the FBI viz a viz the Hilary Clinton 30,000 emails that played such a pivotal role during the 2016 Election. Mr Schmitz was a Trump foreign policy adviser. On top of that, a new book suggests that Melania Trump broke up with DT early on due to his shenanigans.

Sunday 8th April 2018

On the day that a resident of Trump Tower sadly perished in

a fire way up in the building, DT goes after Basha Assad of Syria for conducting an alleged chemical attack on civilians, killing dozens and leaving hundreds seriously injured. Meanwhile, American actor and comic Alec Baldwin describes DT's stay as a 'four-year cash grab.'

Monday 9th April 2018

Another Monday, another Trump spokesperson goes marching off. Michael Anton served as the National Security Council voice for a year, he being the third in DT's time as President. Press Secretary Sarah 'You looking at me?' Sanders says, 'The President is one of the smartest individuals I've worked with.'

Tuesday 10th April 2018

Robert Mueller and his team has undertaken a raid on the offices of Michael Cohen. Mr Cohen you may remember is the DT lawyer who allegedly paid off Stormy Daniels. So, Mr Mueller must feel that there is gold in them thar hills! Meanwhile, DT has reacted to what appears to have been a chemical bombing in Syria. He now threatens action.

Wednesday 11th April 2018

In reply to DT's 'big price to pay' for the alleged Syrian chemical attack, the Russians have responded by saying, 'There was no attack' and have threatened grave consequence to any violence. Meanwhile, the new US sanctions on thirty two Russian billionaires have hit Russian firms and the ruble.

Thursday 12th April 2018

DT tweets that Putin should be more than ready for his missiles; they'll be 'coming fast and smart.' Meanwhile, the President has even become the butt of jokes from none other than HRH Elizabeth II. The Queen has apparently likened the President to a loud helicopter flying above her and David Attenborough.

Friday 13th April 2018

As DT hedges his bets about if and when he launches his fast smart missiles at Syria, *CNN* are reporting that a former Trump building doorman was paid $20,000 to stay quiet to prevent him going public about news that might hurt the Trump campaign. As yet, no news on what this might mean.

Saturday 14th April 2018

We wake this morning to the news that under cover of political darkness, the US, UK and France have carried out bombing raids on supposedly chemical weapons producing factories in Syria. The Russians immediately call fake news loudly and demand a UN answer.

Sunday 15th April 2018

In his new book, 'The Big Fella', James Comey who was famously fired by DT whilst Head of the FBI, has said that he thinks that the POTUS is morally unfit to be President. However, Jan Halper-Hayes, one of DT's former consultants, has said she thinks there are so many more in Congress that are unfit.

Monday 16th April 2018

Sarah Sanders, the White House Press Secretary, has begrudgingly been forced into issuing a statement regarding a tweet she sent out apparently showing the President directing the air strikes from the Oval Office. It was pointed out to her, however, that this was not possible since Mike Pence who was also in the photograph was apparently in Peru at the time the picture was taken.

Tuesday 17th April 2018

As US Ambassador to the UN, Nicky Bomber-Hayley says the US Treasury would formalise additional sanctions on Russia, it transpires that DT has not yet wielded his big black pen to sign off the move. It's alleged that DT has said he's unhappy with the plan and it's in a 'holding pattern.'

Wednesday 18th April 2018

DT sent out a tweet that appeared to say that he felt another tweet about a man who allegedly harassed a porn star to keep her from talking about a sexual encounter with the President was a 'total con job' playing the fake news media for fools. The weird thing about all this is that until he made this statement, few knew this story existed.

Thursday 19th April 2018

Only a couple of days after Mike Pompeo met Kim Jong-un with a view to ultimately meeting DT, the President says, 'Well, I don't see any benefit in meeting him. I won't meet him.' Meanwhile, an ex-Playboy model has been freed from a gagging contract is now free to talk about a possible relationship with the President.

Friday 20th April 2018

Today the *Washington Post* reports that DT is not likely to run for President in 2020. This they say is based on the fact that many previously pro-Trump GOPs are now biting lips and staying silent when asked the question. It also appears that he's been banned from attending Mrs Bush's funeral on the 21st April.

Saturday 21st April 2018

The Democratic National Committee has filed a lawsuit against the Russians, the Trump election campaign and bizarrely, *Wikileaks*. They allege there was a widespread conspiracy to defeat the Democrats through a sustained personal attack on the Democratic nominee Hilary Clinton.

Sunday 22nd April 2018

Yesterday's funeral for Mrs Bush was interesting in that it was attended by four former Presidents and Hilary Clinton and the current First Lady but not DT. Meanwhile, his counsellor Kelly Anne Conway was left fluffing and fuming when asked questions as to why her husband is now sending tweets attacking the President.

Monday 23rd April 2018

On the day that the President of France, Macron, flies into Maryland to meet DT, his support for the current President coupled with possible 2020 campaigning is waning somewhat. Ivanka doesn't think he should run and several GOP members are looking to protect Robert Mueller from a sacking.

Tuesday 24th April 2018

More info is emerging about DT's links to Russia, certainly in terms of trips he made in 2013. DT says, 'I never stopped the night' he told James Comey, but flight recorders coupled with his own social media posts seem to suggest he flew to Moscow on his pal's jet, Phil Tuffin. All this is being pored over by the Investigative Committee.

Wednesday 25th April 2018

According to journalist gossip, DT is apparently visiting the UK in July 2018. The formal arrangement is likely to be made in a couple of days and will be met almost certainly by lots of disapproval. In international detente news, DT is pictured holding hands with the French President.

Thursday 26th April 2018

Wow! An interview on DT's favourite Fox & Friends with the President himself was hurriedly ended when he suddenly went loco bonkers and started ranting about Robert Mueller. Even this pro GOP channel thought he'd gone too far. PS. The UK government has finally revealed that DT arrives on 13th July 2018.

Friday 27th April 2018

It's been confirmed that Angela Merkel will visit the US and meet with DT at the White House. Meanwhile, he is again having to look over his shoulder re. the Mueller investigations, especially since the President may have perjured himself on television.

Saturday 28th April 2018

Despite now promising to visit the UK, it is clear from his very public derision of the new US Embassy in London that he is not particularly enamoured with it. It appears he's mostly looking forward to meeting the Queen.

Sunday 29th April 2018

Lawyers representing 'adult film actor' Stormy Daniels think that DT's attorney will cooperate fully with the investigations into the President. Apparently, DT is in panic mode. Mind you, he appears to be like that even when he's on top.

Monday 30th April 2018

This should be interesting. South Korean leader Moon Jae-in reckons DT should be awarded the Nobel Peace Prize over the shock weekend announcement of the cessation, in principle anyway, of the conflict between the North and South Koreans.

MAY 2018

Tuesday 1st May 2018

DT on the war path today about leaked comments made public from Mr Mueller's investigation team. The President says it was 'disgraceful' that forty-nine questions were published in the *New York Times* on Monday. Questions also being asked about ongoing Israel-Iran issues.

Wednesday 2nd May 2018

It's alleged that a letter made public *before* the Presidential Election highlighting that DT will be the 'fittest and healthiest President ever' was in fact written and crafted by, yes, you've guessed it, DT himself. Doctor Harold Borstein says, 'He dictated the lot. I didn't write it at all.'

Thursday 3rd May 2018

Once again DT's recollection of his Stormy relationship (ho ho), 'I don't recall, there was no payment etc., never heard of it' has been questioned by no less than Rudy Giuliani. He makes it clear that the $130,000 was 'money paid to the lawyer specifically to keep Ms Daniels silent.' Suddenly DT agrees and he says 'it was to stop lies.'

Friday 4th May 2018

DT responds again to the Stormy Daniels issue saying that 'Rudy will get his facts right eventually,' and 'he's a special guy and he's just beginning the job. We love this guy and he really understands that this is a witch hunt.' Meanwhile, John Kelly is finding his position as White House henchman under threat.

Saturday 5th May 2018

As DT sucks up to the NRA again, he does his usual anti-gun dissing speech while theatrically waving his hands around and mock-firing an imaginary pistol like a child. Patchow!, patchow! Boom! Boom! He says, 'If someone had a gun, no-one would have died,' and this regarding the recent shootings in the US. On the UK, DT bizarrely says 'London hospital floors are covered in blood.'

Sunday 6th May 2018

'Rudy Giuliani's comments seemingly implying that President knew all along about the Stormy Daniels pay-off and saying that he'd pay off more women if it was necessary will play into the hands of the Mueller investigation,' says Adam Schiff and that 'Mr Giuliani's words are also deeply hurtful to my client.'

Monday 7th May 2018

Today Boris Johnson has appeared on DT's favourite TV shows, *Fox News* & Friends. His plea to the President was 'Don't throw out the baby with the bath water,' this specifically related to the 2015 Iranian Nuclear Accord. DT has previously called the accord 'insane' having been agreed during the last administration.

Tuesday 8th May 2018

DT's lawyers are putting forward the case that the President being forced to testify to the Mueller team would be a 'serious distraction to his role as President.' This though is the worst defence idea as DT has terrible trouble *not* being distracted from the particularly important job of leading the free world.

Wednesday 9th May 2018

As a precursor to the planned meeting with their new best friends, North Korea has released three US citizens with North Korean heritage, who've been imprisoned in the desolate land. Needless to say, the President and his supporters are happy.

Thursday 10th May 2018

As DT celebrates arguably his best week for since becoming POTUS, the White House announces the date and location of the Summit between the President and Kim Jong-un of North Korea. They will be shaking hands in Singapore on the twelfth June, just a month before DT shakes hands with the UK Prime Minister, Theresa May.

Friday 11th May 2018

While Mike Pence urges Robert Mueller to wrap up the Russian investigation, DT angers the Scots by banning Iron Bru sales at his prestigious Turnberry Golf Course. Apparently, he's concerned over the 'carpet staining properties' of the eponymous drink as the locals might say, 'Yah daft bampot.'

Saturday 12th May 2018

Following the despicable and sly attacks on the dying John McCain, principally by political staffer and writer Kelly Sadler, he has been defended by several people including his daughter who said that, 'he's an American hero who is championing a world view and for that he should be respected.'

Sunday 13th May 2018

Not for the first time DT appears to have caught himself out. He's tweeted that he's trying to sort out the 'issue with ZTE' which is a telecoms company. This is odd given that the White House had banned American companies from selling components to the Chinese company.

Monday 14th May 2018

Steve Schmidt, the Republican strategist, has accused the President of having 'blood on his hands,' specifically with the opening of the new US Embassy in Jerusalem. So far, fifty Palestinians are reported to have been killed by Israeli troops. It's also reported that babies have died from the inhalation of tear gas.

Tuesday 15th May 2018

Poor old Hoopers Island, Maryland. This is a place known for crab fishing, more importantly, seasonal foreign crab fishers that are now being screwed due to DT's latest visa change policy. The so-called H2B visa system has been capped so basically there's no-one to catch, sort and bag up any of the crabs.

Wednesday 16th May 2018

Just when it was looking all peachy for the President, notwithstanding the inconvenient discussion 'Look to Israel' re. his own wall, North Korea are now saying, 'If you're trying to undermine our nuclear capability, we will not make the September meeting.'

Thursday 17th May 2018

As DT celebrates the one-year anniversary of the witch hunt (his words) he also tweeted an unsupported claim that Barack Obama 'embedded an informant spy in my Presidential campaign team.' In California DT convened a meeting that sought to depict sanctuary cities and immigrants as 'a violent threat.'

Friday 18th May 2018

DT ought to be very wary. High profile attorney Michael Avenatti is after him. Basically, he's harassing Rudy Giuliani which is making the tired old Mayor of New York a little loose around the lips. Meanwhile, Bill Gates has claimed that the President once asked him if there was 'a difference between HIV and HPV.'

Saturday 19th May 2018

On the day that Prince Harry married Meghan, an old story emerges. DT once claimed he could 'have sex with Lady Di,' but would have only done so if she'd 'had an HIV test first.' On a political note, DT has been in contact with President Uhuru Kenyatta of Kenya pledging continued support.

Sunday 20th May 2018

Following volte faced by North Korea over the Singapore summit, DT has been chatting to the South Korean President Moon Jai-in in order to get their collective script right, one assumes. All this just as Boris Johnson is bellowing, 'there should be a Nobel Peace Prize for the President.' Kim Jong-un is very cleverly shifting the goal posts.

Monday 21st May 2018

Senator Bob Corker, who to be fair has not had the friendliest of relationships with the President, has turned down an offer to be US Ambassador to Australia. 'That's not the right step for me,' he said. Meanwhile, Peter Rachman clone Ron Gidwitz who's previously been slammed by Barack Obama for slum housing, has been picked as the US Envoy to Belgium.

Tuesday 22nd May 2018

On the same day that DT suggests there is a substantial chance that the summit with Kim Jong-un may be delayed, it also transpires that an actual sinkhole (not a metaphor) has opened up on the White House lawn and appears to be growing by a substantial amount annually.

Wednesday 23rd May 2018

As DT rabidly pursues his paranoid claim that the FBI is/was a conspiring against him, Judge Naomi Rice Buchwald rules that since the President has a very public *Twitter* feed and if he, or his aides blocked anyone it 'violated the first amendment,' that being the exercising of free speech.

Thursday 24th May 2018

Maybe the meeting with Kim Jong-un is still on. Journalists were invited to see what is purported to be the North Korean regime blowing up nuclear tunnels, buildings and a metal foundry. This was presumably to demonstrate a commitment to a reduction in nuclear capability and production.

Friday 25th May 2018

Nope! DT calls off the talks with North Korea, blaming the 'tremendous anger and open hostility.' But what's this? When asked today if the talks could go ahead, DT says, 'We're talking to them. It could happen on the twelfth.' This is very confusing. On the home front, the President is still claiming that his campaign team had an FBI informant placed in it.

Saturday 26th May 2018

Both parties, the US and the North Korea, are bigging up the chance of talks. However, like all of these summits, it's about what's *not* being disclosed that matters. Meanwhile, DT and the GOP are desperately trying to raise funds and are looking at putting twenty five percent on car imports.

Sunday 27th May 2018

Moon Jai-in, the South Korean President, has stated that the Kim Jong-un has declared his commitment to, 'complete de-nuclearization of the Korean Peninsula,' and that the peace process should not be halted. So, after all the bluff and bluster, June twelfth is maybe back on.

Monday 28th May 2018

Rudy Giuliani has admitted that the spy in the camp scandal is simply a PR tactic by the GOP to deflect any news or reporting on anything else that might disrupt the President's main goals. Yet another Republican departs saying, 'Whatever I do, I get asked questions about Donald Trump.'

Tuesday 29th May 2018

DT back on the war path, specifically related to a tweet sent by the Democrats showing immigrant children locked up in steel cages. DT re-tweets his cynicism then states, 'The Democrats must agree to the wall and new border protection. Bi-partisan bill now!'

Wednesday 30th May 2018

Today is MCTD or Melania Conspiracy Theory Day. Two weeks ago, Melania Trump popped out for some minor surgery. The First Lady hasn't been seen since. Various theories abound that go from: she's holed up with the Obamas, cooperating with Robert Mueller or she's moved to New York. But the question is, where is she?

Thursday 31st May 2018

The UK FTSE dips today as the US imposes the long-threatened tariffs on steel and aluminium imports and this has led once again to Europe making threats of commercial retaliation. A German business magazine (*Wirtschafts Woche*) has reported that DT told Emmanuel Macron that he wanted to 'stop Mercedes driving down Fifth Avenue.'

JUNE 2018

Friday 1st June 2018

DT was quick to appear on US national TV to show his people a large letter that he'd received from North Korea. As usual, he bumbled his way through a non-explanation of what the letter was actually about. However, it would appear that the talks with North Korea on the twelfth June are back on again.

Saturday 2nd June 2018

Apparently, Theresa May is going to press DT at the G7 meeting in Canada on his decision re. metal tariffs. What response she's going to get is debatable, but whatever it is, DT will likely change his mind and confuse the issue by talking about other things that have no relevance.

Sunday 3rd June 2018

The protectors of the world otherwise known as the GOP, have withdrawn the Protection Act brought about by Obama's government specifically protecting whales and sea turtles. No explanation from them except 'it isn't relevant at this time.' Neither one supposes are any other laws that might protect the planet.

Monday 4th June 2018

When asked questions about the special investigation into possible Russian involvement during the 2016 election, DT said today, 'Why? When I've done nothing wrong,' adding 'it is unconstitutional and I have absolute power to pardon myself.' Meanwhile, the Supreme Court have upheld the right of a Christian baker not to bake for a gay couple.

Tuesday 5th June 2018

Today DT is involved in all sorts of shenanigans. He's had a spat with the Philadelphia Eagles and 'disinvited' the team's visit suggesting it would be a political stunt. He's still going mad about Robert Mueller while trying to defend off accusations of sexual assault by Summer Zervos, a contestant on The Apprentice. The judge is likely to summon the President for a statement.

Wednesday 6th June 2018

Lots of rumblings in the GOP about last straws. Yes, all things must come to an end and if the grumblers have their way, DT's time might be running out. It's all to do with the steel and aluminium tariffs, a move that really goes against the Capitalist grain for a large percentage of the Republican donors.

Thursday 7th June 2018

DT once again demonstrates his grasp of history. During a call to Justin Trudeau, the President asks the question, 'Didn't you guys burn down the White House?' This, bearing in mind that Canada didn't actually exist when the British set the White House on fire in 1814.

Friday 8th June 2018

As usual, DT comes out with his testing statement of the week. At the G7 summit he says, 'Whether you like it or not, we used to be the G8. So, the Russians should be let back in again.' Meanwhile, DT also cryptically says that he wants NFL players to kneel so they can recommend people 'who have been victims of injustice to be pardoned.'

Saturday 9th June 2018

As the G7 participants all feel the wrath of DT, as in 'we're sick of subsidising Europe,' he also has a pop at Justin Trudeau, this time about the Canadian supply system. DT maintains 'it's very unfair to our farmers with high tariffs. Well, it's going to stop or we'll stop trading with them,' he says.

Sunday 10th June 2018

Who'd trust a President? At the end of the G7 Summit, all of the nation's sign a Communique to trade and then DT tweets 'Canada is weak and dishonest' and promptly cancels. That will work well if he tries that tack with Kim Jung-un in Singapore. Eight-twenty pm and DT has now landed in Singapore. Here we go!

Monday 11th June 2018

Both Kim Jong-un and DT are now ensconced in Singapore; DT was presented with an early seventy second birthday cake while the North Korean President took selfies. Hopefully this meeting goes better than the G7 which was basically DT telling all of his allies that he didn't want to play.

Tuesday 12th June 2018

Well, today will go down in history with a handshake and meetings that were held between arguably the two strangest people on the planet. North Korea has stated clearly that they are committed to de-nuclearization of the Korean Peninsula and the President goes completely off-script saying that the 'US would no longer hold South Korean joint military exercises.'

Wednesday 13th June 2018

As observers throughout the free world try to get a grip on what actually happened in Singapore, DT and Kim Jong-un both claim victories. Be that as it may, back in the US, DT's former lawyer Michael Cohen has said he's likely to cooperate with Federal prosecutors.

Thursday 14th June 2018

Relatively quiet day today, probably due to the fact that the World Cup has now commenced in Russia. The USA, Mexico and Canada have at last become friends. Which they'll need to keep up as they will be co-hosting the World Cup in 2026. The award wasn't really in doubt as the only competitor at the FIFA selection was Morocco.

Friday 15th June 2018

Busy day today for DT. The New York Attorney's General Office is issuing the Trump Foundation with a lawsuit regarding various violations of finance and campaign laws. As DT pushes for a twenty five percent tariff on Chinese imports, he also says 'Crimea must be Russian because the people there speak Russian.'

Saturday 16th June 2018

DT says to an interviewer that 'when Kim Jong-un speaks, his people listen and I want the American people to treat me the same way.' As if to back up his authoritarian dream, the President suggests that the US will withdraw from the UN Human Rights Council. Why?

Sunday 17th June 2018

DT is unhappy with the Court's decision to keep Paul Manifort in jail prior to his trial. This is a little hypocritical when you consider the very many people who the President has deemed should be in jail which they wait to have their immigration rights cleared, with many families separated.

Monday 18th June 2018

Yesterday Roger Stone, long-time associate of DT, says that he met with Henry Greenburg, a Russian, who said he 'had dirt on Hilary during the Presidential campaign.' A copy of a Homeland Security memo is released stating very clearly that if families are identified as seeking asylum, children are likely to be separated from their parents.

Tuesday 19th June 2018

The screams of isolated children being kept in chain-link areas and walled rooms are only drowned out by the shouts of indignation made by DT and his cohorts, 'The US will not become an immigration camp for asylum seekers.' This action is roundly attacked by human rights groups.

Wednesday 20th June 2018

Well, that didn't go so well! Following on from DT's imposition of tariffs on goods from the EU, similar tariffs have now been placed on US bourbon, jeans and motorcycles; from this Friday, a twenty-five percent import duty on US goods. DT of course maintains that 'the EU treats us unfairly.'

Thursday 21st June 2018

During one of his noisy rallies in the town of Minnesota, DT has indicated that he's keeping America great by being strong. He relates this leadership strength to 'othering', i.e., in creating an enemy within specifically immigrants, he is 'transferring power to everyone but himself.'

Friday 22nd June 2018

So, following the global outcry over children being placed in cages and separated from their parents, DT has signed his warrants stopping the process. Mind you, he did say he was damned if he did, damned if he didn't. The EU twenty five percent tariffs are being applied from today.

Saturday 23rd June 2018

So now DT threatens, by tweeting of course, to place a twenty percent tariff on all cars coming from Europe just as US manufacturers are shutting down. In a classic DT move of back-tracking, he declares today that North Korea 'still poses an extraordinary threat,' and because of that, he will extend the national emergency covering that country for another year.

Sunday 24th June 2018

DT calls for a deportation order to basically kick out 'illegal immigrants' without any trial or judicial proceedings. This, as David Bossie, a DT campaign manager tells a black Democrat strategist Joel Payne that 'he's out of his cotton-picking mind.' This is America 2018.

Monday 25th June 2018

On a day that western money markets stepped every closer to the precipice with this morning's FTSE being down two percent, it transpires that not only are DT's poll numbers higher than ever, but he goes on the offensive over Sarah Sanders being kicked out of a 'Red Hen' restaurant in Virginia.

Tuesday 26th June 2018

As tension builds for the non-State visit of DT to the UK Friday 13th, Harley Davidson, that most American of American companies has made comments suggesting that they might move its production system outside the US. Needless to say, DT tweets various threats over tax and 'this company is finished,' etc.

Wednesday 27th June 2018

The Supreme Court has upheld DT's policy of restricting immigration for people from five mainly Muslim countries to which some are now saying 'we have to live as second-class citizens.' Dana M Sabraw a district judge in San Diego tells the POTUS that he's got thirty days to re-unite migrant children with their families separated on the border as a result of the Presidents 'zero tolerance' policy.

Thursday 28th June 2018

DT praises Vladimir Putin and Russia in the way they are handling the World Cup just as both leaders agree to meet in Helsinki on July sixteenth. Meanwhile, DT's comments about various US steel manufacturers 'expanding' appear to be ahem, mistaken, i.e., they're not, and this according to US Steel.

Friday 29th June 2018

Following the dreadful shooting dead of five journalists in Maryland, DT says, 'like any other Americans, they should be allowed to go about their business in safety.' General Motors warns the President that his tariffs on imported vehicles could lead to a smaller General Motors because it will isolate foreign buyers and investment.

Saturday 30th June 2018

James Melville, the US Ambassador to Estonia, has decided to take early retirement after thirty-three years due to remarks made by DT about Europe and NATO which he says are 'factually wrong.' After the historic Summit with North Korea, the mood has changed. North Korea meanwhile appear to be improving nuclear sites, not blowing them up.

JULY 2018

Sunday 1st July 2018

Loads of little things today. First of all, DT urges the Saudis to increase oil output by 2 million barrels a day then Sadiq Khan is barracked by Rudy Giuliani for 'insulting the President.' Black Senator Tim Scott found a discussion on race with DT 'uncomfortable' and thousands demonstrate in the US to abolish the immigration and custom enforcement rules.

Monday 2nd July 2018

ABC has reported that Michael Cohen whose offices were raided three months ago, has said that 'my wife, daughter, son and country have my first loyalty.' This, it seems is Mr Cohen ending his joint defence agreement with DT.

Tuesday 3rd July 2018

Apart from another set of misspelt Tweets, it's a quiet day today with news that apparently, yesterday's meeting with the Dutch Prime Minister, Mark Rutte, went well by all accounts.

Wednesday 4th July 2018

According to *CNN*, a survey seems to suggest that fifty percent of US citizens think DT is a racist. This in itself is a remarkable measure of what people think and what they will tolerate, certainly at this moment. Peculiarly, DT has also allegedly repeatedly considered invading Venezuela.

Thursday 5th July 2018

As if a visit by a very unliked stateman wasn't bad enough, it looks like the British taxpayer will have to foot a £5 million bill protecting DT while he plays golf in Scotland. The Chief Constable of Scotland estimates that a further 5,000 officers will be needed to police the whole area.

Friday 6th July 2018

At a rally in Montana, DT takes a swipe at George W Bush, in particular the odd phrase that he used, '8,000 points of light.' DT said, 'What the hell was all that about?' Many of the previous President's supporters however came out in his defence saying, 'The President's comments were offensive and uncalled for.'

Saturday 7th July 2018

It appears that the all-clear has been given by the London Mayor to fly a blimp in the shape of Baby Trump on the day DT arrives in the UK. The US President will likely avoid the capital at all costs. There's only so many bared arses a man like DT can take when he's on holiday.

Sunday 8th July 2018

Both DT and Mike Pompeo have played down the recalcitrant comment by North Korea who have accused the US of having a 'gangster-like mindset when it comes to de-nuclearization.' Many other commentators are not so favourable, suggesting DT has been played for a fool.

Monday 9th July 2018

The Press, certainly in the US, is having a right old time today with the *New York Times* headlines of 'Trump Reeks of Fear.' This on the day that DT attempts to appoint two of his Supreme Court favourites. Rudy Giuliani, meanwhile, suggests that the White House will 'refuse to meet with Robert Mueller.'

Tuesday 10th July 2018

The President states that prior to his trip to Europe, he recognises that 'Boris Johnson is my friend.' He also said that 'NATO doesn't respect us and that the UK is in turmoil.' What reception the US President will get when he arrives in the UK is anyone's guess.

Wednesday 11th July 2018

After DT goes nuts about NATO suggesting that 'it will be easier to deal with Putin', the EU Council President has responded by saying, 'The US really should respect its allies.' Donald Tusk also added that 'Europeans collectively spend many times more on defence than Russia and China.'

Thursday 12th July 2018

DT arrives to great pomp and celebration. Well, by flying into Stansted the 4th busiest airport in the UK. Now there's pomp. The President starts with claims that 'NATO is much better off now' and that 'Brexit Leave voters 'probably won't get what they want.' The demonstrations in the UK have just started and £10 million of Police security will hold them all back.

Friday 13th July 2018

When history reflects on today, I wonder how many will report information that while DT patronises the Prime Minister, and has tea with the Queen at Windsor, 250,000 Londoners are on the streets making it clear to the POTUS that his brand of leadership is not welcome here.

Saturday 14th July 2018

DT sets off today apparently 'leaving the UK' according to the US Embassy in London. Well actually, he's off to Scotland, ostensibly to play golf at one of his clubs. One assumes he will be well protected from the many protestors who will also seek to advise DT that his presence is equally unwelcome in the Highlands.

Sunday 15th July 2018

DT completes his 'quickie' tour of the UK and sets off for Helsinki where he will meet up with his boss, Bronco Putin. The Scots had come out in force to demonstrate their dislike of the orange invader from overseas.

Monday 16th July 2018

Seven a.m. DT has early tweeted that the US-Russian relationship is at an all-time low. By midday in the delightful Finnish capital of Helsinki, the President, after shaking hands with Vladimir Putin, says, 'We, the US and Russia, are going to have a very special relationship.'

Tuesday 17th July 2018

Following yesterday's interesting response by DT to the question 'Did the Russians interfere with the US Election?', where the POTUS responded by saying, 'No. Vladimir Putin says no, so no,' the links between this and the UK Brexit process just got worse and the police are now investigating.

Wednesday 18th July 2018

Absolutely amazing scenes. The President is sat in front of a camera and almost certainly prompted, makes it clear when asked about the alleged interference in his Presidential campaign that, 'I don't see why it would be in terms of Russian interference.'

Thursday 19th July 2018

After the NATO debacle, several Europeans have expressed concern over the reliability of the US. The German Defence Minister said, 'We can no longer rely on the White House' while a former Polish Foreign Affairs Minister says 'Trump has abandoned the European Alliance.'

Friday 20th July 2018

A bit of a shock for the Director of National Intelligence when he is told that 'The President has invited Vladimir Putin to the US for more talks.' Donald Coats' reaction is a picture as he leans towards the TV journalist Andrea Mitchell on camera and says with wide eyes, 'Say that again,' and then 'That will be special.'

Saturday 21st July 2018

Iran has made several warnings to DT and the US. Hassan Rouhani said, 'Americans should seek the path of peace with

Iran.' He also said, 'Mr Trump shouldn't play with a lion's tail. This would only lead to regret.' The Iranians are no doubt concerned about the continuing effects of the ongoing sanctions.

Sunday 22nd July 2018

DT goes onto *Twitter* to threaten Iran with what some are suggesting is war, 'Never, ever threaten the United States again or you will suffer consequences,' he tweeted. This was balanced with the Iranian Parliament saying, 'A war with Iran is the mother of all wars.'

Monday 23rd July 2018

Yet again DT's personal approval ratings have snaked downwards and don't look as though they're coming up any time soon. This in itself doesn't impact on the President and his popular front. This latest dip will appear to be as a direct result of his last meeting with Vladimir Putin.

Tuesday 24th July 2018

DT has somehow become aware of Russian interference, 'I am very concerned they will look to impact on the 2018 midterm elections and influence the Democrats this time.' DT couldn't provide any evidence for this so could be amateur reverse psychology.

Wednesday 25th July 2018

On the day that DT's Hollywood Walk of Fame star was smashed to pieces, *CNN* announced that they have now obtained a copy of the recording of the President explaining why it is useful to pay off a model that is alleged he had an affair with. Meanwhile, a judge has allowed an emolument case to proceed against the President.

Thursday 26th July 2018

Robert Mueller is investigating tweets of a threatening nature that DT made about James Comey who's now long gone. He thinks these may be grounds of possible obstruction of justice. The claim also includes Jeff Sessions and Andrew McCabe.

Friday 27th July 2018

An *NBC* source has said that Michael Cohen is willing to say to Mr Mueller that Donald Trump Jr. 'told his father about a meeting between himself and a Russian lawyer.' The President has denied any knowledge of this and said 'Somebody's making up stories just to get out of a jam.'

Saturday 28th July 2018

The leaders of the Koch Network, a group of Conservative mega donors who between them make pledges worth millions of dollars to the Republicans, have opened their annual summer summit with a harsh criticism of DT. The main concern is the virulent rhetoric that the POTUS continually spouts, making business extremely difficult.

Sunday 29th July 2018

Using all his political nous and diplomacy, DT says that unless the Democrats agree to vote for the border wall, he will shut down government. The POTUS has previously said, 'If they don't want the wall but we're going to get the wall; even if I have to close the country.'

Monday 30th July 2018

DT has reacted to the Koch brothers' remonstrations saying that they are 'globalist and over-rated.' This is a little odd since the Koch Network is a major Republican Party finance provider. DT has also now sided with Rudy Giuliani's tone that 'Collusion is not a crime' specifically re. the Manafort Trial.'

Tuesday 31st July 2018

DT is pushing for the Treasury Department to consider yet another tax cut for the wealthiest Americans, though through a change that won't need approval from Congress. Basically, the POTUS is keen on the capital gains tax to be adjusted to take inflation into consideration.

AUGUST 2018

Wednesday 1st August 2018

DT claims that 'Americans need to carry their ID cards when they go shopping.' This is incorrect because there are no legal reasons to carry ID cards and maybe this is a little bit of card issue 'nudging.' Meanwhile, the President has tweeted that Attorney General Jeff Sessions should 'stop this witch hunt right now.' This following on from a comment made by Mr Sessions regarding collusion.

Thursday 2nd August 2018

Serious concerns are now being raised that DT's continuous attack on journalists is inevitably going to lead to another violent episode. *CNN* appears to be the main butt of his jokes. And meanwhile, the debt level of government, centrally and federally, is increasing. Trump says tax cuts will help with this.

Friday 3rd August 2018

At a heated press briefing at the White House, the question 'is the Press the enemy of the American people?' was asked of Sarah Sanders. Sarah filibustered and waffled for a few minutes but ultimately refused to respond. These are dangerous times for the Press.

Saturday 4th August 2018

Tough end to the week for the President. Many observers are

predicting a tricky future. The GOP is struggling to keep control of Congress where there is the potential for a Democrat takeover coupled with Robert Mueller and the Russian investigation pursuing impeachment.

Sunday 5th August 2018

DT is now saying that the meeting that Donald Trump Jr held with a Russian lawyer was 'to get hold of Clinton dirt' and was totally legit. This of course is the meeting that DT said he wasn't aware of and then he was. This is yet another contradictory statement from comments made in 2017 and earlier this year.

Monday 6th August 2018

The President has commenced the week by reintroducing some of the sanctions against Iran that were withdrawn by President Obama. These include the moving of dollar notes through Iranian banks and sanctions against gold, aluminium, steel, aircraft and coal. Worse still for wealthy Americans, no more caviar.

Tuesday 7th August 2018

The reintroduction of Iranian sanctions has been enhanced today with DT making a global threat, 'If you trade with Iran,' he said, 'you won't trade with us.' This in effect involves pretty much the rest of the world. What next for the Iranians?

Wednesday 8th August 2018

The Republican-led government has ordered new sanctions against Russia, apparently as a result of the deadly Skripal poisoning in Salisbury, UK. At the same time, rumours picked up through leaked documents suggest Vladimir Putin lobbied DT in Helsinki on arms control. The details are patchy but they could be nuclear-based.

Thursday 9th August 2018

Despite the sanctions imposed on Russia, DT has been unusually quiet about the whole thing. The general opinion amongst aficionados of such things is that any comment from the President may well sponsor a comment back from his bosom buddy Vladimir Putin, re. tales of alleged 'golden showers.' Hmm.

Friday 10th August 2018

Both Europe and the US have had their recent financial gains set back by DT's imposition of tariffs on Turkey. He's doubled tariffs on steel and aluminium already so this is a serious issue for them, probably prompted by Turkey's acquisition of a missile defence system from Russia.

Saturday 11th August 2018

The UK has agreed to work with the EU to try to block the impact of DT's new sanctions against Iran. Odd this at the same time as the UK Prime Minister's hand-holding of the President is pushing for a coming together of Europe and they now have to deal with a deliberate attempt to destabilise it.

Sunday 12th August 2018

A former aide to DT, Omarosa Newman, has released an

audio tape of an alleged conversation with the President which seems to suggest he is unaware of what actually takes place in the White House. She is publishing a 'tell all' book so this will be interesting.

Monday 13th August 2018

Rumours abound that DT has made numerous telephone calls to other world leaders in his time as POTUS, many of which would regularly wake up the unfortunate Premier of that country. These were allegedly carried out by the President with him completely oblivious to differences in time zones. It's been alleged that he simply doesn't understand the spinning of the planet.

Tuesday 14th August 2018

DT goes mad against Omarosa Newman because of her soon-to-be-released biography exposing all book about the POTUS and the White House. He tweets that 'she is no better than a dog and a crying low life.' He also claims 'there are no tapes of me using such a terrible word that begins with 'N."

Wednesday 15th August 2018

Less than three months before the mid-term elections which are ostensibly a referendum on DT's first two years as POTUS, his approval ratings are back into the low forty's. Previous incumbent leaders with similar ratings lost control of at least one house of Congress. Only time will tell if this improves.

Thursday 16th August 2018

Former CIA Director John Brennan issued a robust statement over the decision by DT to revoke his access to top secrets. In his statement, Mr Brennan describes the claims by DT that there was no collusion with Russia as 'hogwash' and that the attempt is another scare tactic for those that might be a threat to the President.

Friday 17th August 2018

Cause and effect, eh? As DT continues to refer to the Press in the US as 'enemies of the people', the Boston Globe today received a bomb threat which was later found to be false, leading some commentators to again voice their fears that the President is promoting violence against journalists.

Saturday 18th August 2018

Tragic news yesterday being that of Aretha Franklin's passing, but even more tragic was the speed in which DT claimed that the afore-said Aretha 'worked for me.' This was based on a brief concert given by the jazz diva at one of DT's casinos in the 1980s. This was clearly not one of those great employer/employee relationships.

Sunday 19th August 2018

During the 1950s the McCarthyite witch hunts caused untold pain and anguish for many US families. DT now claims that the Mueller investigation is akin to these times. Meanwhile, John Brennan is now threatening to sue the President over his security clearance being stripped.

Monday 20th August 2018

DT's position in charge of the administration that he feels is out to get him is looking even more precarious. By tweeting that he thought that John Dean was 'a rat', (John Dean was the chap that brought down Nixon) he's said to be equating Watergate with alleged Russian involvement in the 2016 election.

Tuesday 21st August 2018

Blimey, what a day! After months of tittle tattle politics, Robert Mueller and his team have now started to turn the screw. Both Paul Manafort and Michael Cohen have now been convicted of serious fraud and will likely result in jail terms for both men. What next for the President?

Wednesday 22nd August 2018

With claims that Michael Cohen has put a target on the President's back, DT basically reverts back to tried and tested denial. Manafort's a good man. Nothing to do with Russian collusion. Doesn't involve me. It's all a witch hunt etc. etc.

Thursday 23rd August 2018

As DT goes on the offensive, sort of, Jeff Sessions has actually attacked his boss, sort of, in response to the latest tweet the POTUS. 'While I am Attorney General, the actions of the Department of Justice will not be improperly influenced by political considerations,' he said.

Friday 24th August 2018

The President continues to defend his position by basically

saying, 'Come on then. Impeach me!' His job though could be in jeopardy as Allan Weissenberg, DT's long-time Chief Financial Adviser, has been granted immunity by Federal prosecutors as part of the Michael Cohen case.

Saturday 25th August 2018

DT tries to deflect attention from his issues by sending tweets about supposed 'land grabbing and white farmer genocide' in South Africa. The only problem is no such thing has ever happened. Professor of University at the Western Cape says, 'You get that feeling that we must explain things to the Americans once again.'

Sunday 26th August 2018

With much sadness, the US newscasters announce the passing of John McCain from brain cancer. This plain speaking yet fair man had been a power in the Vietnam war and as a Presidential candidate but some DT followers continually attacked him despite him having the illness and that says a lot about them.

Monday 27th August 2018

In death John McCain has spurned the President by ensuring that he's not invited to the funeral, despite tributes pouring in from senior figures from across the world. Most Republicans failed to criticise DT. Mr McCain will be lying in state for a week.

Tuesday 28th August 2018

So, in mock reverence to his old sparring partner, DT chooses to fly the US flag at the White House *full* mast. A man with the morals of the Ebola virus, he again bad mouths NFL players who continue to kneel during the anthem as a protest against discrimination.

Wednesday 29th August 2018

There's little point listing the officials leaving the White House anymore, but here's another. Don McGahn who is the White House Counsel, is leaving in the autumn. This seems to follow on the back of the promotion of Brett Kavanagh to the Supreme Court. DT says this is nothing to do with said Mr McGahn's chats with Mr Mueller.

Thursday 30th August 2018

The President's approval ratings dip to the lowest of any Presidency; just thirty six percent are saying he's doing a good job. Meanwhile, Bruce Ohr, a senior law maker in the Justice Department, has said that he learnt from British agent Christopher Steel that 'the Russians had DT over a barrel during 2016.'

Friday 31st August 2018

DT was busily backtracking on his opposition to John McCain today by making a speech in Indiana. Sorry, did I say backtracking? I mean butt kicking. He repeated many Nationalist statements about 'respecting the flag, dishonest people, the Democrats held hostage to haters' and all this while Aretha Franklin is put to rest.

SEPTEMBER 2018

Saturday 1st September 2018

Convicted former Trump campaign adviser George Papadopoulos has publicly contradicted Jeff Sessions, the Attorney General, in his sworn testimony to Congress. He claims that both Sessions and DT supported his proposal that the President meet with Vladimir Putin during the 2016 campaign.

Sunday 2nd September 2018

DT has been reminded it's not just Mr Mueller he needs to be worried about. Ongoing investigations into five different business subjects, coupled with a lawsuit brought by two State attorneys into whether the President is in violation of the US Constitution will definitely keep DT on his toes. All he could say in response to the McCain and Aretha Franklin funerals was, 'Make America great again.'

Monday 3rd September 2018

As the President's latest Supreme Court nominee experiences a mini riot due to Democrats and Liberals trying to delay the appointment of Brett Kavanagh, the mid-term election numbers are stacking up against the President. Two months ahead of the vote, disgruntled voters are indicating that they favour a Democrat over a Republican by twelve to fourteen percent.

Tuesday 4th September 2018

According to a fiery new book by legendary reporter Bob Woodward, DT called his Attorney-General Jeff Sessions a traitor and moaned that 'everybody is out to get me.' He also called Mr Sessions mentally unhinged. He was himself called unhinged and an idiot by John Kelly, his Chief of Staff. This is a great book.

Wednesday 5th September 2018

As Ayanna Presley was in Boston yesterday to run for US Congress, DT is getting very twitchy. He still maintains Bob Woodward's book is boring and untrue. The problem is this: POTUS has already created a truth vacuum so anything said by anyone could be accurate, vacuous or even downright false. No-one can tell!

Thursday 6th September 2018

Wow! On top of Mr Woodward's exposé, the seeds of dissent within the White House have blossomed, so much so that DT is crying 'treachery.' One unnamed official is quoted as saying that he 'represents the rise of the Resistance.' This enemy within is describing DT as 'unfit to rule and is a mix of ignorance, ego, pettiness, malignance and recklessness.'

Friday 7th September 2018

At a rally in Montana, DT warns his supporters that it will be their fault 'if I get impeached.' All the while he's making this impassioned speech, a young man is filmed sitting right behind him pulling faces. These facial tweaks seem to suggest a sense of disbelief in the listener. He was subsequently removed.

Saturday 8th September 2018

Barack Obama has unusually made some very public comments about the existing President. He makes the point that DT has 'failed to uphold basic principles of American values while violating a whole host of norms including the Rule of Law, Freedom of the Press and US citizens' rights.'

Sunday 9th September 2018

The double, triple, nay quadruple bluff is clearly now being bandied about. An anonymous news item in the *New York Times* suggests that Mike Pence, the Vice President, is trying to remove DT using the twenty-fifth Amendment which is the inability to discharge the powers of duties of office. Mike Pence has denied this.

Monday 10th September 2018

Bob Woodward says 'I've never seen an instance when the President was so detached from the reality of what's going on.' The latest tweet from DT re. 'Our best GDP unemployment rates in 100 years' has been derided by many as simply untrue. The figures that the President quoted have been seriously tweaked.

Tuesday 11th September 2018

Conspiracy theories linking Brexit and the US election are raising eyebrows over DT's latest message. He has suggested 'there will be violence if the GOP does not win the mid-term elections.' This is much like the rabble rousing from Nigel Farage and others that say the same thing about leaving Europe and the 'will of the people.'

Wednesday 12th September 2018

DT has signed an order today that punishes foreign meddlers in US elections and voting. A little bit late in the day methinks. Meanwhile, with Hurricane Florence on the way to clobber the eastern coast, DT claims credit for the previous storm support but still attacks the Mayor of San Juan.

Thursday 13th September 2018

DT continues with his anti-Puerto Rico rhetoric by claiming that 'not many people died in the PR hurricane. The figures were exaggerated by the Democrats to make me look bad.' The President also helpfully advises citizens that the imminent Storm Florence is 'very, very big and very wet.'

Friday 14th September 2018

Paul Manafort, DT's former campaign manager has indicated he will plead guilty to two counts of conspiracy at his trial. At this stage it isn't known if Mr Manafort will cooperate with Robert Mueller's Special Council investigation into Russian interference in the Presidential election.

Saturday 15th September 2018

Following on from DT's comments re. the Puerto Rico hurricane death toll, Ricardo Rossello has said that he hopes 'you send a message of support to show you stand with the US citizens in Puerto Rico that lost loved ones.' DT responds by saying he's upset by the video still being shown of him throwing towels.

Sunday 16th September 2018
Hurricane Florence having killed fifteen people in North Carolina, has been downgraded to a tropical storm but carries the risk of flooding. DT has declared the area a disaster zone and promises support. Meanwhile, he's once again attacked Robert Mueller again, saying his 'poll numbers are good but could be better if it wasn't for the rigged Russian witch hunt.'

Monday 17th September 2018
Oops! DT's Supreme Court nominee Brett Kavanagh has had sexual assault allegations made against him and this is likely to have an impact on his appointment. The President, of course, has lost his temper although the White House has said they 'wouldn't smear the accuser. They just want to ignore her.'

Tuesday 18th September 2018
DT reignites a trade war with China by setting new tariffs on imports valued at $200 billion. A sliding scale that kicks off at ten percent on Monday twenty-fourth before rising to twenty five percent on the first of January 2019. He's also escalated efforts to interfere with the Russian investigation by releasing interview notes and emails.

Wednesday 19th September 2018
As the President tweets data about the science of atmospherics and meteorology (water is wet, sky is up etc.), the Stormy Daniels exposé looks like a bit of a damp squid with no major scandal except for the main item. Meanwhile, the Polish leader wants the President to build 'Fort Trump in Poland as

a Russia safeguard.'

Thursday 20th September 2018

Blimey, DT must have shares in bricks and mortar as it's reported that he suggested to the Spanish Prime Minister that he build a wall across the Sahara to prevent migrants coming from the Med. Senator Geoff Flake, meanwhile, says that a tweet from Donald Trump Jr re. the Kavanagh accuser is 'sickening.'

Friday 21st September 2018

Following Theresa May's battering yesterday in Salzburg, DT, it's reported is now about to impose tariffs on European vehicles sooner rather than later. Meanwhile, the US Embassy in Battersea, London which DT described as a 'bad deal and in an off location' has been open to the public to great praise.

Saturday 22nd September 2018

So, Brett Kavanagh's accuser has agreed to testify against him in public. The UN Ambassador Nicky Hayley says, 'People shouldn't second-guess what Christine Ford will say.' Meanwhile, the *NBC* News *Wall Street Journal* survey seems to suggest that the GOP will be squashed in 6 weeks at the midterm elections.

Sunday 23rd September 2018

My goodness, here we go! DT, Mr Erratic, is chairing the UN Security Council for the first time. Few people think this will go smoothly. Indeed, the reaction of eighty-four Heads of State, forty-four Heads of Government of the 1983 sovereign states will be very interesting to watch. DT to address the Assembly on Tuesday.

Monday 24th September 2018

Rod Rosenstein, the Deputy Attorney-General, looks as though he's going to have to meet the President to discuss the allegation that he'd suggested 'wearing a wire' in order to gather evidence about the POTUS to invoke the 25th Amendment. Needless to say, there's no telling where that will go. Meanwhile, the Robert Mueller probe may be at risk if Rosenstein goes.

Tuesday 25th September 2018

DT gives his 2018 UN General Assembly speech and receives a chorus of raucous laughter. The mirth from the assembled gathering was a response to his claim that he had 'accomplished almost more than any other administration.' DT also called Iran the world's leading terrorism sponsors and that he turned down a meeting with Tehran.

Wednesday 26th September 2018

On the back of the reports that the Republicans are likely to take a vote of beating at the mid-term elections, DT has now started to accuse the Chinese of interfering. In the meanwhile, the President went again on the attack of Iran at the UN Security Council. He said, 'Patriotism, not Internationalism.'

Thursday 27th September 2018

Scott Law, the US drinks promoter, was going to be working

with the Scots brewer 'BrewDog' but their offer of a free beer to all Trump supporters caused BrewDog to kick them into touch. They said, 'We care about beer and people, not hate.' DT will keep a very wary eye on the Kavanagh/Ford testimony show.

Friday 28th September 2018

The working week ends with high drama in court as it looks like Brett Kavanagh appears to be on the verge of being appointed. The GOP is under tremendous pressure now as the mid-term elections loom. It also transpires that Simon Kukes, a major DT funder, was in Moscow and allegedly boasted that he was 'actively involved in the 2016 election.'

Saturday 29th September 2018

Interesting. A Federal judge has approved a lawsuit alleging that DT's private business is violating the Constitution. 'No-one is above the law,' say the Democrats. Several commentators are saying that the UN laughingstock episode could bounce back. The Brett Kavanagh case is now going to be investigated by the FBI.

Sunday 30th September 2018

While DT speaks of his 'love' for Kim Jong-un, a staffer working for the Democrat candidate Andrew Gillum has been fired after apparently calling for President Trump's execution and wearing a t-shirt with 'Dumbfuckistan' on the front. DT supporters, meanwhile, are saying that Brett Kavanagh's accuser has been paid by the Democrats.

OCTOBER 2018

Monday 1st October 2018

Blimey, the President has secured a massive trade deal with both Canada and Mexico. The settlement revamps the NAFTA and is now being called the US 'Canadian Mexico Agreement.' It was also reported that India is very keen to start negotiations over trade deals, hopefully reducing tariffs to seal the deal.

Tuesday 2nd October 2018

Following yesterday's ups, suddenly it's all dipped down again. It has been reported in the *New York Times* that DT gained millions of dollars using questionable tax strategies. These occurred mainly during the time when he was helping his parents. The POTUS, meanwhile, has started denying visas to unmarried same sex partners of foreign diplomats.

Wednesday 3rd October 2018

DT's sudden but not unexpected verbal attack on Christine Ford re. Brett Kavanagh has been met with disdain by his fellow GOP members who have described his words as simply wrong. It also turns out that it was a financial disclosure by his own sister that led to the *New York Times* report on DT.

Thursday 4th October 2018

A US Judge has blocked DT from ending various protections

that have allowed 300,000 immigrants from four countries to live and work in the US. San Francisco-based Judge Edward Chen granted an injunction stopping the move, saying that 'such a decision would do irreparable harm and hardship.'

Friday 5th October 2018

As DT winds his stumbly, bumbly way up the stairs of Airforce One with what appears to be a piece of toilet paper stuck to his shoe, commentators are asking 'does the President deserve a Nobel Peace Prize?' Meanwhile, a Russian official accused of directing the lawyer who met with DT's election campaign officials in 2016 has been killed in a helicopter crash. The moral? Being a Russian with links to the US may be risky at this time.

Saturday 6th October 2018

Thanks to a Bafta award-winning performance coupled with the capitulation of Messrs Flake and friends, it looks pretty certain that Brett Kavanagh will be appointed to the Supreme Court. It was with some relief that a Nobel Peace Prize for peace has been awarded to anybody but DT and his new pal Kim Jong-un.

Sunday 7th October 2018

DT woke up this morning knowing he was on a roll. Brett Kavanagh was confirmed as a US Supreme Court Judge. He was so happy that he straightaway went on to attack Democrat Senator Elizabeth Warren, referring to her again as 'Pocahontas.' This as she claimed to have Native American Indian ancestry.

Monday 8th October 2018

DT's claim that Melania Trump had done a tremendous job representing the US in Africa, 'like no-one before', has been derided as absurd by *CNN*. In addition, his approval ratings across the country have dropped again. DT's administration meanwhile says, 'If we're (the planet) already doomed, there's no need to worry about climate change.'

Tuesday 9th October 2018

The rewards for supporting the leader can be difficult. Iowa Senator Chuck Grassley, (Rep) has been told that high grade ethanol fuel, which is currently banned by the EPA during the summer months, will be back on the market. Iowa can use this for its corn production for 2019 but at what cost?

Wednesday 10th October 2018

Yesterday Nicky Hayley resigned as the US Ambassador to the UK. This was unforeseen and may have an impact in future UN discussions. However, word on the wire is that she is seen as a sensible Republican member and may well be lined up tactically for the forthcoming mid-term elections as the voice of reason in DT's world.

Thursday 11th October 2018

On a date Mrs Kavanagh is seen uncomfortably supporting her delightful hubby at his Supreme Court ceremony, it transpires that the cost of protecting the President on his UK tour was £18 million, all this on the same day that the Dow Jones Index absolutely tanked. By today, it had lost over eight percent throughout early October due to market fears.

Friday 12th October 2018

DT is for once stunned into silent gawping as bizarre yodeller Kanye West lets rip a stream of foul mouth invective while on a trip to the White House. Meanwhile, Melania is still getting interesting feedback viz a viz her comments suggesting, 'she's the most bullied person on (sic) the world.'

Saturday 13th October 2018

On the day that Trump supporters are touting his 2020 victory, Joe Biden the Democrat is being put forward in some circles as a 2020 candidate. Meanwhile, as DT praises Robert E. Lee in a speech in Ohio, he is unusually quiet when the subject of the alleged murder of a US journalist in Istanbul is raised.

Sunday 14th October 2018

With his cage rattled, DT now says that he will 'get to the bottom of the disappearance of Jamal Khashoggi, the US journalist allegedly killed in the Saudi Embassy in Turkey. The Saudis, however, replied by saying they will 'respond to any threats made by the US with equal action.' The Saudi markets dropped seven percent during these exchanges.

Monday 15th October 2018

At a rally in July, DT said to Elizabeth Warren, 'I'll give you a million dollars if you take a DNA test and it shows you're an Indian.' Mrs Warren did subsequently take the DNA test and it appears to indicate that there was some evidence of Native American Indian ancestry. DT now says, 'I didn't say that to you at all. You better read the email again.'

Tuesday 16th October 2018

As Mitch McConnell, the leader of the House of Representatives announces a $1.5 trillion dollar tax cut, he suggests the national deficit is 'not a Republican problem' but 'Medicare, Social Security and Medicaid (or entitlements as he so lovingly puts it) is.' Melania, meanwhile, attacks Rapper T.I. whose latest video appears to show an apparently fake, naked Donald Trump.

Wednesday 17th October 2018

Assorted US businesses have shown huge profits, hence why suddenly the Dow Jones has seen massive rises this week. Meanwhile, it is suggested in some papers that DT is 'advising Mrs May on the UK's restrictive and unnecessary food standards.' This appears to be opening up the way for US food imports. Oh dear.

Thursday 18th October 2018

DT is hastily planning a meeting with Mike Pompeo following the State meeting with both Saudi Arabia and Turkish diplomats re. the mysterious disappearance of Jamal Khashoggi. In other news, the US is withdrawing from 140-year-old postal treaty that it says lets China ship goods into the US at unfairly low prices.

Friday 19th October 2018

Probably not the time to praise an elected politician who assaults a journalist, but that's what DT just did. Montana Congress member Gregg Gianforte has been charged with assault after he violently attacked a *Guardian* journalist, Ben

Jacobs in 2017 after he asked him a question regarding the Obamacare programme and healthcare policy. DT thinks that Gianforte is 'smart.'

Saturday 20th October 2018

The Saudi Arabians release a bizarre statement saying Jamal Khashoggi was 'involved in a fight in the Saudi Consulate in Istanbul and was killed as a result.' DT says that he accepts this. The recent $100 billion arms deal with the Saudis seems to outweigh the need to carry out any further investigations into the murder of a US citizen.

Sunday 21st October 2018

Never a dull moment with DT. Today he says he intends to end the intermediate range nuclear force treaty that was originally signed by Ronald Reagan and Mikhail Gorbachev. He says, 'Russia has been violating this treaty for years.' The EU have voiced their extreme concerns.

Monday 22nd October 2018

It's clear from DT's comments that he thinks the GOP may be in for a panning at the up-and-coming mid-term elections in November. He still blusters in public but privately he's already planning to point the finger at others. His principal target will be the media and it remains to be seen if journalists will pay a price.

Tuesday 23rd October 2018

DT declares that if no further action is taken by the Mexican authorities, the Hondurans heading for the border will be dealt with by the US Border Force. He tweets that, 'This is a national emergency and I will cut cash support to Mexico, Honduras and Ecuador.' These are tense times down Mexico-way.

Wednesday 24th October 2018

Former White House Communications Director Anthony Scaramucci says, 'The President is a liar and should probably dial down the lying.' All this on the day that suspected IEDs have been sent and intercepted to both Hilary Clinton and Barack Obama. And contrary to yesterday's point, DT has said he has no plan if migrants arrive from Mexico.

Thursday 25th October 2018

Well, well, seven other prominent folks including those mentioned yesterday have now been sent pipe bombs through the post. DT says in a speech that, 'no civilised nation should tolerate violent threats' and then promptly blamed the Press for their fake news. One of the devices was sent to Robert De Niro. Oh, taxi driver, where art thou?

Friday 26th October 2018

Wow! Very swift action as Florida Police arrest Cesar Sayoc on suspicion of sending pipe bombs to a group of people. His white van is covered in Trump stickers and inside right-wing pamphlets. DT now says 'these terrorising acts are despicable and have no place in our country.' The mid-terms are now days away.

Saturday 27th October 2018

DT responds to the terrible Synagogue attack in Pittsburgh that cost the lives of eleven by saying cryptically, 'If he chooses to destroy others, I will seek to destroy him.' The President had said that the massacre was terrible to a rally in Illinois. He also added, 'they should have been armed.'

Sunday 28th October 2018

On the day the *Observer* describes DT's tweets and messages as 'vile rhetoric,' other reports suggest he could lose up to nine of his cabinet members over the coming weeks. There are now attacks on him by members of the acting fraternity like Jim Carey and this might spur on the mid-term voters, but which way?

Monday 29th October 2018

Still desperate to deflect attention, DT accuses the media of 'stoking great anger in the US' and once again says that the media is, 'the true enemy of the people.' The people of Pittsburgh, however, have made their viewpoint very clear. 'He (DT) is not welcome here' they say stressing that he should distance himself from white nationalists.

Tuesday 30th October 2018

DT steps the rhetoric on hard-line immigration restrictions by suggesting he can end 'birth right citizenship.' In effect, this would end the right of citizenship being taken by children born to non-citizens and unauthorised immigrants born on US soil. Any attempt to do this, however, would likely be seen as an attack on the Constitution.

Wednesday 31st October 2018

Sure enough, DT is met with large protests as he pays his condolences at the synagogue in Pittsburgh. Still, that doesn't seem to have dulled his fervour, certainly as far as his continuing attacks on the Media are concerned. He says that the mail bomb story is being dreamed up by his critics. The Republicans are still considering his birth right citizenship threat.

NOVEMBER 2018

Thursday 1st November 2018

DT has gone on the offensive as even he is very much aware of the mid-term kickback. His tweets are focusing on deeply divisive anti-immigration messages, pretty much it seems, trying to frighten voters. His specific threat is that the 'Democrats will let anyone in including cop killers.'

Friday 2nd November 2018

The Trump administration has announced that it's going to reinstate all the sanctions on Iran removed under the 2015 deal arranged by the previous President. Meanwhile, the *Washington Post* has reported that DT has told 6,420 lies and misleading statements as President. This number has risen sharply recently, perhaps linked to the forthcoming mid-term election.

Saturday 3rd November 2018

So, the mid-terms are looming and DT is already laying out the reasons on why the Republicans have lost. Of course, if DT manages to retain Republican control, he'll be cock-a-hoop. Meanwhile, he still continues to push the Mexican 'invaders' scene which may in the short term have a Brexit-type effect on voters.

Sunday 4th November 2018

It's reported in several papers that quite a few previous DT voters are disillusioned over the lack of jobs for blue collar workers. Meanwhile, Obama is rallying for Democrat voters by mocking DT's decision to send 15,000 troops to the Mexican border, calling it a political stunt. 'I believe in fact-based campaigns' he said.

Monday 5th November 2018

As Iran says it will defy any imposed sanctions by the US, *Facebook*, Fox and *NBC* have decided to pull a DT election ad which seemingly suggests the Democrats allow killers to roam the nation. Meanwhile, the singer Rhianna has told DT to stop playing her music at his rallies and novelist Don DeLillo says, 'I'm not sure this country is recoverable.'

Tuesday 6th November 2018

So, finally the mid-term elections are here and the voters are out. The money markets are holding their collective breaths; they think a Republican win, money up; a Democrat win in both houses, money down and everything else, even stevens. The early signs are that young voters are out in force, up by seven percent on previous elections in Tennessee with Georgia also showing big numbers of low-income black voters out despite the rain.

Wednesday 7th November 2018

So, the votes have been counted and sure enough, DT has lost the House of Representatives. There have been plenty of firsts in this election. There's been success for a gay man, a native American and a Muslim woman amongst many other changes. DT is partially happy though as the Republicans increased their strength in the Senate which gives him a slight upper hand.

Thursday 8th November 2018

DT gives a *CNN* reporter a hard time at the post mid-term election press conference, once again calling him 'the enemy of the people.' The POTUS reckons he will win any confrontation with the Democrats relating to the Russia investigation. And Jeff Sessions has 'resigned' (he says he was pushed) as Attorney General.

Friday 9th November 2018

A Federal Judge has blocked the controversial Keystone XL pipeline which is designed to link Canadian and Texas refineries. The Judge, Brian Morris from Montana, said the State Department had ignored crucial issues of climate change and so by doing, had gone against law which 'requires reasoned explanation for a decision.'

Saturday 10th November 2018

Following the devastating fires in California, DT lends his usual erudite and cultured opinion to the debate, tweeting that 'the reason these fires have been so severe is due to the mismanagement of the Northern California forests.' On this he's also threatened to withhold Federal funds as a result which doesn't seem to be very helpful.

Sunday 11th November 2018

As Emmanuel Macron repeated his warnings about the rise of Nationalism and the dangers to peace across the globe, DT finally attended a commemorative ceremony for the 100 years anniversary of the end of the First World War. He said, 'Each of these marble crosses and stars of David mark the life of an American warrior who gave everything.'

Monday 12th November 2018

Usual antics from Donald following the mid-term results which did create something of a stir. The POTUS has repeated baseless claims that voter fraud took place in Florida, this as ballot papers are recounted. Meanwhile, the Democrats have confirmed they will be investigating DT a) to see if he punished the Media and b) regarding his gains at the mid-terms.

Tuesday 13th November 2018

In what must be a US first, *CNN* are suing the President and his top White House aides for barring their White House reporter, Jim Acosta. The lawsuit alleges that both the reporter and the TV company have had their first and fifth Amendment rights violated. DT, meanwhile, mocks France by tweeting 'they learnt German before the US came and saved them.'

Wednesday 14th November 2018

It's Ladies Day today at the White House, well Melania Day anyway. Out of no-where, the First Lady issues a statement saying that Mira Ricardel, Deputy National Security Adviser, with whom she allegedly clashed, was 'no longer deserving of the honour of serving in this White House.'

Thursday 15th November 2018

On the day the White House announces the second North Korea US Summit will take place, the US is still coming to terms with the dreadful fires in California. The death toll is at sixty-eight with hundreds still missing. The mid-term Florida recount meanwhile, is approaching its conclusion amidst continued claims by DT of voter fraud.

Friday 16th November 2018

US Judge Timothy Kelly who was appointed by Donald Trump, granted *CNN* a request to restore the Press pass for James Acosta. This will of course give the aggrieved journalist permission to access the White House grounds to cover events and Press conferences. He did not, however, state whether there had been a violation.

Saturday 17th November 2018

Pictures are currently doing the rounds of the President and his wife holding hands. However, it does look worryingly like Melania is petrified. To be fair, DT looks like he's hanging on for grim death. As the fatalities rise in California, now up to eighty with 1,000 people still listed as missing, DT says he will visit the site.

Sunday 18th November 2018

DT visits California to offer his support and that of the Federal Government. Sadly, amidst the hyperbole, the POTUS again suggests the fires are 'a result of poor forestry management.' How this helps the grieving process for those who have lost loved ones no-one knows. One person whose children had lost their house said, 'the President can kiss my red arse.'

Monday 19th November 2018

Ahh, DT not content with upsetting a grieving State, he now arrives in the devastation of the town of Paradise and in front of the world's media, calls it 'Pleasure.' Some comment that this may be synonym abstraction. He also made a suggestion discussed allegedly with the Finnish President (who did not recall this comment) that Californians should 'rake the floor like they do in Finland.'

Tuesday 20th November 2018

Two weeks after the mid-term elections and GOP celebrations 'were a complete victory,' said DT. It now seems that with all of the results in, the US is much more Democrat blue than before, certainly in California. Four counties fell from the Republicans for the first time in many years. There were wins in New Jersey, Washington, Georgia and Maine for the Democrats.

Wednesday 21st November 2018

News reports today suggest that at one time, DT was going to 'set the Feds' on Hilary Clinton and others with a view to holding a very public trial. My take on this is that it's baloney and the POTUS is a) shoring up his rapidly diminishing tough guy stance and b) deflecting attention from himself regarding investigations.

Thursday 22nd November 2018

Despite the US coming together to celebrate Thanksgiving, DT maintained his attacks on Judges, blaming them for all the 'bedlam, chaos, injury and death.' This followed on from the comments made by a San Francisco Judge who said, 'Whatever the President's authority, he may not rewrite the Immigration Laws imposing a condition that Congress has forbidden.'

Friday 23rd November 2018

Apparently, DT is so concerned about being sued whilst President, attempted to persuade a Judge that he and his family were exempt from this. A New York Judge, however, has said that any allegations raised that 'do not involve any action taken by Mr Trump and any subsequent actions' would not affect his duties as President. In other words, DT, you can be sued while you are President.

Saturday 24th November 2018

The New York State Attorney General has been given the all-clear to proceed with the lawsuit against DT and his three eldest children. Justice Saliann Scarpulla ruled that a sitting President can face a civil lawsuit, 'for actions not taken in his official capacity.' Second time this has happened in as many days.

Sunday 25th November 2018

It's been alleged by the Democrats and others that DT 'lied' when he chose to say that the 'CIA had no evidence' that the Saudi Prince bin Salman ordered the murder of Jamal

Khashoggi in Turkey. The problem with this is that the CIA briefed a number of people saying that they thought the opposite and they had high confidence of complicity re. the Saudi Prince.

Monday 26th November 2018

US border troops fired rubber bullets and tear gas at migrants attempting to cross the border between Mexico and San Diego. DT tweeted 'Move the migrants back to where they come from' and he also said to Mexican officials 'They are not coming into the USA and we will close the border permanently if you don't stop them.'

Tuesday 27th November 2018

Poor old Theresa May. Just as she commends the Brexit bill to the House as the only deal, DT puts in his size twelves. He said, 'Well it's a good deal for the EU but it probably means the UK will not be able to trade with the US', although Mrs May thinks otherwise and is confident of a deal.

Wednesday 28th November 2018

It was again reported that DT has told Robert Mueller that he had 'no knowledge' of the *Wikileaks* i.e., Hilary Clinton's email story of the alleged meeting at Trump Tower between Donald Trump Jr and a Russian lawyer. All this now taking on a whole new and serious flavour as Mr Mueller prepares his final report.

Thursday 29th November 2018

Michael Cohen, DT's former lawyer, appeared again in court

to plead guilty to charges that he'd made four statements to Congress about his efforts to secure a Trump Tower deal in Moscow during the 2016 campaign. This news is dangerous for the President as Robert Mueller closes his case.

Friday 30th November 2018

DT celebrates a bit of good news today with the signing of the new NAFTA with leaders of both Mexico and Canada governments. The only hiccup may be getting the whole process through Congress, bearing in mind the House of Representatives is now controlled by the newly elected Democrats.

DECEMBER 2018

Saturday 1st December 2018

DT along with other ex-US Presidents have led tributes to George Bush Sr who sadly passed away at the age of ninety-four. Meanwhile, Michael Cohen has claimed that he was in 'regular contact' with the Trump legal team whilst in the middle of crafting full statements to the US Congress.

Sunday 2nd December 2018

So far, the second time in a week DT pulls another trade rabbit out of the hat by shaking hands with the Chinese President saying that the US will postpone tariffs on Chinese imports. The Chinese in turn say they will purchase more US goods. DT meanwhile is filmed walking away from the Argentinian President leaving him standing alone in the middle of the G20 stage.

Monday 3rd December 2018

The last month of 2018 is underway and the spectre of the Robert Mueller investigation looms larger over the shoulders of the President. The money markets though are jumping for joy over the decision to delay any tariffs with China. Meetings between DT and the Democrat leaders are cancelled so it looks like another shut-down is on the cards.

Tuesday 4th December 2018

First hints that Robert Mueller is about to reveal the findings of the investigation are filtering out of his office. Reporters are openly making direct comments about cracks in the Trump edifice. Taking into account the lawsuit alleging Constitutional violations and Michael Cohen's situation; how soon, how soon?

Wednesday 5th December 2018

A video emerges of DT signing the NAFTA Agreement. However, the smirks and titters in the background by Mr Trudeau amongst others, illustrated their sudden realisation that the President has signed the document in the wrong place. Roger Stone, meanwhile, claims the 5th Amendment when asked for a dossier of evidence for the Mueller investigation.

Thursday 6th December 2018

So, the great and good assemble for the George Bush Sr funeral with one serving President and two previous incumbents amongst the attendees. All is reasonably civilised, as you'd expect until DT enters the service. At this point everyone in the front row hurriedly scans the Order of Service like commuters reading a newspaper on the Tube during rush hour.

Friday 7th December 2018

It's pick n' mix time again for DT as he makes his decisions about the next Attorney General and UN Ambassador. His choice of Attorney General held the post from 1991 to 1993 so he has form. Heather Nauert who DT is considering for the UN post has absolutely no experience in this field whatsoever. She was, however, a *Fox News* anchor.

Saturday 8th December 2018

Wow! A real change in impetus in the investigation has court filings from Robert Mueller produce the most direct evidence yet linking DT to criminal conduct. This evidence caused DT to go bonkers on *Twitter* as is his usual response, while some Democrats are now openly talking about impeachment proceedings.

Sunday 9th December 2018

CNN reports that although the ever-wary DT resorts to his usual distraction and denial tactics, the threat of a Robert Mueller inspired attack (maybe prosecution, maybe impeachment) prompted him to say, 'Everything they find shows there's no collusion whatsoever.' This is the alternate reality we all live in now.

Monday 10th December 2018

With uncertain times on the horizon, Nick Ayers, who is currently a Mike Pence aide, has declined an offer to be Chief of Staff to DT. Parts of the Mueller report are being leaked and several other reports are saying there is a very real possibility of DT 'doing jail time.'

Tuesday 11th December 2018

DT swats aside any comments about cash paid to his' lady friends' prior and during the 2016 campaign, by simply referring to it as his 'private business.' Meanwhile, he's still desperately searching for someone, anyone, mug enough to be Chief of Staff.

Wednesday 12th December 2018

So, Michael Cohen has been sentenced to three years jail for a smorgasbord of offences. He claims that blind loyalty to the President caused him to behave this way. The lawyer acting for Stormy Daniels says, 'Today Cohen, tomorrow it's Donald Trump.'

Thursday 13th December 2018

DT is pushed very hard to respond to claims that he prompted Mr Cohen to act illegally. The President (still) responds by simply repeating 'No.' One irony that hasn't been lost on the *Twitterati* is a message sent by Mr Cohen in 2016 saying 'Hilary Clinton jail time.' Very ironic.

Friday 14th December 2018

Even the news here in New Zealand is starting to question whether DT is about to be arrested. However, US commentators are questioning the illegality of DT's actions or lack of collusion. They're also saying anything the President may or may not have done is 'not technically a crime' and Robert Mueller must not 'look for sin.'

Saturday 15th December 2018

Just a few hours before DT's imminent announcement about his new Chief of Staff appointment, the appointee decided to withdraw. Not a surprise anymore. DT, meanwhile, goes into meltdown again on *Twitter* re. Michael Cohen and suspected Presidential wrong-doing.

Sunday 16th December 2018

And another one hops off the Good Ship Trump. Interim Secretary Ryan Zinke has resigned following a series of scandals. A Texan High Court has deemed Obamacare as unconstitutional, seemingly because twenty-six other States weren't prepared to go with it.

Monday 17th December 2018

So, Rudy 'Chatterbox' Giuliani now says that DT had spoken with Michael Cohen about a Trump Tower in Moscow as late as November 2016 which is significantly later than the January 2016 date note by the President. The Democrats have jumped on the GOP-led Obamacare case saying 'this is going to be big in the 2020 election.'

Tuesday 18th December 2018

Data released today by the US Homeland Security suggests that the Russians sponsored influencing of the 2016 POTUS election went much further than *Facebook* and *Twitter*. It appears that YouTube, *Instagram* and a whole raft of social media sites were chosen.

Wednesday 19th December 2018

The troubled Trump Foundation charity is being closed down amid allegations that DT and his kids misused funds. In the meantime, Michael Flynn, DT's ex-security adviser, has seen his sentencing postponed until 2019. This has not pleased anti-Trump groups.

Thursday 20th December 2018

DT causes a stir in the Republican Party ordering the withdrawal of all US troops from Syria, stating that the country has 'been freed from ISIS and further threats.' His GOP team disagree and are concerned about the power shift in that country.

Friday 21st December 2018

On Wednesday DT states that he would sign the Finance Bill today thereby preventing the threatened government shut-down. So, why are we then surprised that he's changed his mind at the last minute? He says he will *not* now sign all the while the Democrats ignore his need for a wall across the southern border.

Saturday 22nd December 2018

After yesterday's stir, DT is even more put out by Jim Mattis resigning as Defence Chief. Not surprising really. He does, however, cheer himself up by tweeting that the 'Democrats now own the government shut-down' because the Democrat-led Senate won't pass his wall bill.

Sunday 23rd December 2018

And yet another expert in defence and Middle East conflict decides to accelerate his resignation, such that he won't be the guy to withdraw troops from Syria. DT belittled Brett McGurk's decision as a 'nothing' event adding he was an 'Obama leftover.'

Monday 24th December 2018

Jim Mattis's resignation-come-declaration of early retirement has been accelerated by DT, formerly sacking him. Typical foot-stamping approach from the POTUS and one which is increasingly more likely as he (amazingly!) heads into his third year in charge of the USA.

Tuesday 25th December 2018

DT tweets that 'I'm all alone in the White House waiting for the Democrats to agree to my wall.' A third of the government's departments are now shut down for the foreseeable future and the money markets have dropped like a stone. This is indeed a strange time in the US.

Wednesday 26th December 2018

Still no sign of a shift of position from DT or the Democrats so the shut-down continues apace. As Federal government funds and the Dow Jones continue to dive rapidly with stocks at their worst position for several years. Who will blink first?

Thursday 27th December 2018

When he can surprise, he will. The President and Melania have travelled to Iraq to see the troops posted there. The Dow Jones index, meanwhile, shoots up today, probably because DT tweeted this week that 'now is a good time to buy shares,' principally I suppose because several recent decisions made under his leadership have sent stocks down.

Friday 28th December 2018

While DT signs troops' caps in Iraq, he decides to tweet a

video of himself, naturally, which appears to show the location of US Special Ops teams like Seals. Oops. The POTUS also makes a bizarre claim that he's the only person to 'increase service personnel salaries.'

Saturday 29th December 2018

With his back to the non-existent wall, DT storms on *Twitter* that 'unless I get money for the wall, I will close the border with Mexico.' A news reporter also calls DT's claims of increasing soldiers' salaries for the first time in years as an 'outright lie.'

Sunday 30th December 2018

As a second child dies whilst in custody on the border between Mexico and the US, DT indicates that these deaths are 'the fault of the Democrats with their immigration policy, leaving immigrants thinking they can travel for miles and enter the US without consequences.' Others may think differently.

Monday 31st December 2018

DT ends the year by arranging a pay freeze for all Federal staff. This comes on the back of a current shut-down which has left hundreds of thousands of workers on holiday or working unpaid. Bye-bye Miss American Pie!

Section Intro: 2019 - Year 3

- Newspapers
- Nominations
- Name Calling
- No Man's Land

‘Halfway through the Trump Presidency’ are words I never thought I'd write.

JANUARY 2019

Tuesday 1st January 2019

The President opens the year by saying 'if Obama can have a ten-foot wall around his house for security, why can't I have my wall?' All enormous fun except it's not true Obama doesn't have a ten-foot wall round his house. He's also attacked a retired General for calling him 'immoral.' He says of General Stanley McChrystal, 'He was fired like a dog by Obama.'

Wednesday 2nd January 2019

Two of the President's many GOP critics, Bob Corker and Jeff Flake are leaving the White House very soon on retirement. Who now will take their place and be brave enough to criticise the President? Journalists, meanwhile, are trying to decipher and decode DT's New Year upper case tweets.

Thursday 3rd January 2019

Formal Presidential candidate Mitt Romney has said that he doesn't think DT is 'fit to be President' and 'doesn't wear the mantle.' DT responded in usual fashion by saying, 'He lost to Obama and I won big.'

Friday 4th January 2019

As the shut-down heads into the third week DT is starting to lose any advantage he may have had. Despite his New Year bullying messages to Democrats, they are unmoved and as

Nancy Pelosi takes up the role as House Speaker, things look to get worse for him.

Saturday 5th January 2019

Commentators state that DT will make immigration and the border wall the centre piece of the 2020 election campaign. In the meantime, he also says he may declare 'a national emergency' over the wall issue, bypassing Congress. He says, 'I may do it. We can build a wall very quickly.'

Sunday 6th January 2019

247 of DT's appointees have had their draft pick nominations kicked into touch by the now very strong Democrats. DT still has the upper hand but with 800,000 US citizens rapidly running out of money and patience, he may not have it for much longer.

Monday 7th January 2019

Looks like Donald Trump Jr and Roger Stone may be beginning a walk on a short plank as the Democrats are preparing to hand over evidence to the Robert Mueller investigation. The simple fact is they could be charged with perjury if there's evidence they lied to Congress.

Tuesday 8th January 2019

DT is demanding, and getting, TV airtime to persuade US citizens that he isn't off his trolley in trying to get funding for his wall. As 800,000 citizens try to eat and survive on no money, the Democrats demand equal airtime to respond to his claims.

Wednesday 9th January 2019

Not that it means much but after DT's earlier blustering, but it now appears that he won't be declaring a national emergency over the wall after all. He does, however, make serious claims about 'insurgence and terrorists crossing the border' and warns of the threat of 'beheadings'.

Thursday 10th January 2019

Hey ho, another busy day in DT's 'brain bone' (courtesy of Cletus of the Simpsons). He walks out of a meeting with Chuck Schumer and Nancy Pelosi, calling it a 'total waste of time' adding 'bye bye' as he leaves the building.

Friday 11th January 2019

And so, it continues. Day 20 of the White House shut-down and immovable objects etc. DT rages about *probably* declaring a national emergency while he now denies he said Mexico would pay dearly for the wall. Robert Mueller's report is in the last stages of being written and published, as the Russian collusion case gets stronger.

Saturday 12th January 2019

Yesterday was pay day for many US Federal workers but the shut-down is now beginning to pinch. DT says he has overwhelming support from the people but when you can't feed your family, something must give. Nancy Pelosi doesn't appear to be the one to fold so it will now depend on the GOP Democrat influencers.

Sunday 13th January 2019

As Texas Democrat Julian Castro says he has thrown his hat into the ring to run for President in 2020. DT goes barmy on *Twitter* and vents his fury over a *New York Times* headline that the FBI were looking into whether he's working as a Russian asset. Referring as he often does to the 'failing times', he made several baseless claims into the FBI Clinton investigations.

Monday 14th January 2019

Very disturbing news from various sources that the President ensured that all reports and transcript notes of his meetings with Vladimir Putin were withheld from any files. No President has ever done this and US security commentators suggest this is not only unusual but very serious.

Tuesday 15th January 2019

When questioned again about whether he works for the Russians, DT says 'No' and he 'hasn't been asked a more insulting question.' He calls the FBI 'scoundrels' while the US Federal government is no longer functioning. Steve King meanwhile, a Republican, is kicked off house committees for saying 'When did 'White Supremacist' become an unacceptable term?'

Wednesday 16th January 2019

As the Democrats turn down an invitation to discuss the shut-down, pictures of DT and his generous fast-food table for NFL players and guests at a White House function have been circulating round the globe. Not a very great advert for the President, a man so keen to please, he fills footballers up with junk food.

Thursday 17th January 2019

Whatever happens to DT, his tax changes are already having an effect. The IRS have now indicated they will waive penalties for those that withheld too little of their tax for 2017.

Friday 18th January 2019

On and on. Michael Cohen admits that he paid the polling firm 'Red Finch' to manipulate and bias the figures during the 2016 campaign. He says, 'I did this at the direction of and for the sole benefit of the President. I truly regret my blind loyalty to a man who doesn't deserve it.'

Saturday 19th January 2019

Republicans and Democrats are now saying that if DT told Cohen to lie to Congress, impeachment is highly likely. The President says of Michael Cohen, 'he's a liar and just wants to get his sentence reduced.' DT, meanwhile, has arranged another meeting with Kim Jong-un at a place yet to be arranged.

Sunday 20th January 2019

DT tries to pull a fast one on the nation and the Democrats by suggesting a compromise to the shut-down. He says he'll make 'allowances for the children of immigrants if I get $5.7 billion for a security fence or wall.' Nancy Pelosi says, 'he is just wrong.'

Monday 21st January 2019

As young students in Frankfort, Kentucky wearing 'Make America Great Again' caps mock a Native American elder,

DT rules out any form of concession or amnesty for 'dreamers. The shut-down, meanwhile, continues and both parties are gearing up for Constitutional battle royal.

Tuesday 22nd January 2019

DT honoured Martin Luther King with his presence at his final resting place today, albeit only for a couple of minutes. How Martin Luther King would have reacted to this President on Day 31 of the shut-down we can only guess. 'We're all created equal by God' he once said. 'Some more equal than others' as George Orwell would have added.

Wednesday 23rd January 2019

People wondering why Sarah Huckabee isn't doing so many press briefings have had their question answered. DT told her to stop saying that she was 'being treated rudely' in the White House and he told her 'Not to bother as the word gets out anyway.'

Thursday 24th January 2019

Nancy Pelosi has got her way in blocking DT from making the Annual State of the Union speech. All this as DT is accused of threatening Michael Cohen by Michael Cohen himself.

Friday 25th January 2019

DT's approval rating has hit an all-time low due mainly to the shut-down and this trend will most likely continue as news has been announced that Michael Cohen must now formally respond to subpoenas from the Senate. What questions? What answers?

Saturday 26th January 2019

Well, here's an answer. DT has backed down and agreed to reopen Government for three weeks so that border security discussions can take place. The sort of upbeat timing may be to do with the fact that Roger Stone has been arrested as part of the Mueller investigations.

Sunday 27th January 2019

As Conservatives continue to press for the wall across the US, the Robert Mueller investigation gathers even more pace. He may well have evidence of collusion and corruption, but he is careful to say that once he shows his hand, he must win. DT and Rudy Giuliani, however, simply say 'No collusion.'

Monday 28th January 2019

The Attorney General announces that the Mueller investigation report is imminent and Nancy Pelosi formally asks DT to deliver the State of the Union speech on February fifth, delayed of course by the shut-down.

Tuesday 29th January 2019

Newspaper reports are suggesting that a lot of Americans will not vote for DT at the 2020 election although, given the abstract nature of US politics, this cannot be taken as a given. DT is also talking about 'vaccines and the link to autism.'

Wednesday 30th January 2019

DT is unhappy once again with his spy chiefs after they contradict him on his claim about Iran and ISIS. He says they, 'should go back to school' and 'they are passive and naïve.' He also warns that US citizens 'should not visit Venezuela.'

Thursday 31st January 2019

As Chris Cuomo from *CNN* calls DT a national security threat, Sarah Sanders states that 'God wanted Donald Trump to become President.' Presumably one supposes to bring about the death of small children on hot borders.

FEBRUARY 2019

Friday 1st February 2019

The US finally loses patience with Russia and withdraws from the nuclear weapons treaty with them claiming that 'to this day, the Russians are in breach of it.' There are still six months, however, to save the Treaty.

Saturday 2nd February 2019

Senator Ralph Northam, Virginia, has been seen in a Yearbook of 1984 for the EV Medical School in full Ku Klux Klan outfit accompanied by a blacked-up colleague. In a bid to be granted asylum in the US Natalia Rybka a sex worker from Belarus claims that she's handed information re. US involvement with Russia, to a Russian billionaire.

Sunday 3rd February 2019

DT has appointed his former doctor to be Chief Medical Adviser. This ordinarily wouldn't be an issue; however, Ronny Jackson is currently under investigation for 'extreme drunkenness, over-prescribing drugs and creating a hostile work environment.' Sounds like a perfect guy.

Monday 4th February 2019

DT is claiming poverty saying that he has lost money running the country as President. While in the process of becoming poorer, the country has to wait with bated breath for his unification, or a version of it, when he delivers the

State of the Union speech. Democrats on standby.

Tuesday 5th February 2019

CNN reports that Federal prosecutors have requested interviews with the executives at DT's organisation. Meanwhile, rumours are in full swing that DT's tax returns may well be made public which is panicking a number of Republicans with similar documents.

Wednesday 6th February 2019

As expected, the State of the Union speech was a bizarre mix of pernicious patriotism, selfless references and aggrandising, coupled with security rhetoric. DT referred to the Mueller investigation simply as 'partisan' and investigations that were 'ridiculous' since the US is 'the hottest economy in the world.'

Thursday 7th February 2019

DT back on super form as he declares at the morning prayer session that one of the greatest achievements of the United States has been the 'abolition of civil rights.' Huh?

Friday 8th February 2019

DT's relationship with the *National Enquirer* and his dislike of all things Jeff Bezos has come to the fore with the *National Enquirer* story about Jeff Bezos's alleged affair. JB claims this attack is due directly to his ownership of the *Washington Post* and their recent editorials.

Saturday 9th February 2019

Clearly the build-up to the 2020 election is under way. DT claims 'the Democrats cannot legitimately win the 2020.' This was in response to the grilling that his Acting Attorney General received from the House Judiciary Committee.

Sunday 10th February 2019

While at least one commentator queries whether the State of the Union speech was delivered by a Trump robot, DT once again finds his comments somewhat diluted by the effective work of Democrat-controlled House of Representatives.

Monday 11th February 2019

As DT claims he works more hours than any other President, Donald Trump Jr calls one of his dad's tweets 'savage', referring to DT Snr's dislike of Elizabeth Warren who may or may not be of Native American Indian blood.

Tuesday 12th February 2019

A breakthrough of sorts regarding DT's request for loads of dollars to build the wall, as the Democrats and the GOP come to an agreement to fund a fifty-five-mile section of fencing costing $1.4 billion, about a fifth of the amount needed. All this would suggest that a further Federal shutdown can be avoided.

Wednesday 13th February 2019

DT calls for Ilhan Omar to resign and she responds by saying, 'he has peddled hate his entire life.' Meanwhile, the President is being reported as not happy with the tentative deal being put to him by Democrats, but is however intending to sign the deal, avoiding a shut-down.

Thursday 14th February 2019

DT goes on the front attack foot again by calling out Andrew McCabe, former Acting FBI Chief, saying, 'This poor little angel is a part of the Hilary Clinton scandal and Hope's (Hicks) Russian investigation.'

Friday 15th February 2019

So, despite the mini truths, the President now says he will declare a national emergency regarding his nightmare belief of immigrant hoards crossing the border with Mexico. What this means is that the next time the nation's finances are discussed, the shut-down will happen again unless he gets the rest of his money.

Saturday 16th February 2019

DT indeed declares a national emergency calling on all sides to recognise the great security risk. He also suggests that ISIS volunteers be accepted back by their respective nations to go on trial, 'The US is one mile away from destroying them.' Meanwhile, Heather Navert, DT's UN Ambassador pick, has withdrawn from selection citing family reasons.

Sunday 17th February 2019

Donald continues to rage about ISIS and the European Court, 'If these countries don't take ISIS back and put them on trial, I'll let them all go,' he says. This is bizarre logic. And all this just as Adam Schiff, Republican, says, 'There is evidence in plain sight of Trump collusion with Russia.'

Monday 18th February 2019

The President this morning absolutely spitting feathers after the *Saturday Night Live* broadcast featuring Alec Baldwin. The initial spat has escalated with the POTUS threatening retribution and Alec Baldwin is left asking whether DT's comments could be 'a threat to my safety.'

Tuesday 19th February 2019

With DT's national emergency declaration comes the inevitable counter from eighteen States, including California. The President immediately responds by demanding a return of nearly $3 million set aside for the Californian West Coast bullet train project.

Wednesday 20th February 2019

Jeffrey Rosen, the Deputy Transportation Secretary, appears to have received a bit of a jump in political status, right up to Deputy Attorney General. Meanwhile, it looks like the end may be nigh for Don Coates, the Director of National Intelligence, following, 'disagreements' with DT. Whoops!

Thursday 21st February 2019

The President stays very silent as news of a potential plot to kill some Democrat politicians and journalists comes to light. This at a time when he quickly takes to *Twitter* to support those backing him.

Friday 22nd February 2019

The victory of the Democrats at last November in taking control of the House of Representatives appears to be very important as they seek to terminate DT's emergency declaration. The POTUS, meanwhile, demands a speedy roll-out of '6G technology' which is a little bit difficult since it doesn't actually exist.

Saturday 23rd February 2019

As DT announces Kelly Knight Craft as his UN Ambassador pick, he warns that the situation between India and Pakistan is looking very dangerous. No doubt he will want to have some hand in any peace process. Michael Cohen, meanwhile, says, 'There are irregularities at the Trump organisation.'

Sunday 24th February 2019

Pictures of Kim Jong-un grinning broadly as he hops on a train to Vietnam in preparation for the second meeting with DT. Commentators wonder who will come out on top and whether anything can actually be gained from having two planet-sized egos in the same room.

Monday 25th February 2019

As the Oscars finish, DT claims big news is about to be announced as a result of the more recent US-Chinese tariff discussions. Spike Lee's comments regarding racism and Native American Indian genocide prompted the DT to say, 'This is doing a racist hit on your President.'

Tuesday 26th February 2019

Reports suggest Michael Cohen will call out DT at a public hearing as a 'racist, cheat and conman.' He will also say that the POTUS knew of Roger Stone's *Wikileaks* contact re. the Hilary Clinton tapes during the 2016 Presidential campaign which may be backed up by tape recordings.

Wednesday 27th February 2019

As DT and his bestie, Kim Jong-un, meet over various food stuffs, Michael Cohen, true to his word, does the dirty on his former boss accusing him of all sorts of stuff. Whether the US Electorate pays any real attention to this remains to be seen.

Thursday 28th February 2019

Well, that didn't go down well! The North Korean leader, who says his country was misunderstood and Mr Sparkle himself, finished the talks earlier than planned, sparking all sorts of rumours.

MARCH 2019

Friday 1st March 2019

DT does what DT does best and walks away from the North Korean US talks without flash bulbs and signed documents. 'They wanted all the US sanctions lifted in their entirety and we couldn't do that. Sometimes you have to walk and this was one of those times.'

Saturday 2nd March 2019

The *Guardian* reports today that the US is now headed up by someone 'pathologically incapable of admitting defeat.' These words have a chilling truth and don't bode well for the 2020 election. Whatever the result, Trump reverberations will ripple on.

Sunday 3rd March 2019

The President going totally stone pure bonkers today with an attack on Robert Mueller's case using the politically astute phrase that they were 'wrong people in a couple of positions and they try to take you out with this bullshit.' This two-hour attack was his longest speech by far.

Monday 4th March 2019

As DT tries to figure out how to fend off the Democrats' formal request for sixty associates' documents, he's also facing a potential revolt from Senate Republicans over his decision to declare a national emergency regarding the wall. It never rains but it pours for this President.

Tuesday 5th March 2019

School records about DT were allegedly secretly hidden according to the *Washington Post.* Jeffrey Coverdale the Superintendent of the private school, the New York Military Academy, says he was, 'accosted' by a prominent wealthy person who was one of Mr Trump's friends.

Wednesday 6th March 2019

There's a sea change a-coming it. It appears Joe Biden already may be a front runner in the Democratic 2020 field for the election and forty percent of voters in Florida a key State to win if DT is to win the next election have said, 'We want him back in.' fifty percent of Floridians say 'we don't want him back.'

Thursday 7th March 2019

American citizens are being asked to carefully consider how they see their President since several members of his election team are in prison, going to prison or are avoiding jail by turning Queen's evidence so to speak.

Friday 8th March 2019

Paul Manafort, DT's former Campaign Chairman, has been sentenced to just under four years prison time for tax and banking fraud. Key to this was £60 million earned as a political consultant for the pro-Russian politicians in Ukraine hidden from the US tax authorities.

Saturday 9th March 2019

Interesting turn of events re. DT and his feelings towards Ann Coulter, a previously high regarded Right Winger in the Trump Administration. He now tweets about her, attacking Ms Coulter's comments about his wall funding and calls her 'a wacky nut job' for questioning his success.

Sunday 10th March 2019

As North Korea prepares to launch another test missile allegedly, MSBNC host Chris Matthews accuses the President of committing impeachable crimes in broad daylight. All this as it appears Chinese business leaders have the ear of the President through the influence of Li Yang, a massage parlour owner.

Monday 11th March 2019

As the Democrats describe DT's budget plan, including the request for $8.6 billion for his wall as 'dead on arrival,' the man himself is defending his peculiar reference to Tim 'Apple' when referring to Tim Cook from the Apple corporation. He later said, 'It saves time.'

Tuesday 12th March 2019

DT comments on the terrible 737 crash in Ethiopia by saying, 'Today's planes are becoming far too complex to fly.' Wise words indeed from a man who finds it difficult to close an umbrella. Meanwhile, the New York Attorney General has subpoenaed banks funding Trump projects.

Wednesday 13th March 2019

Usual DT stuff today. A *Twitter* storm over pretty much everyone. Greenpeace gives him a dressing-down because of his climate change denial. Paul Manafort's jail sentence suggests that DT needs to watch his back and the *BBC* asks 'would the President make a good comedian'?

Thursday 14th March 2019

It looks like DT's emergency build a wall or else threat is going to be squashed by his own GOP colleagues. Dissident Republican Senators are looking to thwart him in the Senate vote.

Friday 15th March 2019

The President makes a point that his advice to Theresa May, 'was ignored' and that if she'd listened to him, 'things might have gone a lot smoother.' His own style of leadership would suggest otherwise however. Meanwhile, he offers his condolences to New Zealand for the disturbing terror attack with the words 'I offer my warmest sympathy.'

Saturday 16th March 2019

Following on from yesterday, some commentators are asking why DT, despite condemning the killings, did not like many other national leaders, deliver a message of support for US Muslims who may feel scared that they are at risk simply by attending prayer sessions at the mosque.

Sunday 17th March 2019

Rather than enjoy St. Patrick's Day, DT has once again gone

for *Saturday Night Live* by threatening them with a federal investigation for mocking him; again. His main beef is that they only mock him but they don't take the mickey out of the Democrats. To be fair, he's so easy to make fun of, he has a point.

Monday 18th March 2019

As DT calls Joe Biden a 'low IQ individual', he says 'it's ridiculous that I'm to blame for the New Zealand shootings.' All this despite the shooter saying that Trump was a 'symbol of white identity.' Meanwhile, the Democrats are now requesting an FBI investigation into possible meetings between the POTUS and the founder of a massage parlour and human trafficking group.

Tuesday 19th March 2019

Ted Koppel says that he feels that both the *Washington Post* and the *New York Times* are 'organisations that the President feels are bad for America.' His comments are based on the fact that both papers he says, now 'put out extreme front-page headlines.'

Wednesday 20th March 2019

On the day that Donald Trump Jr claims democracy in the UK 'is dead due to the poor Brexit negotiations', his dad is looking decidedly rattled as the Mueller investigation reveals newly unsealed court documents including Michael Cohen's search warrants.

Thursday 21st March 2019

Bridget McCain responds to DT's continuing attacks on her late father by saying that he is a 'child.' Kelly Ann Conway's husband, George, says 'Donald Trump is a liar' and in great classic American, 'the worst kind of dumb.'

Friday 22nd March 2019

DT back on form today by firstly making his views clear that Israel owns the Golan Heights; the Syrians are not at all happy about this. And he also reckons that people will not stand for the Mueller Report if it makes him look bad. Sound of laughter across the US.

Saturday 23rd March 2019

The Report is out! Well, it's been handed to the Justice Department for their perusal in order to judge what parts can be published, or even if the Report can be published at all. DT and Rudy Giuliani and the Republican hawks are all gloating that no more indictments will be held. The devil however is in the detail.

Sunday 24th March 2019

Despite the Report having been released to the Justice Department on Friday, still no publication of any details from the Attorney General, William Barr. Everyone holding their collective breath as they wait for the main conclusions which may or may not be the end of the President.

Monday 25th March 2019

So, somewhat unsurprisingly DT has appeared to escape any

blame in the Mueller Report, although the author has not cleared him of obstructing justice. There's no doubt though that he will be bolstered by the publicly released information.

Tuesday 26th March 2019

The *Guardian* reports that documents offering a glimpse into the attention paid to DT's real estate companies by the FBI over four decades were published today. DT will no doubt be concerned that names have been redacted. Not.

Wednesday 27th March 2019

Kelly Anne Conway's husband George has made the point that if Robert Mueller's report 'could not exonerate the President then it must contain something pretty damning.' He also said 'The fact that Mueller specified this is important.'

Thursday 28th March 2019

DT now riding on the crest of 'I'm in the clear' wave says 'I've overridden my administration to ensure that the next special Olympics is funded.' Interestingly, it was his idea originally not to fund it.

Friday 29th March 2019

As DT goes rallying with more cries 'the Russians hoax is already dead', many commentators are now saying that DT may well be favourite to win the 2020 election. He also threatened to close large sections of the US/Mexico border next week due to his concerns over illegal immigration.

Saturday 30th March 2019

With the wall still a way off, DT has gone on the front foot regarding the continuing migrant crisis by cutting aid to El Salvador, Guatemala and Honduras in response he says to those countries sending immigrants to the US border.

Sunday 31st March 2019

A new poll suggests that despite the Mueller Report seemingly saying 'No Russian collusion', many US citizens still think he has more information locked away in the Report and that he is not in the clear. Only twenty-nine percent of Americans believe he is innocent while forty percent do not.

APRIL 2019

Monday 1st April 2019

As DT ups the ante re. Brexit with 'the UK will be at the top of the business and trade news with the US', the Democratic Party are already proposing to fund various programmes by reversing parts of the 2017 Republican Tax Law and subsequent changes.

Tuesday 2nd April 2019

Very peculiar from DT who weirdly now claims that his father was 'born in the great country of Germany.' This is not only strange but completely wrong as Fred Trump, his father, was actually born in New York. Whatever next!

Wednesday 3rd April 2019

Following DT's claims that climate change doesn't exist and several other anti-scientific issues today, he apparently suggested that wind turbines create circumstances that not only kill bald eagles but also may cause cancer. Now that's science!

Thursday 4th April 2019

As observers around the world are still puzzled why the President claims German parentage when it's not true, it is suggested that the Mueller Report is far worse for DT than William Barr is saying.

Friday 5th April 2019

Despite approval ratings of less than forty percent on average, several commentators are now publicly saying that DT may well win in the 2020 elections, unless the Democrats can be confident in their chosen candidate and ensure that, if it is Joe Biden, the Democrats are fully behind him.

Saturday 6th April 2019

As New Yorker Patrick Carlineo Jr is charged with threatening to kill US Muslim and Minnesota Democrat Ilham Omar, DT puts out a tweet that seems to put her in the firing line by suggesting that 'she doesn't like Israel. I forgot that.'

Sunday 7th April 2019

There are concerns today that the Democrats will never see DT's tax returns. The principle seems to be voters knew he could or should produce them; he didn't and yet the US voters still put him in charge anyway. This follows last week's request to see his tax returns by the House Democrats.

Monday 8th April 2019

Another day, another tariff. This time the President threatens to place a tax on Mexican cars of twenty-five percent if the flow of immigrants doesn't slow or stop. Meanwhile, DT accepts the resignation of his Homeland Security Secretary Kirstjen Nielsen as he looks to deal with his border crisis.

Tuesday 9th April 2019

DT announces plans to apply $11 billion worth of tariffs against the EU based apparently on the US losses due to the

Airbus subsidies. This coupled with Brexit fears has caused the IMF to downgrade forecasts with 'No Deal' on the cards.

Wednesday 10th April 2019

It's reported that during a visit to Mount Vernon last year, DT apparently chastised George Washington for not 'putting his name on the Virginia cap' and 'You've got to put your name on a cap otherwise no-one remembers you.' Quite.

Thursday 11th April 2019

What's this? A defender of the President! Step forward none other than author of American Psycho, Bret Easton Ellis. He says, 'When did we relentlessly view the world through the eyes of a victim?' Mind you, this was on the day he launched a new collection of essays called 'White.'

Friday 12th April 2019

It appears that DT put a huge amount of pressure on the unfortunate Mrs Nielsen to place immigrants detained at the Mexican border into so-called 'sanctuary cities.' This was done primarily to get back at Democrats opposed to his wall. Nielsen pushed back and the plan was stopped, but sadly so was Nielsen.

Saturday 13th April 2019

As DT moans that one of Obama's advisers is placed under investigation yet isn't reported, the Democrats have said that he must make his tax returns available for full public view by the twenty-third of April. 'He cannot refuse' they say.

Sunday 14th April 2019

As DT tweets celebratory messages to Tiger Woods for his Masters win in Augusta, he maintained his attack on Democratic Muslim Ilhan Omar by tweeting a video of the 9/11 atrocities suggesting she downplayed the incident, all of which is seemingly completely fake.

Monday 15th April 2019

Sure as night follows day, Ilhan Omar has in fact seen a rise in death threats. In Mueller Report world, the Department of Justice has now announced that the full report will be released to the public on Thursday. The only slight issue is much of it has been redacted.

Tuesday 16th April 2019

The Democrats steal a march on the President with tax returns being released for Bernie Sanders and Beto O'Rourke. Meanwhile, DT suggests that Boeing would do well to rebrand the now rather besmirched 737 Max. Good luck with that!

Wednesday 17th April 2019

Nancy Pelosi, the Democrat Leader of the House makes it clear to Leo Varadkar, the Irish Premier, that any trade with the UK post-Brexit would be entirely dependent on how it impacts on the Good Friday Agreement and border issues with Northern Ireland. Any change to this will impact negatively on trade with the US she said.

Thursday 18th April 2019

DT's legal team describe the Mueller Report as 'a total victory,' all this on the day that the redacted version is released. William Barr, the Attorney General, faces very stiff criticism over the way the report has been publicised.

Friday 19th April 2019

The Democrats have today issued a subpoena for full unredacted Mueller report to be released. Jerry Nadler has asked for the Department of Justice to comply by at least May first, this being the day William Barr is due to appear before a Judiciary Committee.

Saturday 20th April 2019

UK comedian John Oliver, now based in the US, makes it clear in his late-night programme that the Mueller Report is a pretty clear 'non-exoneration.' He says the details are incredible, especially the one that has DT allegedly saying 'I'm fucked' when finding out that Robert Mueller was Special Counsel for the case.

Sunday 21st April 2019

On the day that Rudy 'Zip It' Giuliani says, 'there was nothing wrong in taking information from the Russians,' the House Judiciary Chairman, Jerrold Nadler has said that it is impossible to rule out impeaching the President.

Monday 22nd April 2019

Bernie Sanders lays down a glove to Democrats daring them to stop him this time in his run-up to being declared the Presidential runner for 2020. It remains to be seen whether the Party will be able to translate these words into deeds.

Tuesday 23rd April 2019

DT repeats his unproven and controversial comments that the UK used covert surveillance methods at GCHQ not only to spy on the President, but also that they aided and assisted Barack Obama's attempt to stop his tenure as President.

Wednesday 24th April 2019

The big announcement today is the upcoming three-day State visit to the UK by DT in June 2019. Whether there will be any demonstrations for or against his visit is yet to be discussed. However, whatever the plans are, the UK could do without it simply because of security costs.

Thursday 25th April 2019

Vlad 'Smiler' Putin greets Kim Jong-un in Moscow in preparation for the forthcoming summit between DT and the North Korean leader. This is now the fourth such meeting and there are hopes that this one will actually have an outcome.

Friday 26th April 2019

DT's old allies *Fox News* are clearly smarting from previous attacks as Andrew Napolitano launches into a sharp critique of the President. He says, 'The Mueller Report has laid out at least half a dozen crimes of obstruction committed by Trump.' Blimey, this is the news channel that supported the President!

Saturday 27th April 2019

In order to enhance world peace, DT announces that he will withdraw the US from the International Arms Trade Treaty which was signed by Obama in 2013. The US is the world's top arms exporter so this was and has been cheered on by the NRA and other arms makers.

Sunday 28th April 2019

Even though Kelly Anne Conway defends DT's position on white supremacy after the shooting at another synagogue where one woman was killed, it's clear that the POTUS has made it acceptable for ring-wing extremism and fascist behaviour to be tolerated simply with his silence.

Monday 29th April 2019

DT has threatened Cuba with a full and complete embargo over their support for the Venezuelan President Nicolas Maduro. On the day that violence has escalated again on the island, the POTUS took to social media to rant against the country.

Tuesday 30th April 2019

Despite pressure placed on the President re. various aspects of his 'leadership', it is unlikely that impeachment proceedings will ever take place. To that end, they are planning to formally request DT to attend Senate hearings, lots of them.

MAY 2019

Wednesday 1st May 2019

Robert Mueller has specifically gone after William Barr, the Attorney General, accusing him of 'purposefully misleading the Mueller Report summary in its public presentation.' There appears to be a question over the integrity and motive of the Attorney General.

Thursday 2nd May 2019

DT chooses his pick for the Federal Reserve, and lo and behold, the unlucky chap, Steven Moore, does the decent thing and withdraws. Meanwhile, the Democrats are now asking William Barr to resign.

Friday 3rd May 2019

The *Washington Post* suggests that there is a precedent for impeaching Presidents as a result of their 'attempt to thwart or prevent justice with continual harassment.' DT's latest letter describes Robert Mueller's report as 'legally defective, a departure from the law, politically biased and evidence of not following the law.'

Saturday 4th May 2019

The Californian State Legislative voted on Wednesday in favour of leaving DT's name off of the primary election ballots unless he agrees to release his tax returns. Not that this is as simple as it seems since the last time this was attempted, it was blocked by a Democrat who complained of a 'breach of the Constitution.'

Sunday 5th May 2019

George Conway who is an outspoken critic of DT says that Russia has 'probably caught onto the imbecility of the President.' As an example of this, DT makes pointed remarks that seem to suggest he will impose further trade sanctions due to problems with China so shares take yet another tumble.

Monday 6th May 2019

The *Guardian* reports that on of DT's main support groups, the National Rifle Association (NRA), is on a rocky road. The President is imploring the bullet-happy bunch to stop their in-fighting, specifically regarding charges of financial misconduct. It could mean a reduction in GOP election funds.

Tuesday 7th May 2019

Nancy Pelosi has called a speech given by DT's Treasury Secretary which said any requests for the President's tax returns are 'case closed', as a 'stunning act of cynicism and a brazen violation of the oath we all take.' The Democrats smell blood.

Wednesday 8th May 2019

It transpires that DT asserted executive privilege over the entirety of the subpoenaed material in the Mueller Report. It seems that Jerry Nadler's push to hold William Barr in contempt effectively terminated any discussion over what details lawmakers could see.

Thursday 9th May 2019

DT and his inner circle are frustrated that the Republican-led Senate Intelligence Committee has subpoenaed his son and heir. The chief issue is that whatever happens, right or wrong, the Democrats will be laughing.

Friday 10th May 2019

At a rally in Panama City, Florida, someone in the audience shouts to DT that migrants crossing the border 'should be shot.' DT responds by laughing and making jokes about it by saying 'Well, only in the pan-handle can you get away with a comment like that.' He does not rebuke the member of the audience.

Saturday 11th May 2019

Don McGahn, a former White House Counsel named in the Mueller Report on potential obstruction of justice by DT's team, was asked by the President to publicly declare that he doesn't believe that the Trump Administration obstructed justice. Mr McGahn steadfastly refused to do so.

Sunday 12th May 2019

Unsurprisingly, DT goes ape bonkers at Don McGahn. Brian Kolfage, the guy who started the 'Go Fund Me' campaign to build the wall, is, four months after it raised $22 million, now asking 'what's happened to the money?' Many of the supporters who donated are also asking for evidence of 'some bricks being laid.'

Monday 13th May 2019

As DT applauds the very right-wing Hungarian PM for doing 'a tremendous job', US farmers are getting impatient with the President over his continued trade war spat with the Chinese. They say 'This cannot go on' as Chinese tariffs are hitting them hard.

Tuesday 14th May 2019

Iran, having become DT's latest punch bag, has become his focus of attention again well, for the moment. Threatening an ersatz World War Three, he says 'they will suffer greatly if they do anything.' Presumably this refers to the Iranians recently saying 'Yah Boo sucks.'

Wednesday 15th May 2019

The Republican Senator for Utah, Mitt Romney voted against DT's Judicial pick Michael Truncale which was a bit of a surprise. Apparently, this action was as a result of Mr Truncale calling Barack Obama an 'un-American imposter.' It didn't matter though as Mr T still got the vote: forty-nine to forty-six.

Thursday 16th May 2019

Alabama 2019. Twenty-five men vote to make abortion illegal in the State, all this while the top dog declares a national emergency due, he says, to the threat from foreign adversaries, principally Huawei, the Chinese telecom giant.

Friday 17th May 2019

Toyota took the unusual step of rebuking DT's recent

declaration that imported cars 'threaten national security.' The biggest car maker in Japan said that the statement by the President sends a message to Toyota that 'our investments are not welcome and our US employees are not valued.'

Saturday 18th May 2019

Apparently reported plans by DT to send migrant families to Florida was given short shrift by Florida State and Local officials. 'Because of our efforts,' they said, 'we were able to stop what appeared to be a crisis for our community.' It now looks like migrants will now head to San Diego and Del Rio.

Sunday 19th May 2019

As Justin Amash, Republican Senator for Michigan, called for DT's impeachment (gasp) it is reported that anti-money laundering specialists at Deutsche Bank noted in 2016-17 those multiple accounts and transactions involving DT and Jared Kushner should have been reported to the Federal Watchdog.

Monday 20th May 2019

As Mitt Romney describes calls by GOP members for impeachment process as 'courageous,' Iran describes DT's latest tweets as genocidal taunts. DT said 'I was never a fan of Justin Amash,' the first Republican who called for impeachment. The President also threatens to 'end Iran' if they want to fight.

Tuesday 21st May 2019

DT goes all out anti-Fox today saying, 'What's wrong with

Fox News?' At a rally in Pasadena, he continued, 'They're always putting on more Democrats and Republicans. We have a great new Attorney General who will give it a fair look.' This may be a plan to lock up democracy.

Wednesday 22nd May 2019

DT has threatened to blow a hole in the US infrastructure process; that is fixing bridges, roads, freeways etc. unless the Democrats agree to US/Canada/Mexico plan. Meanwhile, the US shoe/trainer's industry has written saying the China tariffs will devastate them unless he agrees to a new plan.

Thursday 23rd May 2019

Nancy Pelosi, the House Speaker, has said that she believes the President is engaged in a coverup. Needless to say, DT goes into major temper tantrum and tweets like a mad Dave the mad man on Mad Day.

Friday 24th May 2019

Typically, of this Alice in Wonderland President, he's now suggesting that Huawei mobile phone company could be part of the discussions with the Chinese re. tariffs. Meanwhile, Nancy Pelosi says that she 'prays for him.'

Saturday 25th May 2019

DT approved an $8 billion arms sale to Saudi Arabia as part of his anti-Iran rhetoric. He was also keen to be nice to his Japanese hosts by seemingly mocking Akio Toyoda, the Toyota President, at the US Residence dinner by calling him 'the boss.'

Sunday 26th May 2019

As DT and his pal Kim Jong-un agree that both feel Joe Biden has a low IQ, the House Democratic Chair, Hakeem Jeffries, said that he has 'reason to believe that the President Donald Trump has committed an obstruction of justice.'

Monday 27th May 2019

DT reflects today on the decisions made by two judges who have both issued their ruling swiftly and decisively over subpoenas demanding documents regarding financial records from the President's accounting firms. Impeach is the word.

Tuesday 28th May 2019

As poor old DT says 'Without Mueller, my ratings would be seventy-five percent,' his trip to Japan continues with the usual Press rants. As he makes his way home, he will no doubt be planning some intervention in UK politics next week on his visit.

Wednesday 29th May 2019

Hell hath no fury like a right-hand man and right winger gone wrong! Steve Bannon describes the Trump organisation as a 'criminal enterprise.' James Comey chips in with 'there's no conspiracy here, just lies and dumb lies at that.' DT goes on the election trail again in Airforce One.

Thursday 30th May 2019

The President is going through a real Homer Simpson moment when he sends a tweet, 'Russia helped me win the 2015 election' then rapidly dismisses this as a joke to reporters. Doh!

Friday 31st May 2019

On the day that DT insists that he will levy a five percent tariff on all Mexican goods due to the ongoing immigration issue, Steven Miller, the White House immigrant guru and professional hatemonger, is laughing all the way to the Eugenics Bank. Also, the President can't meet Mr Farage next week.

JUNE 2019

Saturday 1st June 2019

As promised in March, DT says that India will no longer be allowed to benefit from the trade dispensation system that has allowed India preferential trade rates. He says they've 'done enough already to allow US access to Indian trade.'

Sunday 2nd June 2019

DT doing what he does best. Just as he sets out to disrupt the D-Day Landing commemorations, he says, 'Boris Johnson would make a great Prime Minister and GB should leave the EU without a deal while Nigel Farage does the negotiations.'

Monday 3rd June 2019

And so, begins the next Daliesque performance by this President. DT heads off to the UK. Where he will be hidden behind high fencing, shown the most bare-backsides in history and agonising over pre-Brexit UK politics. Bizarre really for a guy on the brink in his homeland.

Tuesday 4th June 2019

So, DT arrives in the UK, meets the Queen, talks about good great deals and attends a lavish banquet. Strangely, the only Conservative Cabinet member *not* invited to the banquet just happens to be Sajid Javid. At the same time Labour leader Jeremy Corbyn leads a protest.

Wednesday 5th June 2019

DT's UK adventure continues apace with his baby blimp being punctured by a Trump fan. While the man himself has made it clear that any post-Brexit trade talks must involve the NHS, 'all things must be on the bargaining table,' he said to the gathered Press.

Thursday 6th June 2019

The President starts his trip over to Ireland by telling the Taoiseach Leo Varadkar that the border between Northern Ireland and Southern Ireland compares directly (in his mind) to the wall he wants to build to stop people moving from Mexico into the USA.

Friday 7th June 2019

Now that his 'State Visit' to the UK has concluded, DT starts where left off by giving Nancy Pelosi flack on *Twitter*. Mrs Pelosi had the cheek to say, 'I'd rather see the President jailed than impeached.' DT says, 'She's a nasty woman. vindictive, horrible.'

Saturday 8th June 2019

On the back of some severe feedback from US business leaders and politicians, DT has backtracked on his threatened tariff on Mexico goods and services. He boasts that this is down to 'very, very hard bargaining.' And with that, the US breathes another financial sigh of relief.

Sunday 9th June 2019

DT is facing renewed attempts by Democrats to delve deeper

into the Mueller Report, especially the evidence of any obstruction of justice. The House will stage a vote on whether William Barr is in contempt of Congress when he released the report.

Monday 10th June 2019

It's been revealed that the oak sapling planted as a sign of good faith between the US and France, especially the relationship that DT and Emmanuel Macron had formed, has died. The ties that bind us have been cut.

Tuesday 11th June 2019

Mike 'If gays marry, society will collapse' Pence says DT's decision *not* to fly rainbow flags at US Embassies is the right one. The President, meanwhile, is in denial about his devastating polling figures and he just says, 'ignore them.'

Wednesday 12th June 2019

As the President asserts executive privilege once again over documents subpoenaed by the Democrats, Kamala Harris and Alexandria Ocasio-Cortez, have both gone on the attack over his attempts at a blanket defiance of Congress.

Thursday 13th June 2019

Ominous signs of conflict in the Arabian Sea as what is reported to be a torpedo has struck an oil tanker and damaged it, thankfully without too much injury. US Naval Forces are very much in attendance.

Friday 14th June 2019

The situation in the Middle East is tense with DT insisting that Iran is definitely to blame despite their denial. He cited footage produced by White House Security Chiefs allegedly showing a small boat removing a mine from a boat. How this proves it is Iran is anyone's guess.

Saturday 15th June 2019

DT announces that Sarah Sanders will be leaving her post at the end of June. The White House Press Secretary leaves under something of a cloud, not having done any Press interviews for some time but, to be fair this post always looked tricky.

Sunday 16th June 2019

Despite being the head of a nation, whose citizens regularly shoot each other, DT tweets about the London Mayor, his arch nemesis Sadiq Khan, saying he 'is a disgrace' because three more Londoners were killed this week in knife attacks.

Monday 17th June 2019

As Iran warns that in ten days, they will increase their uranium stockpile unless Europe (at the very least) commits to the Nuclear Deal, Conservative Jeremy Hunt says he 'supports' DT's re-tweeting of Far-Right media commentator Katie Hopkins 'Londonistan' tweet, attacking Sadiq Khan.

Tuesday 18th June 2019

As DT sends an extra 1,000 troops to the Middle East again, reports come in regarding how the Democrats will fare in

2020. Apparently, every Democratic candidate will clobber DT at the next Presidential election. Meanwhile, he says he will depart aliens this week.

Wednesday 19th June 2019

So, DT formally kicks off his 2020 election campaign by bad-mouthing the Democrats, the Press and China whilst promising to kick everyone out of the US. This doesn't say very much about his personal achievements, especially the record number of staff he sacked or have left.

Thursday 20th June 2019

News this morning that Iran has shot down a US drone heightens tensions in the Middle East. If war comes, this President's role in destabilising a situation that his predecessor had sought to calm will not go down well in history.

Friday 21st June 2019

Reports suggest that DT was on the verge of deploying missiles in Iran but was dissuaded at the last minute, probably just a psychological delaying tactic but the Iranians seem to be a tough bunch and this probably won't phase them too much.

Saturday 22nd June 2019

DT says to the Press, 'I was about to press 'go' when I thought 150 dead in a few minutes? That would have been disproportionate retaliation.' The Palestinians were not very pleased by DT's Peace to Prosperity Plan either and have said 'The Palestinians are not for sale.'

Sunday 23rd June 2019

Questioned by the Press re. Euro leaders' efforts to uphold the Nuclear Deal forged between world powers (including the US) and Iran in 2015, DT simply says 'I don't care about the Europeans. In France, they're still selling cars to Iran.'

Monday 24th June 2019

The President has gone full Trump today as he suggests that the US 'will stop protecting international shipping.' He also resorted to claiming yet again that California was at the centre of a voting fraud in 2016. This of course is still as yet unproved.

Tuesday 25th June 2019

Following on from the sexual assault claim by E Jean Carroll, DT defends his position on the accusation of sexual assault by saying 'I never met this woman and anyway, she's not my type.' As ever, the President opts for the sensitive and diplomatic approach.

Wednesday 26th June 2019

Pictures of the death of an El Salvadorian father and his young daughter in the Rio Grande River appears to have shocked the world but so far does not seem to drive any change in the US. The Democrats say 'This is evidence of a broken immigration system.'

Thursday 27th June 2019

With his continued threats to 'obliterate parts of Iran', DT has been warned that this continued aggressive rhetoric will lead to genocide in the middle east. The President has yet to respond.

Friday 28th June 2019

All the while DT is being lovey-dovey to Kim Jong-un, he's describing Jimmy Carter as 'a nice man but a terrible President.' This from the President who jokes with Vladimir Putin about US voting when he says to him, 'Don't you go interfering in our elections!' Ho ho.

Saturday 29th June 2019

DT and Chinese leader Xi Jinping have appeared to restart US-China trade talks. No doubt hedge fund cowboys will be milking the system. DT also says in response to questions about climate change 'We have the cleanest water we've ever had and the cleanest air.'

Sunday 30th June 2019

Historic day as DT and the North Korean leader meet and more importantly, shake hands at the demilitarised zone between North and South Korea. He is the first President of the United States to cross into North Korea, by invitation and says, 'Before I was President, there were conflicts. Now, not so many.'

JULY 2019

Monday 1st July 2019

The President's chats with his Chinese mate will be tested with the reported actions of pro-democracy students in Hong Kong. In the meantime, the President has been attacked for nepotism as Ivanka Trump has been given a role of some importance at the next G20 summit.

Tuesday 2nd July 2019

As we approach the 4th July celebrations, DT has formally requested that the Chiefs of the Army, Navy, Airforce and Marines stand next to him during the special event. In a nod to other despots, he's been promised a parade of US tanks.

Wednesday 3rd July 2019

Some commentators have described DT's Independence Day jamboree as a narcissistic travesty. It is reported that he has set aside $2.5 million for the military march past which will include jets and tanks with the President smack bang in the middle. Obviously.

Thursday 4th July 2019

Strangely, on the day DT wanted to be basking in the glory of his military march past, a US Court of Appeal Circuit Judge has upheld a freeze on funds being redirected to be used for 'purposes other than those for which they were previously allocated, i.e., he can't spend the money on the wall.

Friday 5th July 2019

What was interesting about DT's fourth of July speech was the bizarre claim that during the Revolutionary War, the continental army fighting against the British 'took over the airports.' Nobody's quite sure whether he was being funny or liberal with the truth but, let's face it, the War of Independence did occur 143 years before the invention of flight.

Saturday 6th July 2019

The President says firmly that he will continue to pursue a way of adding a 'citizenship question' to the US National Census, despite the Supreme Court rejecting the original rationale stating that it was contrived. The question is controversial as it will likely stop immigrants in the US from filling in the Census.

Sunday 7th July 2019

The Mail on Sunday reveals that Sir Kim Darroch, the UK Ambassador to the US, had described the Trump Administration as 'inept, incompetent and insecure.' The Foreign Office calls the story 'mischievous' but definitely one that is intended to create tension. Now why would the *Daily Mail*, a Trump supporting paper, print such a story?

Monday 8th July 2019

Despite Theresa May's assurances that she has full faith in the UK Ambassador Sir Kim Darroch, DT says 'We're not big fans of that man.' Tom Tugendhat, the now furious Chair of the UK Foreign Affairs Committee, has launched an investigation to find the source of the leak.

Tuesday 9th July 2019

The President makes it clear that the UK has 'not behaved itself very nicely' so he's refusing to work with the US Ambassador Kim Darroch at any cost. During the 'next Prime Minister's TV debate', Boris Johnson and Jeremy Hunt are both asked if they would keep him on as UK Ambassador to the US when they are Prime Minister. From Boris Johnson, no answer.

Wednesday 10th July 2019

And on the back of the spineless response from the UK, Sir Kim Darroch has now resigned his post in the US, creating some serious backlash. What is clear is that with Brexit looming, no-one in the UK government wants to upset our future trading partners.

Thursday 11th July 2019

In a speech made re. a campaign to tackle kidney disease, the President strangely says, 'the kidney, it has a special place in my heart.' All this as he jokes that he may serve 'fourteen more years.'

Friday 12th July 2019

After yesterday's retreat in the face of a Supreme Court ruling about citizenship questions on the 2020 Census, coupled with Mr Gorker's abuse of a *Playboy* journalist Brian Karem, 'You're a punk, not a journalist,' today has been relatively quiet. I wonder what happens tomorrow!

Saturday 13th July 2019

E Jean Carroll who accused the President of sexual assault says she now sleeps with a loaded gun by her bed. Meanwhile, as Hurricane Barry approaches Louisiana, DT starts a *Twitter* storm by presenting his new golf club and laying into *New York Times* journalists.

Sunday 14th July 2019

The President decides to go full-on rabble-rousing today by saying some Democrat Congress people should 'go back to the broken and crime infested places they come from.' It has been suggested he was referring to Alexandra Ocasio-Cortez and Ilhan Khan, Democrats and both women of colour.

Monday 15th July 2019

As the President defends himself against accusations of racism even from the UK Prime Minister, commentators around the world and the US have condemned his 'go back home' comments as 'xenophobic and unacceptable and clearly meant to divide our nation.' His comments come straight from the '50s. The 1750's.

Tuesday 16th July 2019

The President continues to ride rough shod over any debate about his debates re. 'Go back home.' He derides 'The Squad,' his new nickname for the four Democrats who've gone on to refer to him as the 'Man occupying the White House.' Only US voters will know how the future goes.

Wednesday 17th July 2019

The House of Representatives have formally voted by 240 to 187 condemning the comments made by DT. Nancy Pelosi was, however, reprimanded herself for referring to his tweets as 'racist' and her words were struck off the Minutes. Frankly, if it walks like a duck, sounds like a duck, etc.

Thursday 18th July 2019

An attempt to have DT impeached for disgracing the Presidency was quashed in the House of Representatives. The same House, however, blocked the President's attempts to sell $8 billion worth of guided missiles to Saudi Arabia.

Friday 19th July 2019

The President now says 'I really don't like 'Go Home' chants at a rally' but TV images showing him waiting a very long drawn out thirteen seconds before quietening the crowd down, despite his claims that he stepped in very quickly to get the audience to stop.

Saturday 20th July 2019

DT desperate to carry favour with home-grown youth and all-Americans says he's offered to stand the bail for a rapper – ASAP Rocky – jailed in Sweden for fighting. Swedish PM Stefan Löfven has warned the President he cannot influence the Swedish justice system.

Sunday 21st July 2019

Democratic representative Alexandria Ocasio-Cortez has said that DT's recent tweets re. 'Go back home' is 'putting millions of Americans at risk to either home-grown or exported violence.' In other news, DT is selling the idea that the US should continue to sell plastic straws since, he says, the paper ones don't work.

Monday 22nd July 2019

As the President calls the four Democrat women (I won't say squad) 'racist troublemakers', it seems two unofficial envoys who report directly to the President have been in contact with Ukrainian officials to help discredit the Democrats and Robert Mueller.

Tuesday 23rd July 2019

As the government looks to take 3.1 million US citizens off food stamps, the government of Kabul has asked the President to clarify the comments he made to a TV interviewer where he said, 'I can easily win a war involving Afghanistan but I don't want to kill 10 million people.'

Wednesday 24th July 2019

With DT calling the new UK Prime Minister Boris Johnson the 'British Trump' (Brump?) Robert Mueller says that the President 'could be charged after leaving office as he has not yet been cleared of obstruction.' DT has repeatedly downplayed this but it is a tricky situation for him.

Thursday 25th July 2019

As DT uses his veto to unlock a billion dollars-worth of arms sales to Saudi Arabia and goes bonkers at reporters saying 'read his correction.' Robert Mueller says it was generally true that the President's sworn answers given to the investigation team were incomplete and untruthful.

Friday 26th July 2019

Apple has been threatened along with other tech companies with tariffs while Google has the Presidential threat of an investigation into its *Twitter* activities. This, one supposes is to deflect the continual comments being made by Robert Mueller which, as you'd expect, has not gone down well with the President.

Saturday 27th July 2019

Talking briefly on the tricky subject of Brexit, DT claims he's always in discussions with Boris Johnson re. a substantial free trade agreement which he says will be 'three times better than the EU.' This, however, is a false economic statement. It has been suggested that there will be an across-the-board increase in trade of only nought point two percent compared to a reduction of six-point seven percent with the EU.

Sunday 28th July 2019

Today DT does his best to make friends with his own citizens by calling Baltimore a 'rat-infested place where nobody wants to live.' This probably won't go down well with the leader of this proud city.

Monday 29th July 2019

While DT attempts stand-up comedy by joking about 9/11 and a collapsing stage, Baltimore's Reverend Sharpton responds to the 'rat' comment by saying, 'Frankly, he can't help it. He's like a child with a particular venom for blacks and people of colour.'

Tuesday 30th July 2019

DT on fire today, i.e., toys and prams, as he makes an unfounded claim that the *Washington Post* is a Russian asset, suggests that African-Americans are 'happy with what I'm doing,' and reacts to the French plan to put a three percent tax on Google, Apple, *Facebook* and Amazon by taxing French wine.

Wednesday 31st July 2019

The new UK Prime Minister has been bigging up the possibility of a UK/US trade deal if there is a No Deal Brexit, but Congressional leaders have warned that any deal will be blocked if it affects the Irish peace process.

AUGUST 2019

Thursday 1st August 2019

As support with Democrats surges for impeaching the President, Gary Cohn, DT's former Chief Economic Adviser says, 'The trade war, mainly tariffs, is affecting the US economy while failing to damage that of China.'

Friday 2nd August 2019

Supporters at a DT rally are a bit surprised when one of their number stands up and unfolds a banner saying, 'Immigrants built America.' Needless to say, Trump supporters swiftly take this banner down. Meanwhile, the US market has gone down swiftly DT as reiterated his threat to hit China with tariffs.

Saturday 3rd August 2019

Many have been celebrated on stamps over the years but maybe none as peculiarly historic as the most recent series of stamp issues from the North Korean Post Office. These feature DT and Kim Jong-un shaking hands and signing Agreements. A real crowd-pleaser!

Sunday 4th August 2019

DT's anti-everybody rhetoric seems to have proved dividends with last night's shooting that claimed thirty-four lives in four separate incidents. One in particular focused on a shooter saying 'I want to kill as many Mexicans as I can' just before the shooter was killed himself. DT to Sadiq Khan 'Hold my beer.'

Monday 5th August 2019

After weighing up the impact of the many deaths in El Paso and Daytona, DT goes public with the usual platitudes re. 'mental illness' and 'no place for racism in the US.' All this after delivering his continual stream of anti-Latino invective.

Tuesday 6th August 2019

As the President names the wrong city involved in the killings in Ohio, the Republicans try to blame the Democrats with the shootings which is bizarre. DT plays down the China response to his tariff threats, even though China may stop buying farm goods.

Wednesday 7th August 2019

Even before Joe Biden had finished the speech in which he condemned the President for having fanned the flames of White Supremacy, the POTUS was hammering *Twitter* with his usual 'Sleepy Joe Biden. The US will do poorly with him (as POTUS).'

Thursday 8th August 2019

In a peculiar turn of events, DT suggests that the Ohio shooter was a fan of Antifa and a supporter of the Democrats as though this was a factor in the person shooting a group of strangers in a bar.

Friday 9th August 2019

DT gives the cameras his best TV thumbs up while his wife Melania holds up a baby apparently orphaned by the El Paso shooting. Even though I fundamentally know that this is a

President who is different from other people, sometimes writing this diary is very difficult.

Saturday 10th August 2019

The ongoing tariff debate continues all the while Xi Jinping declares that he wants to turn China into one of the world's leading economies by 2050, however ambitious. DT maintains his position that the $300 billion tariffs will be applied no matter what.

Sunday 11th August 2019

As the world reels from the news that Jeffrey Epstein has apparently hanged himself in jail while he was being held on sexual assault charges, DT helps himself to some free publicity, re. attacking his old enemies, the Clintons. He says it's all linked!

Monday 12th August 2019

William Barr went all '…failure by jail staff' when Jeffrey Epstein was found dead in his cell and followed this with 'his co-conspirators should not rest easy. The victims deserve justice.' How close might this get?

Tuesday 13th August 2019

As if by magic, DT has delayed imposing tariffs on mobiles, laptops, footwear and clothing, this apparently after China and the US had a chat. Apple shares go nuts and it seems China now say they will buy into farming in the US.

Wednesday 14th August 2019

As DT prepares to close the latter half of the 2019 with a leap into an election year, it looks increasingly likely that the US may head into recession. This is something that up until a little while ago was unthinkable and fantastical.

Thursday 15th August 2019

Ken Cuccinelli, Acting Director of US Citizenship suggests that the Statue of Liberty's quote 'Give me your tired and poor etc.' applies only to those coming from Europe, not apparently from black countries.

Friday 16th August 2019

On the day that Denmark said that they will not be selling Greenland after the President half-seriously offered to buy it, his old buddy Scaramucci has said he thinks the President has finally lost his marbles. In other serious news, the Democrats are still pushing for impeachment.

Saturday 17th August 2019

Following the UK decision to release the Iranian tanker from Gibraltarian waters, DT's reaction is to launch a legal appeal to impound the ship. There's no comment yet from him on how the US might undertake the arrest of a boat.

Sunday 18th August 2019

As the President comments on weird changes happening at Fox, Tim Cook, the Apple CEO, has apparently made a very compelling case that any future China tariffs will hamper the Apple corporation's ability to compete with Samsung.

Monday 19th August 2019

In the run-up to the 2020 election, DT has accused Google of manipulating the 2016 US election in favour of his Democratic rival Hilary Clinton. Many observers are suggesting that as he nears the election, he will make this claim many, many times.

Tuesday 20th August 2019

With the 2020 election gears being oiled, the Trump Administration is considering abandoning all together the on/off tariff as that's threatening to bring about a recession in the US, just as the President wants to go on the road to say how great the US is.

Wednesday 21st August 2019

DT has called the Danish Prime Minister's comments re. buying Greenland 'nasty and inappropriate.' He added 'I thought it wasn't very nice. They could have just told me no.' One wonders who started this whole silly idea.

Thursday 22nd August 2019

After DT was likened to the King of Israel by a right-wing conspiracy theorist, he was happy, but wasn't so pleased with the *New York Times* front page image headlined 'The last whopper.'

Friday 23rd August 2019

Several commentators are now openly questioning the sanity of the President. Notwithstanding his more recent foray into property purchase i.e. Greenland, there was his at times, unintelligible speech to the veterans which was interspersed with rambling incoherent words.

Saturday 24th August 2019

With China threatening to place another $75 billion on US goods as tariffs, DT announces new higher tariffs on Chinese imports. He says the Chinese action was politically motivated. Meanwhile, Donald Tusk has launched a scathing attack on DT at the G7 summit.

Sunday 25th August 2019

DT livens up *Twitter* by sending a message that the 'media is destroying the free press.' Meanwhile, at the G7, both the President and Boris Johnson say that are friends and DT says of Johnson 'He needs no advice. He's the right man for the job', adding 'We're looking at a very, very big trade deal, the biggest we've ever had.'

Monday 26th August 2019

At the G7 summit the President continually points at our Prime Minister saying, 'Do you know who this is?' while making the point to everyone that next year's G7 event will be held at his very expensive golf resort in Florida, so long as he's still President.

Tuesday 27th August 2019

Several rival Republican members are already putting their lines in the sand for the 2020 Presidential election. Joe Walsh says, 'As Donald Trump is unfit to be President, I am the natural choice to run.' Not everyone agrees. Meanwhile, the three-way Joe Biden/Elizabeth Warren/Bernie Sanders Democrat fight is accelerating.

Wednesday 28th August 2019

With DT's 'I'm an environmentalist, better than anyone ever' words still ringing in their ears, Deutsche Bank suggest they have copies of bank statements that might belong to the President. Meanwhile, as the UK Prime Minister suspends Parliament like a latter-day Charles 1st, DT says 'He's the right guy for the job.'

Thursday 29th August 2019

It's reported today that DT allegedly proposed Presidential pardons to any officials breaking the law in building the wall on the Mexico border. It is imperative to his 2020 campaign that the wall exists.

Friday 30th August 2019

Apart from Ivanka Trumps' personal assistant being fired, DT has said that the US wasn't involved in an explosion on a launch pad in Iran. On top of this, he's now apparently suggesting that the next war will be in space. A very odd Friday.

Saturday 31st August 2019

Fox News Network host Neil Cavuto has felt the lashing tongue of DT as the President attacked the news channel. Fox has hit back by saying, 'Mr President. We don't work for you.' This after DT tweeted, he was looking for a new network.

SEPTEMBER 2019

Sunday 1st September 2019

So, on the pretext of monitoring the Federal response to Hurricane Dorian as it speeds towards the US, DT cancelled his trip to Poland which was planned to coincide with the Second World War commemorative services. Instead of this, he played golf in Maryland.

Monday 2nd September 2019

Probably not a wise move to hack off the Poles as they have immediately said that they 'will oppose any bid to allow Russia back into the G7.' DT, meanwhile, states that 'I'm not sure I've heard of a category five hurricane,' this despite having four of them hit the US on his watch.

Tuesday 3rd September 2019

We meet two Republicans today who don't think very much of DT. This isn't good news for him as more information comes to light regarding so-called 'Stripper-gate' pay-outs made to silence girl talk by his legal team.

Wednesday 4th September 2019

After last night's drubbing in the UK House of Commons for the Prime Minister, DT tweets a message supporting the under-fire leader by saying, 'I like Boris Johnson. He's a fighter and will come back fighting.'

Thursday 5th September 2019

On a day Jason Greenblatt, DT's US Envoy in the Middle East, resigns, *Twitter* has gone into overdrive re. the President and his hand-drawn map, seemingly showing Hurricane Dorian going to Alabama – which it did not.

Friday 6th September 2019

Lots of Sharpie ink pen jokes are the flavour of the day today following DT's very public display of a weather forecasting map highlighting the wrong weather in the wrong place. All this as the President and his team look to re-evaluate how foreign aid is distributed around the globe.

Saturday 7th September 2019

The US Congressional Committee is investigating potential conflicts of interest with the President (again), and military spending at the Scottish airports near DT's golf course Turnberry, where it appears that the United States Military has allegedly spent $11 million on fuel there since October '17.

Sunday 8th September 2019

The news that DT has cancelled peace talks with representatives of the Taliban wasn't the issue. It was the fact that they were supposed to be secret and that he managed to piss off both Doves in the Democrats and Hawks in the Republicans.

Monday 9th September 2019

The Democratic Committee team have formally requested records from the White House and State Department that may show that DT's White House tried to manipulate the

Ukrainian government into digging up dirt on Democrat Joe Biden.

Tuesday 10th September 2019

As DT claims he has sacked his Security Adviser John Bolton, he (Bolton) denies this saying he 'resigned.' Meanwhile, the President has again had a pop at John Legend and his other half Chrissy Teigen, calling her a 'filthy-mouthed wife.'

Wednesday 11th September 2019

DT claims that Mr Tough Guy Bolton made 'some very big mistakes. He also tweeted about claiming a third term as President which is impossible and all this while the rest of the US commentators commemorate 9/11. His input to that occasion is to say, 'On the day, I got people out of the rubble.'

Thursday 12th September 2019

In a sort of blow to DT's kudos as a man for all, Don Creale, the guy the President once referred to as 'My African-American' has finally lost patience, had enough and decided to leave the Republican party.

Friday 13th September 2019

On the back of DT's recent decision to backtrack on getting rid of inefficient lightbulbs, he's now saying that 'every efficient LED lightbulb I stand under makes me look orange.' Meanwhile, a Federal Appeals Court has said that a lawsuit examining Trump Hotel profits can now be examined.

Saturday 14th September 2019

Several commentators are now suggesting that DT may be posing as a 9/11 hero, 'I helped dig them out,' which is apparently known as 'stolen valour syndrome.' Also, three separate border wall projects appear to have been cancelled as there were insufficient funds for the twenty miles planned.

Sunday 15th September 2019

As more allegations of sexual misconduct against Brett Kavanagh surface, DT says that, 'Maybe he should start suing some people.' All this as the *Guardian* describes the President as, 'seriously and frighteningly unstable.' They also suggest that with DT in charge, the world is 'in danger.'

Monday 16th September 2019

With Iran saying, 'it wasn't us' regarding a Saudi oil refinery attack, the US responds by sending a message that they are 'locked and loaded.' It also seems that States like Iowa may turn towards the Democrats because of DT's approach to ethanol where it is now causing damage to the corn belt.

Tuesday 17th September 2019

DT's desperate need to oversee, partake in or at least vicariously sneer at the Schadenfreude moment of Middle East countries kicking the shit out of each other, may be fulfilled soon. Mind you, none of that seems to matter since DT appears to consider war in those countries, a given.

Wednesday 18th September 2019

After DT's 'Who do you prefer, your country or Hispanics?'

comment to Steve Cortez, shouts of racism are flying from all directions and just in case anyone's confused, he's retweeted more stuff from noted UK right-winger Katie Hopkins. DT tweets that the attendance of 20,000 at the Elizabeth Warren rally in New York, 'could be done by anyone.'

Thursday 19th September 2019

Serious accusations are breaking that a whistle-blower has accused DT of 'speaking to a foreign leader and making a promise.' This was then told to the National Intelligence Agency. However, it seems to have been blocked by the Department of Justice.

Friday 20th September 2019

Much mirth and amusement today as commentators review the bizarre *CNN* interview with habitual gossip or Rudy Giuliani as he's known. When asked the question was there a link between the whistle blower story and DT, Rudy Giuliani said, 'What about Ukraine? *CNN* covered it up and did I investigate Joe Biden through Ukraine? Yes, and I'm proud of it.'

Saturday 21st September 2019

Following yesterday's RG revelation, the *Wall Street Journal* scoops with 'President seeks foreign government help to damn a US candidate.' The whispers of impeachment that became loud conversations in corridors have now become the clarion call by people from all sides: impeach the President now!

Sunday 22nd September 2019

While Mike Pompeo says, 'It wouldn't be appropriate to release transcripts of the phone call to the Ukrainian President,' DT says, 'I'm not looking to hurt Joe Biden but he did a very dishonest thing.' This in relation to a dormant investigation into Joe Biden's son, Hunter.

Monday 23rd September 2019

As Karen Pence sends messages to the US voters to support DT to 'Make America Great Again,' many don't agree with her. Impeachment talks, meanwhile, intensify as the Democrats are saying that Ukraine-gate, 'really ups the ante.' It depends now on Joe Maguire and the House Ethics Committee.

Tuesday 24th September 2019

So, DT makes a speech at the UN. The world reacts to his somewhat petulant, 'She (Greta Thunberg) seems like a happy young girl.' And the Democrats are now on the front foot re. impeachment following disclosures that the President allegedly withheld cash for Ukraine immediately before his now infamous phone call.

Wednesday 25th September 2019

Breaking news! An impeachment, 'will be announced shortly.' The Ukrainians say, 'We don't want to be involved in any US election process.' The phone call is released and it shows that the President pressured Ukraine for Joe Biden information whilst stressing that military US support for Ukrainians may be restricted. More soon!

Thursday 26th September 2019
As the details come to light re. the whistle-blower complaint, it becomes ever-clearer that the allegations of trying to coerce a foreign agent to assist in the US election have disturbing and troubling connotations. DT says, 'it's all a hoax.'

Friday 27th September 2019
New York Times in a bit of bother today as they revealed the whistle-blower's job. He's a CIA agent. DT calls him, 'a sort of spy' which you could say is true. Meanwhile, the President has taken time out to explain his lack of grammar in his tweets. He blames it on *CNN* though.

Saturday 28th September 2019
As DT tweets and sweats in equal measure, the US Special Envoy to Ukraine, Kurt Volker, has resigned. This just a week before he's due to appear before the Congress to answer accusations that he allegedly helped Ukrainian President Volodymyr Zelensky navigate through Trump's demands.

Sunday 29th September 2019
Despite reservations by the Democrats that the Republican ruled Senate may block any impeachment, it seems that they would be beholden in allowing any impeachment trial to go ahead. Robert De Niro says, 'Get him out!'

Monday 30th September 2019
As lawyers suggest that DT has put the whistle-blower in danger, the President demands to meet him or her. The comedian John Oliver meanwhile, has labelled the scandal as,

'The Stupidest Watergate. The President says 'I've done no wrong' then releases a phone call that seems to show that he has done the complete opposite and that can't help the President's case.'

OCTOBER 2019

Tuesday 1st October 2019

Just to add a bit more fuel to the simmering embers of impeachment, it transpires that DT also asked the Australian Prime Minister to 'help me look into the Mueller investigation.' Apparently, and a little surprisingly, the Aussie PM agreed to this, hence the reason why Robert De Niro now says, 'He shouldn't be President, period.'

Wednesday 2nd October 2019

On top of the news that DT allegedly asked Boris Johnson for help in undermining the Mueller investigation, commentators are now saying that he is dangerous accusing the President of 'unhinged depravity.' This after he quoted a Far-Right preacher warning of civil war.

Thursday 3rd October 2019

DT's alleged plan to shoot Mexicans in the legs to slow them down wasn't met with much enthusiasm. So, he went back on attacking Greta Thunberg saying, 'She's not an activist, she's an actress.'

Friday 4th October 2019

Following yesterday's press conference melt-down and the handshake flip from the Finnish Prime Minister, the impeachments got real again in that fifty-one percent of US citizens surveyed say, 'We support a formal impeachment of the President.'

Saturday 5th October 2019

The impending impeachment process has accelerated with the Democrats issuing a subpoena to the White House demanding that they hand over all documents relating to the Ukraine-gate phone call. They are surely stalling for time and want to press home their advantage.

Sunday 6th October 2019

So, the view is now either a) DT continues to rant and rave, calling everyone traitors while admitting asking foreign bodies to assist him in effectively winning the 2020 election or b) gets impeached. Either way, he may come out smelling of roses and continue on his unhinged Presidential way.

Monday 7th October 2019

Uh oh! A second whistle-blower is about to be made public and in response DT goes completely bonkers in a tweet that says, 'In my great and unmatched wisdom.' This, of course, elicits many responses on *Twitter*, many of them not so complimentary. Most suggest that the President is mad.

Tuesday 8th October 2019

On the day that DT's administration seemingly prevents an EU ambassador from testifying to Congress, more rumours abound that he may quit rather than be impeached. It also transpires that the Turnberry Golf Resort in Scotland is now heading for a loss in the $millions, the fifth year in a row.

Wednesday 9th October 2019

As seems to be the way in western democracies these days as the White House has simply said, 'We won't comply with the processes setting out the impeachment.' DT's Administration are making accusations against Adam Schiff once again, claiming that the Democrats 'want to reverse the 2016 vote.'

Thursday 10th October 2019

Mike Pompeo rejects the notion that the US agreed to Turkey invading Syria and attacking the Kurds. DT now says the road traffic death of a UK citizen (Harry Dunn) by a US Diplomat's wife in the UK was because, 'we (the British) drive on the wrong side of the road.' STOP PRESS! Two associates of Rudy Giuliani have been arrested on charges of funnelling foreign money to US politicians in a bid to affect the Ukrainian/US relationship.

Friday 11th October 2019

At a Minneapolis rally, DT spurs on his supporters to chant 'Lock Him Up' when referring to Joe Biden. Mick Romney, meanwhile, has stepped up his own plans to take on the current President at next year's election. DT responds but at seventy-two, the Utah Senator has heard it all before Ukraine gate so insults clearly won't phase him.

Saturday 12th October 2019

As a former US Ambassador to Ukraine accuses DT and Rudy Giuliani of targeting her, lawyers acting on behalf of the whistle-blowers say that they are acting to defend the second one as well. DT has postponed a tariff on Chinese goods sending stocks up.

Sunday 13th October 2019

As even safe sites like Iowa become embroiled in questions about impeachment, these are also being asked about the appointments that DT has made to diplomatic posts, many of whom have little or no qualifications but are listed as donors to the Republican Party.

Monday 14th October 2019

As DT disavows himself from a mocked-up video of him killing journalists doing the rounds on social media, his nemesis Robert De Niro says, 'he's too stupid to be evil.' DT, meanwhile, has defended Rudy Giuliani who is also now under investigation. Fiona Hill who sits on the National Security Council will be speaking to the House panel this week.

Tuesday 15th October 2019

A new book by Ronan Farrow claims that the *National Enquirer* 'shredded sensitive documents about DT just before the 2016 election.' John Bolton, meanwhile, has said he tried to warn Fiona Hill to tell the White House about alleged pressure on Ukraine.

Wednesday 16th October 2019

With DT calling any impeachment illegal, both Rudy Giuliani and Mike Pence have refused to cooperate with the official inquiry. All this as a third Rudy Giuliani associate has been arrested and the Democrats suggest members have endorsed Bernie Sanders as a potential Presidential candidate.

Thursday 17th October 2019

The President states that the US and Italian nations have 'had a relationship for many thousands of years going back to the Roman times.' Yep. On national television Nancy Pelosi shakes her finger at him and the picture goes viral.

Friday 18th October 2019

Turkish leader Recep Erdogan says DT's somewhat short letter 'about being a bully' was 'not respectful.' Meanwhile, James Mattis has spoken out about his former boss as having, 'earned his spurs from a doctor, mine from a battlefield.'

Saturday 19th October 2019

With the intervention of Mike Pence and the now infamous 'Don't Do It' letter to the Turks, there is a ceasefire between Turkey and Syria of sorts. DT, of course, claims victory saying, 'this ceasefire has probably saved many thousands of lives, or many more.'

Sunday 20th October 2019

Despite DT's attempts to stop the 'Mueller coup' via *Twitter*, impeachment plans are still steadily pushing ahead. DT probably smarting at the decision to cancel plans of holding the next G8 summit at one of his hotels. He thinks it's the work of those nasty Democrats.

Monday 21st October 2019

Nancy Pelosi distributed a new factsheet outlining alleged abuses of power, including a 'shake-down of the Ukrainian President and a cover-up.' DT, meanwhile, says that, 'it was me who captured the ISIS terrorists.' He forgets to say, however, that by allowing Turkey to attack the Kurds, they promptly let all the ISIS terrorists go free again.

Tuesday 22nd October 2019

US Diplomat Bill Taylor has been in front of the Impeachment inquiry saying, 'We thought it was crazy to withhold security assistant for help with a political campaign.' Trump, meanwhile, calls the whole investigation a 'lynching.'

Wednesday 23rd October 2019

DT on full blast with a weird claim of 'building a wall in Colorado' and saying that 'people cried as I signed the Bill and Executive Order', which wasn't true. All this as a mob of Republican Congressmen carried out a five-hour delay to the Impeachment Enquiry by protesting.

Thursday 24th October 2019

Right Wing Christian pastor, Rick Wyles says that supporters of the President will, 'hunt down Democrats and bring violence to America once the President leaves office. This will be carried out by vets, cowboys and mountain men.'

Friday 25th October 2019

The US Justice Department investigation into the origins of the FBI Robert Mueller probe into the alleged Russian hacking kicked off by William Barr is now a criminal enquiry. DT, meanwhile, has been accused yet again of sexual assault by a former Apprentice candidate, Summer Zervos, in 2007.

Saturday 26th October 2019

Summer Zervos has now presented evidence in court that she says corroborates her claims of sexual assault while appearing on The Apprentice. Kamala Harris has pulled out of a South Carolina forum as shortly before, the same organisers had given DT a Justice Award.

Sunday 27th October 2019

The White House has released a Press Statement saying that the President is about to make a 'major statement.' Commentators are suggesting that this will be the announcement that ISIS leader Abu Bakr Al-Baghdadi has been eliminated in a US-led Special Operations raid.

Monday 28th October 2019

DT and his wife appeared at the opening of the World Series baseball game. Once they were shown on the fan cam, the crowd booed and almost as one started cheering 'Lock him up.' Looks like the Baghdadi effect hasn't worked.

Tuesday 29th October 2019

Bernie Sanders has added a few percentage points to his Democratic Presidential campaign candidacy with Elizabeth Warren close behind. The Department of Justice, meanwhile, filed a motion to appeal a federal court ruling ordering the agency to provide impeachment data.

Wednesday 30th October 2019

Just as DT was planning a jaunt to Chile to sign a first-step trade deal with China, the Chilean President Piñera, has decided to cancel the global summit amid concerns that his own Administration is struggling to control the growing unrest over inequality in his own country.

Thursday 31st October 2019

The US House of Representatives is set to vote on how the Impeachment Enquiry should proceed. The discussion will also set out the rights that lawyers acting for DT will have. BREAKING NEWS! four o'clock. By 230 votes to 196, impeachment has been confirmed!

NOVEMBER 2019

Friday 1st November 2019

With US and UK officials still smarting over an apparent phone call from DT to Nigel Farage, the POTUS is putting together some form of defence re. the upcoming impeachment trial. 'I've done nothing wrong!' he said while Nancy Pelosi has described the whole process as, 'a very sad time for the United States.'

Saturday 2nd November 2019

A rule proposed by DT that would have required immigrants to prove that they were in the process of obtaining medical insurance within thirty days of arrival, has been blocked by a US Judge. The Judge said, 'The potential damage to families justified a US-wide ban.'

Sunday 3rd November 2019

DT was looking forward to his visit to Madison Square Garden for a boxing match yesterday but was met however, not only by an anti-Trump demonstration outside, but was also greeted with a chorus of booing inside, mainly from the New York fight crowd.

Monday 4th November 2019

As the Appeal Court rules that DT must provide his tax statements to the New York State Criminal Division, E Jean Carroll has begun sue proceedings against the President regarding her allegation of sexual assault two decades ago in a New York department store.

Tuesday 5th November 2019

Wow! Lev Parman, an indicted businessman linked to the Ukraine scandal, has now agreed to provide testimony and records to the impeachment process through Congress. Antony Scaramucci, meanwhile, says, 'DT will be forced out by March.'

Wednesday 6th November 2019

Gordon Sandland, the US diplomat loyal to DT, has now changed his stance on the Ukrainian scandal. Previously he'd made it clear he wasn't aware of any phone calls or schemes to use foreign policy to seek political advantage. He's now saying he knew about it all along.

Thursday 7th November 2019

Just as DT was maybe hoping that the pressure might ease a bit, Rudy Giuliani has stepped back into the limelight. Even stalwart Mike Pompeo says, 'Yes, all of this is something we have to deal with.'

Friday 8th November 2019

DT doing what he does best by making a comment in the middle of the impeachment avalanche that he is 'considering accepting Vladimir Putin's invitation to attend Russia's military parade in May 2020.'

Saturday 9th November 2019

In order to give the whistle-blower some degree of protection, a 'cease and desist' letter was sent to the White House. This was ignored and subsequently DT has maintained his repeated calls to have the whistle-blower unmasked. This, of course, would obstruct any future prosecution process.

Sunday 10th November 2019

Donald Trump Junior had to walk away from his own book launch as he was being super-heckled by attendees at the Los Angeles campus. But weirdly, the heckling was by supporters of his dad. They wanted a 'question and answer' session with him but this wasn't granted.

Monday 11th November 2019

DT faces a tough-ish week as public impeachment hearings begin. One problem appears to suggest that Rudy Giuliani directly tied Ukraine's frozen military aid to an investigation into Joe Biden's son, Hunter. This becomes a *New York Times* headline.

Tuesday 12th November 2019

While the President watches his back, the EU Trade Chief, Cecilia Malmström, has rejected an approach by the US to sign a mini deal. The EU says this is ridiculous given DT's push for crippling tariffs on European car exports.

Wednesday 13th November 2019

As the hearings re. impeachment get under way; Diplomat Bill Taylor drops a real bombshell by saying that a 'staff member' told him of another phone call indicating DT further personal involvement by the President re. the Hunter/ Biden pressure issue.

Thursday 14th November 2019

As the hearings continue, the *Washington Post* reports that DT has backtracked on his commitment to bring in gun control following the shootings in El Paso and Daytona. This is presumably to retain support from the 'gun nut' vote.

Friday 15th November 2019

DT is on his way back to the UK just before the election, December second to the fourth, apparently as part of a meeting with NATO Alliance leaders. Meanwhile, Maria Yovanovich, the ex-US Ambassador to Ukraine, continues to say she is the victim of a concerted effort against her.

Saturday 16th November 2019

Roger Stone, DT's former adviser, has been found guilty of obstruction, lying and witness tampering. DT, meanwhile, makes his impeachment a bit worse by interrupting Ms Yovanovich's testimony by tweeting aggressive messages which are, as you'd expect, not received very well.

Sunday 17th November 2019

The President not happy today as his Republican-backed Congressman Eddie Rispone has been beaten by John Bell Edwards (Democrat) in Louisiana election. This second term victory was despite serious backing from the President over the last 2 weeks.

Monday 18th November 2019

Stephen King, the author, tweets 'Trump used blackmail and coercion in order to torpedo the candidacy of the man he saw as his chief roadblock to a second term as President. Case fucking closed.' Now that's a quote!

Tuesday 19th November 2019

DT hears that the Supreme Court have temporarily blocked the release of his tax returns, at least until the end of the public hearings. This as four new witnesses are set to give evidence on camera. An important week for the President.

Wednesday 20th November 2019

Interesting debate happening at the moment. Coupled with the ongoing madness of King Donald, viz a viz impeachment, there are now reports that the fittest President ever may have had some form of medical set-back. DT this week has attended an un-diarised medical.

Thursday 21st November 2019

The world waits on the impact of Gordon Sandland's impeachment statement yesterday; the man who may well being about the end of the President. Today Fiona Hill gives evidence and the outcome could be important, especially for the President.

Friday 22nd November 2019

The Democrats say they are undeterred by the White House preventing witnesses from testifying before the Committee. Today's witness reports from Fiona Hill and David Holmes seem to have cemented the future of the President. Impeachment seems inevitable.

Saturday 23rd November 2019

As Ivanka defends DT by tweeting a quote that wasn't, Joseph Bandy representing Lev Parnas who was an indicted Soviet-born American, has said he is willing to tell Congress about meetings Mr Parnas has with Ukraine prosecutors last year.

Sunday 24th November 2019

As everyone prepares for the second week of public hearings, Rudy Giuliani warns DT that, 'throwing me under a bus is not a good idea because I have insurance.' He did, however, say that he and the POTUS 'have a very good relationship.'

Monday 25th November 2019

As some commentators, i.e., Rick Perry, suggest that DT is the chosen one, others are less enamoured with his tenure. Despite this, even though the President is accused of withholding $400 million that was due to go to the Ukrainians, the Republicans are hanging onto their President.

Tuesday 26th November 2019

As the US comes to terms with DT's sacking of the US Navy Secretary for the handling of a Seal prosecuted for war crimes, Judge Ketanji Brown has told the President that they 'are not kings' with regard to Don McGahn giving evidence to the Committee.

Wednesday 27th November 2019
As the *New York Times* says that many more US citizens now want DT removed from office, two more Presidential appointees resign as a direct result of the fund freeze to Ukraine. In response, the irascible President sent tweets suggesting that all of this was 'B.S.'

Thursday 28th November 2019
As sacked Navy Secretary Richard Spencer calls DT out over his shocking and unprecedented intervention re. the Seal who the President absolved of any war crimes; it emerges that DT's golf trips have allegedly cost the US taxpayer $115 million since he started his job. Ouch!

Friday 29th November 2019
DT recovering from a surprise jaunt to see the troops in Afghanistan says, 'There's no-where I'd rather have been,' and then went on to suggest that the impeachment is a result of 'Barack Obama maybe ordering spies to infiltrate my campaign group.'

Saturday 30th November 2019
As Denmark places Greenland on its high security risk register due to the President's continued interest in buying it, it's revealed that though DT is getting a mixed reception down south, he's still preferred to Lincoln he says.

DECEMBER 2019

Sunday 1st December 2019

With the Presidential trip to the UK imminent, Boris Johnson is being warned to be very afraid of the effect on his own general election campaign, mostly because of the President's unpredictability and let's say interesting take on the truth and reality. Hold onto your hat, it's going to be a bumpy ride.

Monday 2nd December 2019

As DT boards Airforce One to head across the pond yet again, demonstrations and marches are being planned to greet him as he walks around the country. Meanwhile, You Tube has removed a series of pro-DT campaign ads; the reasons for this are unclear.

Tuesday 3rd December 2019

At his first news interview on this UK trip, DT says, 'The NHS is *not* part of the negotiations,' all this despite it 'being on the table' when he stood next to Theresa May in June. He also says that he isn't interested in the election but 'Boris is a good man and will do great.'

Wednesday 4th December 2019

In London, DT does his level best to zip it rather than mess up the PM's election campaign. Back in the US, the Democrats meet today to choose the path of impeachment or not.

What may cloud the issue is the suggestion that the President's mental state is getting worse.

Thursday 5th December 2019

Boris Johnson is a little disappointed with DT leaving the NATO Summit early but the Democrats are upping their game so it's probably best he goes home.

Friday 6th December 2019

DT goes all climate change-ish by trying to explain how the average US citizen uses the toilet and washes their hands. Meanwhile, several people have been filmed rapidly climbing up and over a section of the unclimbable Mexican wall along the US border.

Saturday 7th December 2019

A seminar on NATO due to be held in Copenhagen is likely to be cancelled due to interference from the US blocking a US academic from speaking as he had previously criticised DT. The Danish Atlantic Council say they will no longer hold the event.

Sunday 8th December 2019

New York Times runs with a story that puts Rudy Giuliani at the heart of the reason that DT is about to be impeached. Indispensable in 2016, Mr Giuliani is now seen very much as a 'for profit pedlar for access and advice' to the President.

Monday 9th December 2019

A protestor shouts 'Treason' at the Democratic Leadership as they prepare to impeach the President. North Korea has described DT as, 'an erratic old man' and Jewish Democrats are furious that the President has said, 'You must vote for me' suggesting the Republicans will protect their wealth, while calling the Israeli American Council 'brutal killers' and 'not nice people.'

Tuesday 10th December 2019

The press conference today re. the article of impeachment gets – from the President – a weak tweet simply saying, 'Not True.' The two main charges are abuse of power and obstruction of Congress. Chair of the House says, 'He is accused of high crimes.'

Wednesday 11th December 2019

With the news that DT has engineered the shut-down of the World Trade Organisation, whoever the Prime Minister is on Friday will have trouble in a year's time if post-Brexit positions are not made clear. The President's impression of Thanos gets him called a 'pompous fool.'

Thursday 12th December 2019

The Senate's Foreign Relations Committee have voted unanimously for a bill that prevents DT from withdrawing the US from NATO. Although he hadn't approved it, there was a risk, however unlikely, that this could happen.

Friday 13th December 2019

Following on from a bizarre image of DT's head on a picture of Sylvester Stallone as 'Rocky', he's been at it again, only this time a cut-and-paste job on the Time cover picture of Greta Thunberg. Very odd! Melania, meanwhile, says, 'Greta Thunberg deserves to be attacked.'

Saturday 14th December 2019

DT tweets today that, 'we have agreed a very large trade deal with China. This includes massive purchases of agricultural products, energy plus much more.' China agrees a deal's been made though they say it's not so much a deal, more of a pause in the tariff war.

Sunday 15th December 2019

With the new Populist government in power in the UK, some in the US are suggesting that the 2020 Presidential campaign may not be as clear-cut as they thought. Any links, for instance, to what may be defined as Socialism or Neo-Nazism will definitely impact on US voters.

Monday 16th December 2019

DT starts the week by losing is temper against his opponents, mainly *Fox News*, who have indicated that half of all US citizens want him removed from the White House. Nancy Pelosi and Adam Schiff took particular tweet venom from the President.

Tuesday 17th December 2019

As Rick Gates, a former DT aide, is sent down for forty-five days for lying to the FBI, the President sends a scorching letter to Nancy Pelosi basically accusing the House of a war on democracy. In other news, DT contradicts a Senate vote saying, 'The Armenians were not massacred.' To placate Erdogan one supposes.

Wednesday 18th December 2019

Today's the day when Congress decides whether to formally proceed with the impeachment. While DT talks about a coup, the Democrats and Republicans are heading into six hours of debate that ultimately will decide the future of the US and its President.

Thursday 19th December 2019

Historic date. So, the die is cast. The Senate has voted to impeach the President for only the third time in history. They said, 'The President has demonstrated that he will remain a threat to national security and the Constitution if he is allowed to remain in office.'

Friday 20th December 2019

As *Christianity Today* headlines with 'Trump should be removed from office,' Nancy Pelosi's plan to withhold the impeachment documents temporarily, has got DT very hot under the collar. He's demanded an immediate trial.

Saturday 21st December 2019

As Jeff Flake tells the Republicans that the impeachment process 'puts the Republican Party on trial as well,' DT is accused of interfering in European energy matters as he signs off US sanctions against companies building a pipeline from Russia to Germany.

Sunday 22nd December 2019

Documents released late on Friday show that the White House halted the aid to Ukraine directly after the phone call between DT and the Ukrainian's President. The email specifically states that 'Congress must not be told' which is damaging information indeed.

Monday 23rd December 2019

The Earth Group says that DT was heard using the phrase 'I know windmills very much' which is very peculiar. They add that the President claims that, 'we're in a battle to save this nation from these people (Earth Group) and their Green Deal.'

Tuesday 24th December 2019

As DT says he 'may give North Korea a beautiful vase as a Christmas gift,' he also says their threats re. sanctions will be dealt with. For Christmas, it appears that US tax gifts have certainly been very beneficial to wealthy Americans.

Wednesday 25th December 2019

Those rumours about DT and his cognition have not gone away and have been enhanced this Christmas with his new words. Speaking to a live audience, he begins a sentence which includes a word that when uttered seems to spell 'beautifewel.' When he says this, he stops, looks at the crowd then waffles.

Thursday 26th December 2019

There's more data coming in which seems to suggest that

public support of DT to be removed from office has reached its highest point, fifty-five percent up from forty-eight percent last week. The US skin is wearing thin.

Friday 27th December 2019

When asked about his Christmas gift to Melania, DT responded by saying, 'Oh, that's a tough question. I picked a very beautiful card. We have a great relationship like few do. I'm still working on the present.' US commentators suggest that's 'nothing then.'

Saturday 28th December 2019

DT revels in this Christmas by connecting with published comments that say that the President is 'heaven-sent' followed by praising a cartoon where Jesus appears to be saying, 'Barack Obama kicked me out of the US, but Trump invited me back.' How very odd.

Sunday 29th December 2019

Vladimir Putin thanks DT for a US security force tip that apparently foiled a New Year's terrorist attack. A reported threat to St. Petersburg was thwarted and two Russian citizens have been detained by Russian Security Forces. They gave no further details.

Monday 30th December 2019

The President seeks to carry opinion by tweeting a message suggesting that US citizens 'come together to fight and end the scourge of anti-Semitism' after the attack in New York. Bearing in mind his support for groups making anti-Jewish messages, this does seem a little at odds. Greta Thunberg, meanwhile, says she thinks the President is 'scared of me.'

Tuesday 31st December 2019

Republican Lindsey Graham says he cheers DT's response to the attacks on the US Embassy in Iraq as, 'putting the world on notice, there will be no Benghazi's on his watch.' In the meantime, the leading consumer electronics trade show is facing criticism after picking Ivanka Trump to be its key note speaker; this after being accused of overlooking women in the field of technology. Ivanka? Really?

Section Intro: 2020 - Year 4

- Virus
- Voter Fraud
- Violence
- Victory

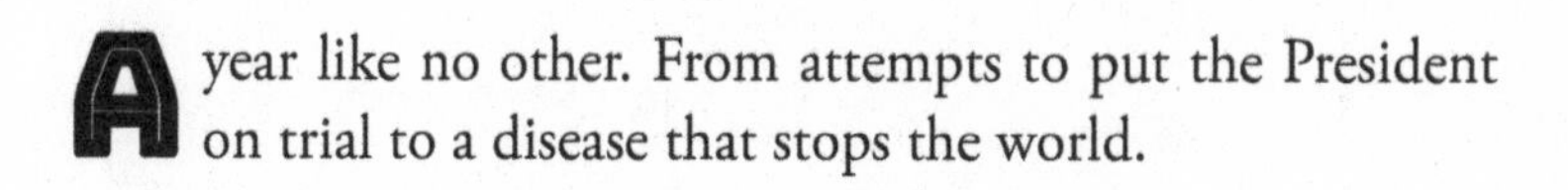

A year like no other. From attempts to put the President on trial to a disease that stops the world.

JANUARY 2020

Wednesday 1st January 2020

As reporters ask Melania Trump 'What is your New Year's resolution?', she responds by saying, 'Peace in the world' which in itself is pretty trite. However, DT then jumps in saying, 'I'm not sure you're supposed to say a resolution out loud.' The POTUS appears presumably to have mixed up birthday wishes and resolutions. This from arguably the most powerful man on the planet. All this as Stuart Stevens, a GOP strategist, says, 'The Republicans are the 'Character doesn't count' party.'

Thursday 2nd January 2020

DT goes on the impeachment hunt by openly suggesting that the trial features as many witnesses that will, 'protect sleepy Joe Biden,' meaning that even during this difficult period for him, he still sees 2020 election campaign positives coming out of his trial. Bernie Sanders leads the Democrat field by declaring $34.5 million has been raised for his campaign in the last three months.

Friday 3rd January 2020

Following the news that Iranian Qasem Soleimani has been assassinated by US Forces while he was in Baghdad, Iranian agencies are threatening extreme retaliation. Commentators have also noted that only a few years ago, DT was sending messages that suggested 'Obama is willing to start a war with

Iran in order to get re-elected.'

Saturday 4th January 2020

By all accounts the UK Parliament is livid with US Security Forces for shooting dead an Iranian citizen in Iraq, meaning that British troops in Iraq are now in danger. Still, we do have that great 'special relationship' with the US.

Sunday 5th January 2020

With the new UK Prime Minister still sunning himself in the Caribbean, the trend on most social media sites is when does World War Three start? Many of the social media commentators are pointing out the safest and most dangerous places to go if it all goes belly-up.

Monday 6th January 2020

As Wall Street markets react badly to the increased tension in the Middle East, Iran places a bounty of $80 million on DT's head, attached or not presumably. Oil prices head skyward and the UK tries to distance itself from the US threat to Iran's heritage sites. Back on impeachment soil, DT may well have to sit through John Bolton giving testimony to the court if he is subpoenaed. Nancy Pelosi has still to release the articles.

Tuesday 7th January 2020

Rather than entering into diplomatic talks, Iran attacks two airports in Baghdad with rockets. Although they were quick to show aggression, first reports are that there were no casualties and the attack was dealt with easily. Sadly, a Ukrainian Air 737 has crashed killing 176 people on board as it approached Tehran Airport. No group has claimed responsibility.

Wednesday 8th January 2020

It seems gunboat diplomacy is the order of the day with DT suggesting that Iran has been 'standing down' after yesterday's somewhat underwhelming attack. He went on to claim that 'no Iraqis or Americans were harmed.' Meanwhile, air crash experts have been clear that last night's 737 crash may have been as a result of an engine failure or other mechanical fault.

Thursday 9th January 2020

Peculiar turn of events as the US says that the 737 that crashed 'may have *accidentally* been shot down by Iran.' Commentators, meanwhile, have raised concerns the POTUS was somewhat confused when making his latest TV announcement; some saying that his fitness for office has been compromised. Meanwhile, Slovenia has decided to mock DT by burning a statue of him.

Friday 10th January 2020

Video footage would seem to suggest that the Ukrainian airliner was shot down, possibly by Iranian Forces. They've denied this but it does seem more likely. As the world watches the unfolding Middle East story, DT says that he, not Ethiopia's Abi Ahmad, should have been awarded the Nobel Peace Prize; presumably because he hasn't started World War Three yet.

Saturday 11th January 2020

Well, there's a surprise. DT's decision to take out Qasem Soleimani appears to have been self-serving. Clearly, the assassination kept impeachment off the front pages of most papers. North Korea, meanwhile, doesn't see any benefit from new talks with the US.

Sunday 12th January 2020

The effects of the attack and assassination of Soleimani has rippled and various groups are reaching for guns and bombs. Despite his continued complaints about no Nobel Peace Prize, it seems unlikely that anyone's mind will be changed about him not being awarded it.

Monday 13th January 2020

A tweet sent out on the authority of the President that indicated the 'first snow over the White House,' was despite the fact that Washington is unseasonably warm and not snowing. This now seems par for the course and *CNN* reports that DT has in effect uttered about 15,000 lies via social media during his time as President. DT has also claimed that Saudi Arabia has deposited $1 billion in a bank account for more US soldiers.

Tuesday 14th January 2020

Another storm brewing with a conflicting news report that 'Soleimani was planning attacks on four US embassies' and that 'his assassination was justified.' The problem is not that this was carried out; it's the fact that none of this was mentioned at the Capitol Hill briefing last week which has left many scratching their heads as to the truth about the security and safety of any US establishment.

Wednesday 15th January 2020

Bernie Sanders and DT go at it again; this time debating the issue of Democrat candidates rise in the polls. The incumbent President asked, 'What does this all mean?' leading Mr Sanders to respond, 'It means you're going to lose.' Meanwhile, Justin Trudeau has laid the blame of the Ukrainian air crash squarely at the feet of the President. Canada's Premier says, 'US escalation of the breakdown in relations with Iran has created all of this turmoil.'

Thursday 16th January 2020

Commentators are still coming to terms with DT's bizarre rally on Tuesday that again covered subjects as diverse as light bulbs, toilets, showers, war crimes, locking up former Presidents and sending at least one of them to hell. On a Presidential front, DT formally signed a trade agreement with China which has a) rattled global markets and b) given the President's profile a lift.

Friday 17th January 2020

Yesterday's Lev Parnas interview comments are sinking in and suggest that the forthcoming impeachment will make Watergate look like child's play. With that, formal proceedings have now kicked off with the appointment of the Senate Judges who will oversee the trial of one DJT. His response as you'd expect is disdainful but he needs to be very much on his guard.

Saturday 18th January 2020

The President gives a minute-by-minute breakdown of the assassination of Soleimani to a Republican donor event. He accuses the Iranians of saying, 'bad things about our country.' This type of name calling now seems to carry a death sentence.

Sunday 19th January 2020

Questions are now being asked about the depth to which DT's own money and that of his organisations are linked. Law suits filed by the President to block subpoenas may fail. Whatever the case, any investigation is going to clash with the election.

Monday 20th January 2020

As Lara Trump once again steps into the limelight and is castigated for mocking Joe Biden's gentle stutter, it is feared that the CIA and NSC may be holding onto further key evidence regarding Ukraine scandal. All this as the President's lawyers tell talk show hosts that he 'cannot be removed from Office on abuse of power grounds.' This is quickly derided by Adam Schiff and Jerrold Nadler as 'absurdist and arrant nonsense.'

Tuesday 21st January 2020

The day the trial of the President begins. While the world waits on the full impact of the impeachment, DT called for, 'a rejection of the predictions of the Apocalypse while speaking to the audience at the 2020 World Economic Forum in Davos, Switzerland. With Greta Thunberg in the audience, he said, 'These alarmists always demand power to alienate transform and control every aspect of our lives.' Great Thunberg responded by saying, 'In case you hadn't noticed Mr President, the world is on fire.'

Wednesday 22nd January 2020

With both sides glaring daggers of steel at each other across the Senate, it is clear that the man himself, DT, may well be the architect of his own downfall; at least, his voice anyway. Blaring out to all those present, he said the following things: 'Article two says I can do whatever I want. I want to find Hilary's emails. If you're listening in Russia. China should start investigating the Bidens,' he says to ABC News. 'If a foreign power had election dirt, I'd want to hear it' and to *NBC* News, 'I fired James Comey because of the Russian investigation.'

Thursday 23rd January 2020

Following on from Adam Schiff's impressive, 'if right doesn't matter, we're finished' speech, many in the Senate are suggesting that the President will be up against it. Even some Republican members are saying that Adam Schiff makes a good case. As you'd expect, DT responded by saying, 'the Democrat case was false, lies and shifty Schiff was angry and deranged.' A tape of DT calling for the removal of Marie Yovanovitch from Ukraine has not helped.

Friday 24th January 2020

The Democrats wrapped up their case and called on the Republicans to, 'give USA a fair trial; she deserves it.' This might be problematic as it is alleged that some Republican senators have been moved to say, 'Vote against the President and your head will be on a pike.' Most agreed with Lindsey Wise who said, 'DT did a lot of damage to his credibility by insulting Senators. We're complicit unless we vote for impeachment,' and this by John Cornyn, Republican from Texas.

Saturday 25th January 2020

DT's Defence team sets out its stall mainly basing the case on the fact that there's 'no collusion, no obstruction, Adam Schiff is a liar and the whistle blower should be here.'

Sunday 26th January 2020

Adam Schiff responded to the messages sent by DT as vindictive and deliberately intending to intimidate. To be fair, that's the modus operandi of the President. Mr Schiff went on to say, 'This man has not paid the price yet for what he's done to our country.'

Monday 27th January 2020

More pressure today being applied by a report in the *New York Times* suggesting that a recent report seen says the President ordered the former National Security Adviser John Bolton to keep military aid to Ukraine frozen in a bid to coerce political favours. The key point here is that Mr Bolton may now be called upon as a witness to the impeachment trial thereby delaying the hopes of DT for a swift acquittal.

Tuesday 28th January 2020

It seems the White House Defence is focusing on their

assumption that the impeachment is somehow a 'Democrat plot led by supporters of Hunter Biden.' The Democrats' response was described their Defence as 'non-sensical, absurd and incredibly surreal.' DT, meanwhile, has gone nuts at comedian Don Lemon for laughing at him on *CNN* News. The President called him, 'the dumbest man on TV.'

Wednesday 29th January 2020

Following the presentation by DT of his new Middle East peace plan, the Palestinian State Leader, Mahmoud Abbas, described it as a game and a conspiracy and he again went on to say that 'Palestinians' rights are not for sale and are not for bargaining.' All this after the President had said that 'This may be the last opportunity for Palestine.' As he speaks, Israelis looked to annex thirty percent of the occupied West Bank: UN Human rights team say this is 'illegal.'

Thursday 30th January 2020

As part of DT's wall on the Mexican border blows down in a 37-mph wind, the President's Defence team try a novel and breath-taking legal argument: that the President's personal interest is in the national interest specifically regarding his re-election in 2020. Their logic is this. The President believes his re-election is in the national interest, therefore whatever he did or does is acceptable. This approach however may not be enough.

Friday 31st January 2020

As the Republicans reject calls by the Democrats for witnesses to attend the impeachment trial suggesting that this is the first stage in the President' Acquittal, there appears to be a real threat to the US from the coronavirus. Up till May 2019, there was an 'overlord' in place to deal with global pandemics but as the position of Senior Director of Biothreats was apparently abolished by DT, there's no-one in that office specifically to address a potential global threat to health.

FEBRUARY 2020

Saturday 1st February 2020

As the impeachment game plays out, DT appears to admit that Qassim-al Rimi, the leader of an Al-Qaeda affiliate group in Yemen, was assassinated by a US drone strike in the centre of the war-torn nation.

Sunday 2nd February 2020

Bernie Sanders has decided to focus on DT in his final pre-caucus push. The Presidential hopeful believes he is the best electable candidate to take on the Trump election team.

Monday 3rd February 2020

'Well done to the great State of Kansas for winning the Super Bowl!', says the President. The only thing was the Super Bowl was won by the Kansas City Chiefs; a team based in the city of Kansas in Missouri. Meanwhile, the problem with the Republicans denying the entry of witnesses to the impeachment is that the John Bolton observations of DT putting the squeeze on the Ukrainians to investigate Biden Jr. will now take centre stage.

Tuesday 4th February 2020

DT is revelling today in the warm glow of embarrassment radiating from the Iowa caucus where the Democrats were all assembled, planning to announce the new Presidential nominees. Sadly, the whole process descended into farce when no results were made public meaning all of the candidates had either won or lost.

Wednesday 5th February 2020

With Nigel Farage sitting in the balcony of the Senate, DT delivers his State of the Union speech. As he draws to a close his rhetoric about 'making America great again' causes Nancy Pelosi, the Speaker of the House to tear up her paper copy of his speech, much to the delight of observers. On the final day of the impeachment trial, the President is criticised for spouting a manifesto of untruths to an assembled group of Senators.

Thursday 6th February 2020

Newsflash! DT has avoided both impeachment charges by fifty-two to forty-eight votes and fifty-three to forty-seven votes. Reports suggest that this has emboldened the President even further. And just to rub it in, he said in response to Mitt Romney's position on his impeachment; 'I don't like people who use their faith to justify their position.' He also slammed Nancy Pelosi by saying, 'I don't like people who say, 'I pray for you' when they know that's not so.' At this point he held up headline newspapers announcing his acquittal.

Friday 7th February 2020

It's been reported that an American citizen has died from the C-19 virus. Reports out today would suggest that DT went apoplectic with rage when he heard that Boris Johnson gave Huawei the go-ahead to invest in the UK 5G system and told him as much over the phone. No doubt the UK will hand over the nation's health system to the US in reparation. Bernie Sanders has thanked his team after a good showing in the Iowa caucus though there's work to do.

Saturday 8th February 2020

DT continues his night of the long knives by sacking both the US envoy to the EU, Gordon Sondland and Lieutenant Colonel Alexander Vindman, each for their role in giving evidence to Congress against the President. 'They are evil,' he said.

Sunday 9th February 2020

A bizarre photo is released showing DT with what can only be described in an orange mac was 'photo-shopped' says the President. However, the photographer, William Moon, said it was not photo-shopped but simply adjusted using an iPhone.

Monday 10th February 2020

As DT pushes to move $2 billion over to his wall project, he's being taken to task for destroying sacred Native American sites. This has allegedly happened as a result of the blasting by construction crews of an oil line. Meanwhile, the lawyer for Alexander Vindman said that comments made by the President were 'obviously false' and that he was in a campaign of intimidation. David Pressman was making very public that Vindman was sacked for telling the truth.

Tuesday 11th February 2020

A scene from the TV show Curb enthusiasm has apparently

gone over the head of the President, specifically the one where Larry avoids being attacked by a crazy biker by wearing an MAGA baseball hat. DT tweeted the scene thinking it was a clear view of the advantage of being a supporter of MAGA. An IPSOS poll suggests that the incumbent President will lose to Bernie Sanders, Michael Bloomberg or Joe Biden.

Wednesday 12th February 2020

With even *Fox News* suggesting that Bernie Sanders is now the anti-establishment juggernaut, the various opinion polls are also making it clear that he is likely to be a genuine rival to DT. Mr Sanders made a statement of intent after winning the Democratic caucus in New Hampshire. He said, 'This victory is the beginning of the end for the most dangerous President in modern history of this country.'

Thursday 13th February 2020

According to The *Guardian*, DT apparently has a fascination with badgers. Not sure why but hey, nothing to see here. Meanwhile, William Barr has made it clear that he is his own man and won't be bullied by anyone, including the President. He goes further saying that his job is impossible to do because of the daily tweets that he's sent by DT. 'I think it's time to stop tweeting about Department of Justice cases, he said.

Friday 14th February 2020

Whilst tweeting a not so nice message denigrating Michael Bloomberg, DT calls upon his supporters to 'keep American great.' Keep American Great. KAG. Now that's one that rolls off the tongue. Not sure how good this will be for the 2020 campaign. Boris Johnson has allegedly cancelled his US trip because the POTUS slammed the phone down on him when the UK approved the Huawei deal.

Saturday 15th February 2020

Ukrainian President Volodymyr Zelensky said today that DT's claim Ukraine is corrupt is nonsense. When asked about the US/Ukraine phone call that brought about the impeachment, he said, 'No corruption in our country. In Kiev we fight corruption every day.'

Sunday 16th February 2020

All pathways signposted for Joe Biden appear to be pointing to the nearest exit. Bernie Sanders is building up a head of steam and the Democrats will soon be right behind him. That being said, Mr Bloomberg has the attention of the party despite the 'baggage' re. financing his campaign.

Monday 17th February 2020

As 1,000 legal advisers demand that William Barr is removed from office, DT was attending the wedding of a white Nationalist. The President's senior aide Stephen Miller was holding his nuptials at DT's hotel in Washington DC. In the meantime, the President was defending his almighty wall, despite it falling over in a breeze. 'This was no-one's fault. It was just wet concrete' he said.

Tuesday 18th February 2020

Following the tweet sent by Barack Obama re. his signing of the 2009 Recovery Act, DT has lashed out at his predecessor saying, 'He's trying to take credit for the economic boom that is taking place under my administration.' Bernie Sanders, meanwhile, has responded to critics of his own supporters by posting pictures of Michael Bloomberg playing golf with the President. 'There's no difference between them,' he suggests.

Wednesday 19th February 2020

US Justice system falls lower into the sleaze pit as the President faces criticism for pardoning white collar workers and criminals for various crimes including Rod Blagojevich, convicted of trying to sell off a Senate secret. DT also pardoned Michael Milken who was convicted of conspiracy to hide stocks and tax fraud. William Barr, meanwhile, is threatening to resign because of interference.

Thursday 20th February 2020

DT kicking off after criticising a journalist for a typo made in a report over a war hero...dog! Pots and kettles are the theme today. He's also called the FBI 'dishonest, scum' at a rally in Phoenix, Arizona. Elizabeth Warren, meanwhile, has attacked Michael Bloomberg calling him a 'billionaire who calls women fat broads and horse-faced lesbians.' Mr Bloomberg has yet to respond.

Friday 21st February 2020

Roger Stone has been sentenced to fourteen months jail for his part in Ukraine scandal. So far, DT hasn't put forward any suggestions to pardon him. Is it too soon? US intelligence agencies have warned that they believe Russia is attempting to get DT elected again in response the President has sacked the acting Intelligence officer Joseph McGuire. That's that problem solved then. DT also says that the Democrats will use this against him.

Saturday 22nd February 2020

In caring health news, DT goes mad at the news that several Americans have been let back into the US despite contracting the coronavirus on a trip to Japan. The patients are now in isolation.

Sunday 23rd February 2020

Bernie Sanders goes from strength to strength, winning the Nevada caucus and says, 'This is a clear point from the voters, especially Latinos based in this State.' A new gallop poll, however, has seen a jump in the popularity of the President up to forty-nine percent.

Monday 24th February 2020

As DT begins his official tour of India, his nation's stock market along with every other country's financial institution, has been absolutely clobbered by the impact of the coronavirus. His thirty-six-hour tour that started with a rally attracted 100,000 people appears to be going well. He was very impressed with the Taj Mahal, describing it as 'incredible, truly incredible.' DT has hinted at a $3 billion defence deal with India.

Tuesday 25th February 2020

Mark Ruffalo, the US actor, has said that, 'the world should consider my President as public enemy number one.' He added, 'what we do in the next ten years will be crucial to the future of the planet.' As DT is feted by India on his tour, seven of their citizens have been killed during protests over the new Citizenship Amendment law. Many people see this CAA as an anti-Muslim law and isn't likely to quieten down any time soon.

Wednesday 26th February 2020

DT gets to the end of his tour of a bit of India and while the US and India have reached an agreement on the multi-billion-dollar defence deal, twenty more people have died as a result of the continued rioting. The President, meantime, has appointed Mike Pence to run the Coronavirus response team. 'The team is brilliant,' he said. 'Mike will be working with doctors, professionals and everyone.'

Thursday 27th February 2020

According to the President, 'Coronavirus is a bit like flu. People die from flu, right? So, the virus is a bit like flu but yeah, different. We've got it all under control.' Well, that's that sorted out. Nancy Pelosi has made it clear that the Democrats are unified and will support the nominee, whoever it is, as Bernie Sanders continues to gain in voting strength, especially from black voters.

Friday 28th February 2020

As Mike Pence sets about reassuring the US public that the coronavirus is under control, it's been highlighted that those affected in the States seemingly haven't been abroad and have somehow contracted the illness in the US. John Colbert the television presenter meanwhile has a field day in response to the meaning of DT's messages of 'we need a miracle' and 'who knows what's going to happen.' On his nightly broadcast, John Colbert simply and calmly announces 'plague.'

Saturday 29th February 2020

Yesterday we had a calming message from DT re. coronavirus, 'a lot of people are getting better. The fifteen people likewise we have them down to a much lower number. One of them is not doing well.' With top-down leadership like that, I think we need to be very afraid.

MARCH 2020

Sunday 1st March 2020

The main reports are focusing on the mixed messages about coronavirus. Despite sixty cases now known in the US, it seems very confusing as to what the Trump Administration will actually do to help its citizens. The Presidents mixed messages 'undermine public trust' says Georges C Benjamin, executive director of the American Public Health Association.

Monday 2nd March 2020

As Mike Pence 'he can deal with the virus' and bows his head with his entourage in prayer, the rest of the US is relying on effective controls and medicine. The VP meanwhile, also has to defend Donald Trump Jr for his comments that 'the Democrats hope the virus kills millions of people.' Mike Pence says, 'he was merely pushing back.' He ought to pray that DT and his family keep their comments to themselves.

Tuesday 3rd March 2020

As it is announced that Pete Buttigieg has formally withdrawn from the 2020 election, DT delivers a news conference on the coronavirus accompanied by Anthony Fauci, the Director of National Institute of Allergy and Infectious Diseases. As the President tries to convince the viewing public that there will be a vaccine in six months to a year, Mr Fauci stops him in his tracks saying, 'I don't think there will be anything developed for eighteen months.'

Wednesday 4th March 2020

Following on from yesterday's Democratic debates that show Joe Biden taking a giant leap forward, Michael Bloomberg has, despite oodles of cash to keep going, decided to withdraw from the 2020 campaign. Interestingly, he says he will now place all his support for Joe Biden. Jeff Sessions, meanwhile, has now got DT on his back regarding the Alabama run-off election.

Thursday 5th March 2020

The third Democrat contender after Bloomberg and Buttgieg to pull out of the race is a little surprising, Elizabeth Warren. Sad really as she seemed to be a competent and eloquent politician who would have been a great leader, I think. DT, meanwhile, has reacted angrily to the criticism levelled at him after he called a *Fox News* show to say that 'I think the WHO three-point four percent death rate is false. My hunch is that based on conversations I've had that it's only one percent.' By some measure it's difficult to fathom how the President is an expert in these matters.

Friday 6th March 2020

The US health authorities have announced that they don't have enough C-Virus test kits for their citizens. The President, meanwhile, suggests plans to cut medicine and social security payments which has brought about a furious response from Joe Biden and Bernie Sanders. DT's Attorney General, William Barr, has again come under fire for his handling of the Russia report. Judge Reggie Walton said, 'He'd made misleading public statements.'

Saturday 7th March 2020

At the same time as DT was replacing his Acting Chief Staff Mick Mulvaney with Mark Meadows a North Carolina law maker, he was bad-mouthing the Democrats and *CNN* while praising his security team. He is also continuing to take flack for his coronavirus comments this week.

Sunday 8th March 2020

On a day when it was revealed that an attendee at the American Conservative Union (the CPAC Conference) had tested positive for the virus DT, who had been an attendee with Mike Pence said, 'I'm not concerned at all about the virus getting closer. We've done a great job.'

Monday 9th March 2020

DT goes full angry emperor today, blaming the fall in the US stock market on fake news despite almost everyone else actually quite concerned at the rapid rise of the C-virus in the US. Even the White House Press Secretary, Stephanie Grisham, has lost the plot. When asked by *Fox News* what impact the epidemic might have on the nation and how the President is going to deal with it, she said, 'He doesn't sleep. Works fifteen hours a day and is fine and healthy.'

Tuesday 10th March 2020

As Joe Biden opens up a substantial poll lead over Bernie Sanders in a number of key States, the President is allegedly fretting over the C-virus. *Vanity Fair* reports that DT is just waking up to the fact that this is bad but he doesn't know how to respond to it. In addition, the White House has said the President hasn't been tested for the virus despite coming into contact with several Republicans who may well be infected.

Wednesday 11th March 2020

DT is up very early this morning tweeting scornful messages accusing Elizabeth Warren of splitting the progressive vote. This all the while Joe Biden was winning Idaho, Michigan, Mississippi and Missouri and improving his chances at the 2020 election. Concerned US citizens are still amazed that DT and Mike Pence are shaking hands despite calls to limit contact. In the US the C-virus has now passed 1,000 in cases.

Thursday 12th March 2020

DT finally recognises that the coronavirus is an issue and makes a speech to the US public. Unfortunately, this presentation seemed to focus on European foreigners spreading the bug within America. To this end, the President stated that all flights to and from Europe are banned. Apparently though, this doesn't apply to the United Kingdom, presumably because of the presence of Trump golf clubs in Scotland and Ireland.

Friday 13th March 2020

A Christian journalist with some considerable followers has called out DT on his claim that 'anybody who wants a C-virus test can get one.' The journalist said, 'this was false information, then and now. This is a major failure.' He also went on to say that 'being a great leader has many attributes but confusing people is not among them. The way the President has handled this is sloppy and dangerous.' Blimey, even the Evangelists are narked with this President.

Saturday 14th March 2020

DT finally announces that the US is being placed under National Emergency despite only this week saying that 'the C-virus will fade away.' The death toll in the US is forty-nine. With no White House initiatives, this is likely to get worse.

Sunday 15th March 2020

The physicians for DT have said 'he has been tested for C-virus and the results are negative.' On the back of the manner in which the President has dealt with the crisis so far, his approval ratings are forty five percent to fifty two percent disapproval. This may be a testing time for DT and his hopes for 2020 re-election.

Monday 16th March 2020

German media has reported that DT allegedly asked a pharmaceutical manufacturer developing a vaccine for the C-virus to ensure that, 'this is for use in the United States only.' The company involved and Die Sturm, have confirmed the authenticity of this story. As America's top infectious diseases experts warned that many thousands of US citizens could die unless everyone chips in to stop the virus, DT says the 'virus is under tremendous control.' Deaths today up to sixty-five.

Tuesday 17th March 2020

DT now moving very rapidly away from his fake news and Democrat attack version of the C-virus, to now asking Congress for substantial funds to control the expanding illness. San Francisco and New York are the latest cities to go into lockdown. The Chinese, meanwhile, are kicking off because the Trump Administration are openly calling the virus 'the Chinese flu' which seems counter-productive.

Wednesday 18th March 2020

It looks very much like Bernie Sanders race is run with Joe Biden picking up three more States for his 2020 campaign. *Fox News* has also adopted a more socially responsible line by now suggesting the virus is a crisis, not fake news and they've even started practising social distancing on camera and asking their viewers to follow suit. This only three days after Ainsley Earhardt, a *Fox News* reporter, saying it's 'actually the safest time to fly.'

Thursday 19th March 2020

Despite the introduction of an amendment to the Bill designed to help fund the speedy response to the virus put in by Kentucky Senator Rand Paul, it does look like finally the President is taking control of the situation. DT, meanwhile, has spoken of his disappointment that the virus has had an impact on the US economy with numbers now passing the 10,000 mark which had doubled in twenty-four hours. The Mayor of New York has asked that military medical teams are used in the city.

Friday 20th March 2020

The President has said at a press conference that shortages in ventilators, masks and gowns for medical staff could not have been foreseen. This, though, seems to be in error as medical experts in the public health arena have said for years that the US would face severe shortages if ever a pandemic hit the country. Since the beginning of the crisis, DT and his team have obfuscated and misled the nation in what was happening on the ground.

Saturday 21st March 2020

The *Washington Post* reports that US Intelligence warned DT last January and February all the while he was discussing the virus as a hoax. When asked 'what will you do to save Americans?' DT simply resulted to type by saying, 'You're a terrible reporter.'

Sunday 22nd March 2020

DT has written to the North Korean leader saying that the US is prepared to assist them to eradicate the C-virus. This is a little odd given that only a few weeks ago, the President was tweeting the bug was fake news.

Monday 23rd March 2020

As DT makes light of the report that Mitt Romney has tested positive for coronavirus, a conservative website has denounced him and Mike Pence for 'repeatedly lying about the virus.' Both leaders have consistently said that 'millions of tests have been sent out' when in actual fact they are not arriving or were missing crucial elements. The failure to test suspected cases has made it impossible to determine how many people are infected or how fast it is spreading.

Tuesday 24th March 2020

DT's regular c-virus briefings are now turning back in on themselves as he again seems to be downplaying the pandemic. Most observers are suggesting this is simply down to finances. The Stock Market is on standby having plunged by millions of dollars. Looks like he may cut back on the federal safety protocols and travel restrictions much sooner than planned which is a dangerous plan given the rise of the virus.

Wednesday 25th March 2020

And just to prove my point yesterday, DT now wants to stop the restrictions in time for Easter. It's his vision, he says, 'to see US citizens crowded together in churches on Easter Sunday.' The Senate, meanwhile, has approved a $2 trillion stimulus package to ensure that business and finance institutions are kept afloat.

Thursday 26th March 2020

Unemployment figures for the US have gone up by a factor of four with 3.25 million citizens now claiming benefits. This is on the back of the President's hopes to 'open the US back up for business by Easter Sunday.' Various commentators are saying that halting the social distancing and isolation rules early may bring about a resurgence in the disease. DT appears to be ignoring the government's own pandemic guidance that states this will prevent, slow or mitigate the illness.

Friday 27th March 2020

On the day that the US overtook China in the number of c-virus cases now identified, DT is still telling a tale of great and many successes of the government, mobilising front line healthcare workers and taking time out to lash at Democrats, who are channelling appeals from overwhelmed healthcare staff. All this as Anthony Fauci says, 'Only the virus can set out a timeline for reopening the country.'

Saturday 28th March 2020

As DT visits the USS Consort in Virginia before it journeys to New York to bolster their ICU beds, the President may well be on the verge of placing New York, New Jersey and Connecticut into a quarantine where 45 million people will be shut in.

Sunday 29th March 2020

DT responds to his own quarantine comments by telling himself that he won't be placing these States in isolation after all. The President was a little put back by the change of heart that that he himself has had. However, he's agreed to follow his own rules.

Monday 30th March 2020

With Anthony Fauci's words ringing in his ears of '100,000 to 200,000 deaths,' DT has had a change of heart re. the 'ready for Easter Sunday' with crowded churches comment. The President has also ramped up the issue of social distancing and isolation in various States. On a Royal note, he says, 'I'm a friend of the Queen,' but adds that 'the US will not pay for the security of Prince Harry and Meghan.'

Tuesday 31st March 2020

As the number of C-virus dead passes the 4,000-mark, Mike Pompeo has warned US citizens who are abroad that they should come home immediately. Al Gore, meanwhile, has told DT that 'you can't gaslight a virus' as the President seeks to protect an image of unity and bi-partisan approval. All this as DT manages to estimate the South Korean population at 28 million less than the actual number despite him saying 'I know them better than anyone else.'

APRIL 2020

Wednesday 1st April 2020

DT's latest C-virus scheme is to wear a scarf. 'Many people have scarves and scarves are good' he says. All this as he warns the US population that 'we are facing a hell of a bad two weeks,' warning that 'we're going to lose thousands of people.' Cases to date number 190,000 with the virus and 4,076 people have sadly died. Ultimately, the President may will need to explain how his supposedly fake virus killed a quarter of a million of his own citizens.

Thursday 2nd April 2020

New York is suffering dreadfully with hundreds catching the virus every day and dying. Florida starts testing its citizens using drive-thru medical units. DT goes on full war footing saying, 'we're at war with the virus.' Following a telephone call with Russia, they have sent stocks of PPE and ventilators directly to the US. DT has also turned on his old pals at *Fox News*, namely John Roberts, for an alleged fake story. He also threatened Iran again and questioned China on their virus data.

Friday 3rd April 2020

The US death toll now beats any other nation with nearly 1,200 in twenty-four hours. New York in particular has lost 500 victims to the virus in the last day. Advice is being given to citizens to wear cloth masks. Forecasts are still predicting between 100,000 and 250,000 victims, even if lockdown advice is observed. Jared Kushner, meanwhile, says that the 'Federal governors who say they haven't been given what they need should look to their own resources.'

Saturday 4th April 2020

Following Jared Kushner's speech where he used the term 'us' to indicate where medical suppliers were intended, DT quickly denounces journalists who dare to question this, describing comments as simply using his words as a 'gotcha' moment to the news-hounds.

Sunday 5th April 2020

Following a slight lift in his popularity recently, the handling of the virus by DT has had an impact on this and it now stands at forty four percent approval and fifty six percent disapproval. It maybe that he's hit his popularity wall a bit early.

Monday 6th April 2020

After yesterday's weird intervention by the President to cut off Anthony Fauci's response to a question about the efficacy of the anti-malaria drug, hydroxychloroquine, DT has continued to praise the various drugs that are on offer where they have been neither tested or approved. The New York Governor has said that the State may well have started to hit the apex of the virus, although the 'stay at home' instructions still remain very much in force.

Tuesday 7th April 2020

DT's least favourite paper, the *New York Times* has alleged that he has a 'small personal financial interest in the French drug company, Plaquenil,' which is the company that manufactures the afore-said hydroxychloroquine. In addition to this, the largest shareholders include a company run by a major Republican donor, Ken Fisher. A chorus of Trump supporters have backed the drug despite it not yet being accepted by the FDA.

Wednesday 8th April 2020

Questions no doubt will be asked about the report suggesting that Peter Navarro, a White House trade adviser, warned in January and February that the virus could be devastating, both economically and in death rates. He apparently also warned the lack of immune protection, a cure or vaccine would leave Americans defenceless. Despite DT now saying the virus is 'very painful for the US,' where he'd originally said, 'the virus is under control,' and this a day after the warnings.

Thursday 9th April 2020

DT takes time out from the C-virus to sign an EO to allow the US to mine the moon. On the C-virus front, the President once again attacks the WHO, specifically the fact that they are, he says 'China-centric.' This while New York declares more cases than any country, 151,000, outside the US. Yesterday Bernie Sanders withdrew from the 2020 race to become the presumptive Democrat nominee.

Friday 10th April 2020

With both the US and the UK apparently mishandling the

virus, commentators are saying there's a real risk of genocide in both countries. They still plod along regardless with the promise that 'We'll be open by Easter.'

Saturday 11th April 2020

DT is making it clear he's not particularly keen on postal votes at the next election. He's previously said that he thinks it's open to fraud. Most commentators have, however, pointed out that fraud in postal and other means of voting where people are not physically present at the ballot box are extraordinarily rare.

Sunday 12th April 2020

Not surprising that a comment made by Anthony Fauci that suggested, 'earlier action by the White House could have saved lives' as met with a re-tweeted 'Fire Fauci' message sent out by the President.

Monday 13th April 2020

As the death toll in the US from the C-19 virus passes 22,000, DT has lost his temper over a report suggesting social distancing had been delayed too long. In addition, many governors around the country have made it very clear that it is 'they' that will bring about an end to the lockdown principles. DT, of course, has said that 'it is the decision of the President' and for many good reasons. A lockdown-off looms.

Tuesday 14th April 2020

Absolutely blistering press conference where not only does DT say to the US public that, 'I, as President have absolute power to close or open the nation,' but he also wheeled out a TV and promptly illustrated how well he was doing dealing with the virus. That was going okay until DT went into total meltdown when a CBS reporter, Paula Reid said, 'How is this rant supposed to make people feel confident?'

Wednesday 15th April 2020

DT's mad session went viral and he followed this up with the announcement that he has ordered his team to withhold payments to the WHO for their 'China-centric' approach. All this as the death toll rises fast although figures suggest that there may indeed be a levelling of the corona spread. However, it's worth noting that experts suggest the virus seems to lie dormant in the body for several weeks.

Thursday 16th April 2020

Demonstrations took place today in a few States around the country where armed people looked to perhaps frighten the governors into shutting down their local lockdowns so that they can 'regain our freedom.' The peculiar thing is that despite the ever-growing list of dead from C-19, the twenties Depression-style collapse in the economy in the US has frightened many more than the possibility of dying in a hospital bed.

Friday 17th April 2020

Bizarre messages coming from DT on the back of yesterday's shenanigans in Ohio and Michigan. He tweets, 'Freedom. Open up America again.' By implication he's stirring up the locals, at least the ones with guns anyway, to take to the streets at a time when the US death rate has topped 35,000. It beggar's belief that anyone listens to him but yes, they still do.

Saturday 18th April 2020

At a press conference DT is asked about his pro-anti-virus groups. He says, 'they are good people and they've been treated a bit rough.' US death toll total now stands at 36,000 and rising fast, but a Florida beach was very busy.

Sunday 19th April 2020

I'm not sure how much longer I can keep up this diary. It appears that the Federal Government has erected a supply chain blockage, pretty much preventing medical equipment being delivered to their own citizens. In effect, each State is in a bidding war with the government. This is very sad and strange.

Monday 20th April 2020

US death toll total is now 40,000 and heading up fast with cases up to 800,000. All the while this is happening, DT once again uses his press conference to a) big himself up and b) slag off the FBI as 'human scum.' He also once again defended US citizens who are protesting against the shut-down and demanding 'Freedom or death,' which is a wish ironically, that may be answered one way or another. There's also talk of similar unrest now taking place in other countries around the world.

Tuesday 21st April 2020

For no known reason, DT claimed in an exchange with PBS correspondent Yamiche Alcindor that he 'hadn't left the White House in months except to send off a ship to New York.' When reminded that he had attended rallies in February and March, he said, 'I don't know. Did I hold a rally?' As it turns out, DT of course did hold rallies, five in fact, in February and March. He also claimed he'd 'banned the Chinese and Europeans from coming.' No, he didn't.

Wednesday 22nd April 2020

In order to make it clear to US citizens how they will get through this challenge, DT tells them that 'If Iranians attack our ships, I've ordered them to fire on them and shoot them down.' I'm not sure how much relevance this has on the virus. On the subject of the virus, reports seem to suggest that hydroxychloroquine is not only *not* beneficial but also appears to have the distinct disadvantage of killing people suffering from C-19 more quickly. Always read the label.

Thursday 23rd April 2020

No mention today of said drug by DT so he may have been tipped off not to say any more I suspect. On the virus, DT is still dreaming that he's been brilliant in dealing with the pandemic despite deaths now topping 47,000. My guess is that any number under 100,000 will be seen as triumphing over the virus. Still on the hydroxychloroquine question, Dr Rick Bright says he was 'fired because I asked for more rigorous testing of the drug.'

Friday 24th April 2020

This is not a sketch or satire. At a press conference the President made mention of a possible chemical way to deal with the virus which was by, and I quote, 'using a chemical like disinfectant to clean out the lungs and maybe big infections. We can look into that.' A doctor sitting nearby is filmed looking at though she thinks he has completely lost it. This is a most bizarre speech by a very bizarre President.

Saturday 25th April 2020

Total US virus deaths now top 50,000 and DT has taken to ending his press conferences by walking out early before he can be asked any more questions regarding the unfortunate bleach injection issue. The New York governor, however, is on the ball when he tells New Yorkers 'Staying in saves lives.'

Sunday 26th April 2020

Following on from DT's decision not to hold any further press briefings, he says he stopped them because 'the media spread lies,' it seems he is looking to fall back on the tried and tested xenophobic rhetoric to kickstart his now battered election plan. Still, he has unfollowed Piers Morgan on *Twitter*.

Monday 27th April 2020

As the coronavirus cases in the US reach 1 million proven cases, DT says he's the 'hardest working President in history.' This apparently is despite missing out on delivering any more Covid-19 briefings. In addition, the *New York Times* has questioned the President on his general fitness and eating habits. The President's response was to go bonkers on *Twitter* by suggesting that 'the Nobel Prize Committee take their prizes back' and 'I work late into the night, generally eating French fries, Diet Coke and hamburgers.'

Tuesday 28th April 2020

US virus casualties are now 55,426 but DT still aims his barbs at the Press. All this as he fends off accusations of promoting the consumption of disinfectant and bleach as a result of his bizarre news conference last week. The President has also said, 'I have never thought of changing the date of the election this year. Why would I do that?' And 'I look forward to the election.' This gaslighting is odd really because the President can't legally change the election date anyway.

Wednesday 29th April 2020

DT has said that he believes 'China wants me to lose the election.' This may be based on his trade war that he's waged and the virus. However, it's more likely an attempt to get more votes from 'It's only flu' types. He's also trying the gas lighters' favourite, 'I don't believe the polls when they say Joe Biden will win.' It should be noted that so far, no extensive polling has even mentioned this.

Thursday 30th April 2020

Early this morning DT is waging further war, this time with various TV news anchors, saying for instance of Joe Scarborough, 'He wouldn't know the truth if it was nailed to his head.' This is probably a deflection tactic as the death figures in the US have now risen to 60,000. He also had to refute a claim he'd only made yesterday that the testing campaign would hit the 50 million mark soon.

MAY 2020

Friday 1st May 2020

63,871 are now the number of US people who have died so far from the virus and there's no end in sight. In order to deflect attention, DT casually mentions the recent accusations of sexual assault by Joe Biden on his aides. He then goes on to say, 'He's gonna have to fight it.' This despite over twenty women having accused the President himself of similar assaults. The White House press office says, 'DT will never lie to you.'

Saturday 2nd May 2020

DT's suggestion for a possible four-step plant for a for a return to normality. Step 1: income support. You will need to work. 2: Hide the facts. 3: Pretend it's about freedom. 4: Protect business re. insurance claims. How will he fare in November?

Sunday 3rd May 2020

Regardless and maybe because of the main topic of discussion being C-19, the latest IPSOS poll reports a substantial lead over DT by Joe Biden. The polls seem to suggest that the Democrat candidate leads DT forty five percent to thirty nine percent and this importantly is larger than the lead that Hilary Clinton had over DT in 2016.

Monday 4th May 2020

A bizarre conversation between DT and the *MSNBC* host Joe Scarborough again who took a swipe at the President re. the virus. DT responded by saying that he (Joe) should be 'investigated for the murder in 2001' which is all very odd. The President also congratulated himself on the great reviews he and his government are getting for the response to the virus. This is as even he is predicting 100,000 deaths. The facts suggest he might be being a little conservative in his estimates.

Tuesday 5th May 2020

Nancy Pelosi has taken a swipe at the Trump Administration because of the move by DT to restrict members of the C-19 virus task force from testifying before Congress this month. 'I would hope that they would spend more time on the crisis instead of the President's daily shows.' The speakers concerns follow on from the limits placed on Anthony Fauci reporting to Congress. US C19 deaths 69,925.

Wednesday 6th May 2020

As rumours grow that DT is looking to disband the C-19 task force he responds by saying that they would in fact continue indefinitely. The death toll has now topped 70,000 and it is estimated that 20.2 million jobs have been lost. It's also been reported that volunteers recruited by Jared Kushner to obtain medical supplies had no relevant experience and managed to bungle their jobs. The President, meanwhile, goes back on the road shaking hands and smiling.

Thursday 7th May 2020

DT goes full-on war footing comparisons saying that the virus had been 'a worse attack on the US than Pearl Harbour and 9/11.' Having said that, he was quick to put down a nurse's concern about alleged sporadic supply of PPE for staff. He said, 'sporadic for you but not sporadic for a lot of others.' He also added that the 'shelves were empty of PPE because the previous Administration didn't put anything on them.'

Friday 8th May 2020

It's clear that the DT supporting press are gunning for China, specifically it seems to ensure that the current President remains in position after 2020. In the meantime, he goes on to make a wild and largely unheard-of claim that Barack Obama and Joe Biden had 'tried to undo' his 2016 win. He didn't explain how they tried but did add that once the virus had been dealt with, and despite catastrophic job losses, he would 'bring back the US economy.'

Saturday 9th May 2020

US death toll has now risen to 77,000 and shows no sign of slowing down. A second staff member at the White House has tested positive for the virus and DT says he doesn't know what happened. She was tested negative then, positive. He says it shows the tests are 'no good.'

Sunday 10th May 2020

As members of the White House now start to self-isolate including Mr Fauci, the Atlanta Mayor has slammed DT for his erratic leadership. This just after Barack Obama said, 'it has been an absolutely chaotic disaster.' DT just said of Barack Obama, 'He's being a bit political.'

Monday 11th May 2020

DT dons his fighting gloves and hits back at the former President by attacking him in his handling of the swine flu outbreak more than a decade ago. He also hits out at Joe Biden. At the same time that the current President is still claiming the high ground in holding the pandemic at bay his economy adviser Kevin Hasset said that 'working in the small and crowded White House is very scary.'

Tuesday 12th May 2020

At a White House committee meeting, Anthony Fauci has testified that he believes an early lifting of isolation and social distancing measures would have serious consequences. In a response to Bernie Sanders, Mr Fauci also said that he felt that a death toll may well rise about 100,000 though he couldn't say exactly by how many. DT, meanwhile, is keeping a low profile after he suddenly walked out of a press conference for effectively racially abusing a journalist who was of Asian appearance.

Wednesday 13th May 2020

With Paul Manafort being released from jail, the US Supreme Court has heard various arguments over DT's tax returns. Two Congressional committees and New York prosecutors have demanded sight of these papers. The President's lawyers say that he 'enjoys total immunity while in office.'

But all of the court activity is being played out while US citizens still die in their numbers and DT's own approval rating is down to forty-one percent.

Thursday 14th May 2020

The President is on his guard today as not only has he once again faced down his expert medical director Mr Fauci, so that schools can reopen; he also has to respond to a whistle blower who has revealed details of how the President tried to promote the use of the untested drug Hydroxychloroquine. Meanwhile, the Rock group Guns 'n' Roses have released a single called 'Live and Let Die' to raise funds for musicians affected by the virus.

Friday 15th May 2020

Following on from DT's recent attempt to trip up the previous President by saying the word 'Obamagate' on *Twitter*, Barack Obama has responded by simply tweeting the word 'Vote.' Sometimes less is more. The President's more recent TV presentation contained the statement 'We know there are a lot of virus patients because we're doing a lot of testing. If we didn't do a lot of testing, we wouldn't have so many people suffering from the Covid virus.' Bloody hell.

Saturday 16th May 2020

With the virus still causing havoc, DT goes on *Twitter* to tell people about a new weapon being developed, 'I call it the super-duper missile.' Observers of such things are taken aback by the somewhat immature language used by the US President.

Sunday 17th May 2020

Aside from the rather surreal series of tweets featuring DT on the face of the President in 'Independence Day', the blockbuster movie, the main news of the day is the sad data update indicating the US death toll is now 90,000 and again shows no sign of slowing down.

Monday 18th May 2020

The Trump family must be concerned about the opposition in this year's Presidential election because Donald Trump Jr chooses to tweet false accusations of 'Joe Biden being a paedophile.' Disgusting behaviour really but is anyone surprised by the Trump family antics? As the Trumps continue to lark about, the death rate in the US is tremendous with 2,000 people sadly dying on Sunday alone. 'We are facing our darkest winter' says Rick Bright, an immunologist from the US.

Tuesday 19th May 2020

With DT sharpening up the deflection techniques in re. Obama-gate (whatever that is), he declares publicly at a press conference that he himself is taking hydroxychloroquine despite the fact that it is usually prescribed only for Lupus and may well have fatal side effects. Well, he's been accused of many things but never passive suicide.

Wednesday 20th May 2020

The US death toll now stands at a dreadful 94,000. It remains to be seen how long the nation will tolerate the seeming inaction of the leadership. Member States of the World Health

Organisation have backed a resolution strongly supportive of the organisation, despite yet another attack by the President. His attack coincided with a twelve-day WHO Assembly backing a resolution supporting an 'enquiry into the C-19 virus.'

Thursday 21st May 2020

Fox News has produced an interesting tweet clip seemingly saying that 'This man is unfit to be President.' Following on from his revelation that he 'Yep, I'm taking hydroxy-chloroquine etc.' It's been revealed that use of the drug around the world may have increased death rates in C-19 patients. The President, meanwhile, seems happy to continue to take the tablets, probably at the behest of his Republican team mates.

Friday 22nd May 2020

An effective press picture out of the blue is doing the rounds illustrating the President actually wearing a mask as he tours a factory. The latest polls seem to suggest that Joe Biden leads DT by several percentage points, anywhere between forty and forty eight percent. DT then decides to walk out of a press conference whilst recommending that churches should open this week.

Saturday 23rd May 2020

DT continues to press home his wish that the US 'reopens' in regard to places of worship. He says, 'I may override the governors.' However, this is a power he doesn't actually have. Not that this will bother him.

Sunday 24th May 2020

The virology lab in Wuhan, China, was apparently working on three strains of bat coronavirus but none of these apparently match the C-19 pandemic virus. The Chinese have responded to the US claims that C-19 leaked from the lab by saying that these rumours were pure fabrication. They said, 'How could it leak if we never had it in the first place?'

Monday 25th May 2020

DT going mad again today following Joe Biden's comments that the 'President plays golf while people die' advert on television. He rants on *Twitter* about Joe Biden, Hilary Clinton, Barack Obama, Nancy Pelosi and pushes conspiracy theories. At least one Republican, Adam Kinzinger, responded by saying he should, 'Just stop, stop spreading it. Stop creating paranoia. It will destroy us.' Ann Gaulter is more to the point. She said, 'You are a complete blithering idiot and a disloyal, actual retard.'

Tuesday 26th May 2020

In previous days I've quoted DT as saying that the reason he was unable to deal with the virus was due to 'Obama leaving the cupboard bare. He left us nothing.' The *St Louis Despatch*, however, has reviewed the Trump Administration's own budget and finance demands and they clearly show that the current President has sought to reduce public health expenditure by half a billion dollars. They also say that Obama clearly left the cupboard full but this President has swept it clean.

Wednesday 27th May 2020

Minneapolis has once again stepped into the headlines as it appears that on Wednesday a young black man was forced onto the floor by police officers, one of whom knelt on his neck until he died. A few weeks ago, US citizens stood on the Governor's building steps with Kalashnikov rifles and were applauded. Now with black demonstrators on the streets, the police are happy to fire rubber bullets into the crowds. DT, meanwhile, calls a journalist 'politically correct' for wearing a face mask.

Thursday 28th May 2020

As Joe Biden commiserates with the US as it reaches 101,000 deaths, DT was busy signing an Executive Order pursuing social media giants like *Twitter* which is a little odd as it's the principal source of data for most MAGA types. Obama-gate has still yet to make itself plain to anyone interested. The President suggested his predecessor was part of a 'deep State plot' to frame him for colluding with Russia to win 2016.

Friday 29th May 2020

As the riots continue in Minneapolis following the death of George Floyd, the President sends out a message that 'Once the looting starts, the shooting starts' and gives full permission for Police and the Military to shoot people stealing. Meanwhile, his country continues to suffer the effects of the pandemic and the death toll now reaches 103,000. No-one's cheering.

Saturday 30th May 2020

Cities across the United States are on fire with angry African-American citizens on the streets, desperately trying to come to terms with the terrible killing of George Floyd. The President is simply unable to lead his nation in grief but Joe Biden does.

Sunday 31st May 2020

As America reaches boiling point, the death toll hits 105,000. The Black Lives Matter groups are ignoring the curfew and heading out onto the streets. The violence from Police has brought civil war to the very shores of the United States.

JUNE 2020

Monday 1st June 2020

An anti-DT group of Republicans called 'The Lincoln Project' have paid for a TV ad that rips into their fellow GOP for his supporters' use of the Confederate flag at his rally events. The main drive of the ad is that 'The men who followed this flag 150 years ago knew what it meant: Treason against their country. The death of the United States.'

Tuesday 2nd June 2020

As riots hit almost every State in the US, DT says, 'I'll call out the Military on protesters.' Previously when addressing Xi Jinping the Chinese President about Hong Kong, he said that he should meet protestors personally and there would be a happy and enlightened ending. This seems to show an alternative view to that of the United States. The vision of a 'United States' is rapidly crumbling as the leader hides and the Police hand out hidings.

Wednesday 3rd June 2020

Another Republican group, the 'Republican Voters Against Trump' launched last week to highlight the voices of disaffected party members, has been running an ad on Fox & Friends that uses the President's own words against him. The key line on the ad is 'This American carnage stops right here, right now' and it makes it clear that DT's actions during the pandemic coupled with the fury of the death of George Floyd 'is dividing us.'

Thursday 4th June 2020

As the US Secretary of State for Defence, General Mattice, called the actions by DT 'not right', others close to the President have also come out against him saying that this would breach the US Constitution. The key issue is the difference between the use of National Guard and the Military to act as security. Whatever happens, the idea of US democracy is now in question.

Friday 5th June 2020

TV audiences have been appalled by the violence meted out by sections of the US Police that far exceeds that of a force who are there to 'protect and serve.' This as officers of the Minneapolis force are being charged re. the death of George Floyd. Members of the Armed Services have made it clear that threats made by the President to use the Military to enhance law and order are unacceptable and damaging to the democratic processes in the land of the free.

Saturday 6th June 2020

Strange really that as all the news discusses George Floyd and Covid-19, the announcement that Joe Biden has formally been put forward as the Democrat Party nominee to take on DT in the November Presidential elections, takes second stage. He says, 'I want to win the battle for the sake of the nation.'

Sunday 7th June 2020

As DT rails against Joe Biden and the Democrats, accusing them of representing 'the hard Left', many Republicans are actually turning against their leader and chief. Old GOP members like George W Bush, Mick Romney and Colin Powell have all said they will vote for Joe Biden.

Monday 8th June 2020

A *CNN* poll conducted nationally has Joe Biden on fifty-eight percent with DT on forty-one percent. It will take something dramatic to bring about a swing back to the President but he is a canny and crafty player so don't be surprised for a sudden 'Ooh, this just in about Biden' headline. The death toll, meanwhile, continues to rise and now stands at 112,000 which is by some measure currently the world's worst. All this as New Zealand says it is 'now Covid-free.'

Tuesday 9th June 2020

Michael Cohen confirms that he took steps to undermine Hilary Clinton and was involved in hush money, however more importantly DT allegedly knew all about it. The Attorney General William Barr has also contradicted the President regarding the 'stint in the cellar episode.' When asked whether DT had hidden in the White House bunker during the recent riots, William Barr said, 'The Secret Service felt the life of the President was at risk so they rushed him to the bunker.' DT not amused at any of this.

Wednesday 10th June 2020

The bonkers statement by the President that the 75-year-old

man knocked over by Police in Buffalo was 'deserved because he was an antifa activist,' has dismayed many Republicans. Martin Gugino seemingly walked towards police officers and was unceremoniously sent flying backwards, knocking himself out as his head hit the pavement. What made it worse was this was all on camera and showed the sight of tens of officers stepping over Mr Gugino's prone body.

Thursday 11th June 2020

With DT calling demonstrators in Seattle 'anarchists' and threatening to 'take back Seattle', several politicians have made the point that perhaps it would be best if the President 'went back to his bunker at the White House and kept out of local business.' One of the Generals, Mark Milley, who was filmed taking part in the infamous walk from the White House to the St John's Episcopal church steps by the President, has apologised saying, 'I really shouldn't have been there.'

Friday 12th June 2020

Once again reaching out to his many admirers, DT had already said that the US Police Forces 'dominate with compassion.' This a little oxymoronic as he then went on to soothe his rally attendees by saying, 'If you turn up at the rally in Tulsa, Oklahoma, you won't be able to sue if you catch the virus.' As far as the virus stats go, the US now has 2 million cases with deaths now totalling 116,000.

Saturday 13th June 2020

Hoping to hold his first post-lockdown rally in Tulsa, DT has agreed to move the date so that it doesn't clash with the date nineteenth June that commemorates the end of slavery in the US.

Sunday 14th June 2020

It's getting very tricky for the President at the moment. DT is scrutinised walking down a flight of stairs and it's like he's tiptoeing on a mine field. Strictly speaking, it was a ramp, however it does look like he's on roller skates.

Monday 15th June 2020

With the sad yet predictable news that another black man, Rayshard Brooks, has been shot dead by Police in Atlanta, the President's week starts on the back foot. The Supreme Court has refused to deal with a gun-related case brought by supporters of the Second Amendment of the Constitution, and both the NFL and NASCAR have both said they will support those that take the knee, much to the chagrin of DT. All this as a tweet emerges of DT knocking Barack Obama for inelegant stair walking.

Tuesday 16th June 2020

Ron Perlman or 'Hellboy' as we all know him, has retweeted a comment allegedly made by the President where he said, 'People are dying from the virus who've never died before.' DT, meanwhile has a problem with a family member. Twenty years after a feud with his niece Mary Trump, she is now waiting to release a no-holds barred book that is apparently harrowing and solacious. The book is out on the twenty-eighth of July.

Wednesday 17th June 2020

As political polls release data that shows Joe Biden with a 2020 election lead of thirteen percent (forty-eight percent to thirty-five percent), DT has threatened to sue his niece Mary over her tell-all book. He says, 'She signed a non-disclosure agreement.' The President signs an EO restricting choke holds by the US Police Forces and goes on to suggest that 'Barack Obama did not reform policing.' This is untrue. In fact, the current President tore down many of the changes.

Thursday 18th June 2020

The news that over 120,000 US citizens have died will likely be overshadowed by the reports of John Bolton's revealing book which has been leaked to the *New York Times*. With DT looking over his shoulder as the book release looms, his niece Mary's book is also about to hit the stands and he also takes a hit in the High Court as Supreme Court Judges have blocked the President's attempt to rescind the Obama era DACA programme. The former President now says, 'Let's elect Joe Biden.'

Friday 19th June 2020

For the third time this month, *Twitter* has accused the President of manipulating the media as they censure DT for his video seemingly suggesting *CNN* and other media outlets were racist. On top of this, *Fox News*, yes even them, now appear to show Joe Biden twelve points clear of the President and this just five months to go till the election. He doesn't help his cause by saying that 'no-one had heard of Juneteenth (abolition of slavery) before I came along.' C19 Deaths – 121,113.

Saturday 20th June 2020

DT today apparently suggesting to the *Wall Street Journal* that the reason he chose not to go into St. John's Church was that 'I didn't think it was exactly the right time to pray. They had a lot of insurance reasons. You know, the church was boarded up.'

Sunday 21st June 2020

DT's first rally in three months didn't so much go down a storm, more like a damp squib selling way less than very few tickets. On top of this, most of his speech was spent talking about 'walking down a ramp,' demonstrating drinking a glass of water and dishing more dirt on Joe Biden.

Monday 22nd June 2020

Following on from DT's recent appearance before an estimated 6,200 of his supporters, he's gone on the attack today suggesting that the 2020 election will be interfered with by foreign powers and that the vote will be rigged. All this, as latest polls show that the Joe Biden Democrat camp are at fifty percent while support for the President has dropped to thirty percent. John Bolton's book, meanwhile, is going down well in the rooms of the chattering classes. He says, 'DT has no strategy and no philosophy.'

Tuesday 23rd June 2020

The WHO reports a record increase in C-19 cases in North and South America and if that isn't bad enough, DT has to respond to questions about his comment that he, 'demanded to see virus testing was slowed down.' His reply, 'I don't joke.'

Problem was, White House aides had already previously said, 'Oh no, The President was only joking.'

Wednesday 24th June 2020

As Joe Biden continues to gain ground in the early 2020 election polls, Doctor Anthony Fauci says, 'There are disturbing resurgences of the virus in the southern States that came out of lockdown too quickly, Texas and Florida,' adding that 'The next few weeks will be critical in tackling the virus.' While some GOP members have been embarrassed by the Tulsa gig, Kellyanne Conway defends the term 'Kung Flu' used by the President. All this as *Twitter* again warns the President over his use of threatening language against Washington DC activists.

Thursday 25th June 2020

CNN leads with the story that DT is facing a catastrophic defeat at the forthcoming election. The *New York Times* has carried out a new survey that indicates the President trailing Joe Biden by between eleven and six points in many so-called swing States. The concerning thing for DT is that these are the States that he won, all of them, at the 2016 election. Still, he's taken the bull by the horns; asking the statue of Confederate General Albert Pike, to be put back up again.

Friday 26th June 2020

As US Covid cases increase at an alarming rate, DT has asked the US Supreme Court to 'quash the Affordable Care Act known as Obamacare.' DT speaking to a rally in Wisconsin says, 'Joe Biden is unable to put two sentences together and he's a candidate that will destroy our country.' He also for some odd reason criticised crime rates in Chicago saying, 'It's like living in hell and worse than Afghanistan.'

Saturday 27th June 2020

It has been suggested that if DT wins his bid to repeal the Obamacare Bill, Covid-19 sufferers may lose their right to health insurance. As a number of States reimpose lockdown due to C-19 spikes, DT has ordered that all statues are protected from mob rule. Disturbing really since it is the living that are suffering. US death toll now stands at 128,000.

Sunday 28th June 2020

Reports of DT having Covid appear to be off beam as he's been spotted dressed and ready for a game of golf. This in reaction to a report that says Russia paid the Taliban to kill allied troops. Nancy Pelosi says, 'This is as bad as it gets.' But DT still finds time to re-tweet a white power message.

Monday 29th June 2020

Yet another Supreme Court judgement goes against the Conservatives and the President as they strike down abortion restrictions made by Louisiana as unconstitutional. DT meantime, re-tweets a picture of two people presenting their weapons to peaceful protestors in St Louis.

Tuesday 30th June 2020

DT continues to deny that he knew anything about the alleged story that Russians were paying the Taliban to shoot US and UK troops. Anthony Fauci has also been testifying before the Senate on the government's C-19 efforts mainly due to White House comments that the outbreak has 'been reduced to embers.' 'We are not even *beginning* to be over this,' said Doctor Anne Schuchat. *The Atlantic* reports that something has shifted. After months of Joe Biden leading by single digits, he is now building a sizeable lead.

JULY 2020

Wednesday 1st July 2020

US death toll now at 130,000. Joe Biden says, 'The President doesn't know what's going on,' as DT claims the Russian bounty story is all a hoax. He also refuses to wear a mask even as the numbers of C-19 cases gets ever higher and this is causing many of his allies to desert him. Even Mitch McConnell said, 'The wearing of a mask must not become a stigma. Wearing a mask is not about protecting ourselves; it's about protecting everyone else.'

Thursday 2nd July 2020

On the day the President claimed that he has put out the flames of the virus and denied access by Congress to the documents featured in the Russian debate, Ghislaine Maxwell, Jeffrey Epstein's paramour, has been arrested. DT has now also 'remembered' that he was briefed on the Russian bounty story but wasn't sure when. Joe Biden, meanwhile, has attacked the President for a hidden vulnerability, mainly the EU ban on American tourists travelling to Europe.

Friday 3rd July 2020

DT has arranged an event at Mount Rushmore where $600,000 worth of fireworks may well threaten lives some say. The Sioux Nation President says, 'The President is not welcome here.' In a weird turn of events, Donald Trump Jr is actively spreading doubts about the effectiveness of wearing masks at precisely the same time as his dad is actually *finally* starting to encourage people to wear them. This may well have come a little too late for DT and the US.

Saturday 4th July 2020

A group called 'Vote Vets' now says 'Step aside Benedict Arnold. Donald Trump is America's number one traitor.' He has also taken flack over his flagrant self-promotion on the day when the US usually remembers its fallen.

Sunday 5th July 2020

As Vladimir Putin and Xi Jinping place themselves in unassailable positions, i.e., in charge for ever, the US is in a very weak and fractured position, not dissimilar to the UK with their 2020 election just weeks away. It is not looking good for DT and is now predicted to lose heavily.

Monday 6th July 2020

It appears the President's love affair is finally over, the one with *Fox News* that is. He's riled because the channel is showing him trailing in the polls to Joe Biden by some margin. Joe Biden, meanwhile, says, 'Teachers are very important,' whilst the President says, 'All they teach our children is Left Wing Fascism.' Still too many commentators in the US are suggesting that the virus is either not serious or that the testing in the US is good enough to maintain control. The key though is the data. US death toll is now at 132,000.

Tuesday 7th July 2020

It is noted in a number of media outlets that the Republicans have made a commitment to protect a particular structure for some reason, Brazil's Christ the Redeemer. Why this is no-one can really say. New York Mayor, Andrew Cuomo, has accused the President of being a co-conspirator of Covid, and suggested DT had worsened the crisis by making up facts and declining to set a mask-wearing example. Mary Trump releases her explosive book next week in which she claims that the President suffered child abuse at the hands of his father.

Wednesday 8th July 2020

Tricky situation for DT, both on the domestic and political front. Mary Trump's book makes all sorts of searing historic points about the President and his upbringing. Another report suggests DT's relationship with Vladimir Putin seemingly meant that the President allegedly pushed the CIA into giving intelligence to the Kremlin, all while taking no action against the Russians for allegedly arming the Taliban basically to fire on UK and US troops.

Thursday 9th July 2020

As medics blame an upsurge in the virus cases in Oklahoma on DT's comeback rally, New York prosecutors have been given the go-ahead by the Supreme Court to view the President's tax returns. The queen of quotes, Kellyanne Conway, has had her comments re. 'Joe Biden saying some really creepy things' turned right round as an ad shows DT responding to the question 'What do you think of your daughter?' with, 'Well, if I wasn't her father, I'd probably be dating her.'

Friday 10th July 2020

Death toll 136,000 and still rising. DT draws a veil over this by saying he 'aced an IQ test' recently, although he is a little set back by the WHO news that the pandemic is not going anywhere just yet. He's so put out that he cancels his New Hampshire rally. DT, however, seems to suggest that he has done so because of a storm. Joe Biden, meanwhile, has urged DT to ironically put America first by backing his plan to invest $700 billion as an investment to kickstart the US economy.

Saturday 11th July 2020

Mick Romney makes a point, 'Unprecedented corruption as an American President commutes the sentence of a person (Roger Stone) who was convicted by a Jury of lying to shield that very President.' The Lincoln Project goes on to the front foot with more anti-Trump TV ads.

Sunday 12th July 2020

Today DT is actually filmed wearing a mask. He said, 'I never had anything against masks. They have their place and time.' The time here appears to be three months too late. Robert Mueller has castigated DT's decision to release Roger Stone as 'terrible.'

Monday 13th July 2020

DT has made it clear that since the 2016, he said, 'I would be only too happy to release my tax returns to the public but I'm being audited by the IRS.' This is all very plausible but Rudy 'put foot in here' Giuliani now reveals that all these tax return audits have already been carried out. Poor old Anthony Fauci is having to fend off a smear campaign being allegedly driven by the White House. Adam Schiff, the House Intelligence Committee Chairman, described this as 'atrocious.'

Tuesday 14th July 2020

DT is questioned on the safety of US children as he urges schools to reopen. He says, 'Kids should go back to school. They want to go back to school.' As Covid numbers head skywards, parents aren't convinced that this the best way forward. The President also confusingly added that, 'You're losing a lot of lives to the virus by keeping things closed.' On a different front, the fact-checking team on the *Washington Post* reckon it's taken the President 267 days to tell 20,000 lies.

Wednesday 15th July 2020

Yesterday's press conference by DT in the Rose Garden at the White House lit up social media and TV, mainly because the President a) used it as an election campaign and b) went off on an incomprehensible ramble that nobody could understand. At one point he seemed to suggest that 'all US citizens can get a test if they want' which is incorrect. Mary Trump, whose bombshell book is a number one seller says, 'He's utterly incapable of leading the country and should resign.'

Thursday 16th July 2020

CNN runs with another story re. Joe Biden and his polling performance. They say he has a fifteen-point lead over DT. Fifty two percent of voters now suggest they'll vote for the former Vice President while only thirty-seven percent are going for the existing President. The main issues to US voters are economy, race relations and the Covid-19 virus inaction. Meanwhile, it appears that the White House C19 team has quietly shifted hospital bed information over to a different department namely, Health & Human Services.

Friday 17th July 2020

As the virus numbers soar DT, for reasons only he can explain decided to retell his story of 'stopping the abuse of the clean water act.' He also repeated the comment that 'many people cried like babies when I signed the legislation and brought back incandescent light bulbs.' He also made the point again that 'dishwashers have more water in them than they used to have before.' In the real world, 72,000 new Covid cases have been reported and the President's approval ratings have plummeted.

Saturday 18th July 2020

100 days to the election. With every US State now sharing increasing C-19 data and the death toll now standing at 142,000, the President has a real job on his hands, principally to try and keep at least a few of his loyal supporters as we approach the election.

Sunday 19th July 2020

When asked by Chris Wallace of *Fox News* how DT had wrongly claimed the virus would 'just disappear,' the President responded by saying, 'I'll be right eventually. I will be right eventually.' On that basis, every human being would be right eventually.

Monday 20th July 2020
Disturbing news that DT has in addition to Portland, Oregon, turned Federal military troops onto the streets of Chicago to deal with 'gang violence.' The President has also had something of a 'road to Damascus' moment re. face masks which he now says, 'are patriotic.' This is a bit late with the C-19 pony many miles away from the stable.

Tuesday 21st July 2020
On the back of comments by DT pretty much saying the 2020 vote will be a fake, Nancy Pelosi says, 'There is a process. It's nothing to do with if the certain occupant at the White House doesn't feel like moving and has to be fumigated out of there because the Presidency is the Presidency.' She added, 'Whether he knows it or not yet, he will be leaving.' The virus is taking its toll on everyone including the President who know wears a mask every day.

Wednesday 22nd July 2020
When asked what his thoughts were regarding the forthcoming trial of Ghislaine Maxwell, the President said, 'I wish her well. I've met her but I'm not following the trial.' 'Not following' is curious for someone who's been filmed in the company of said Ms Maxwell, accompanied by the now-deceased Mr Epstein. Fifteen US Mayors have signed a letter asking DT to withdraw Federal troops from Portland. Woody Johnson, US Ambassador to the UK, was apparently asked by the President to get the British Golf Tournament the Open, moved to Turnberry but this failed.

Thursday 23rd July 2020

What is likely to go down in history, certainly in future US history studies, are the words of the current President. In a bizarre TV interview, DT makes the case for his cognitive skills by outlining questions that were put to him during a mental agility test. 'Person, woman, man, camera, TV,' he said. 'I was told that as I got them in the right order, I would get more points.' So, there we have it, the leader of the US can remember and quote five words in a row.

Friday 24th July 2020

In another interview DT says, 'The other thing we've done is introduce a space force. We have a new force. We have the oh so important Army, Navy, Airforce, Marines, Coastguard and now we have a Space Force.' DT, meanwhile, cancels the Republican Convention just as the UN has warned US police forces not to use disproportionate force against protesters and journalists amid growing scrutiny over the recent Black Lives Matter protests. Joe Biden's support is still growing in suburbs and with Latino voters according to recent polls.

Saturday 25th July 2020

As the famous US Freedom of Speech mantra is once again abused by a cable TV network highlighting the term 'plandemic' and using it as a pejorative basically to attack Anthony Fauci, one of the key sponsors of the President's 2016 campaign Robert Mercer, has made it clear he won't be doing so in 2020.

Sunday 26th July 2020

Portland, Oregon, is fast becoming a battle ground as the Feds under the control of the White House continue to pepper spray protestors including Army vets and others defending their own city. At the same time, the President seems to be ignoring so many crises in order to go golfing.

Monday 27th July 2020

As a storm blows down a section of DT's indestructible wall along the Mexican border, one of the President's key advisers, Robert O'Brien, has tested positive for C-19. The National Security Adviser has 'mild symptoms' and is not apparently a threat to the President. Things worsen in Portland with a college lecturer being shot in the face, although she has survived. Mary Trump, meanwhile, says that she feels pretty sure that DT failed his 'cognitive test.'

Tuesday 28th July 2020

The President is none too happy to hear that his son has been blocked by *Twitter* for showing a video that was spreading fake virus information. This was a video that DT himself had shown until it was removed. William Barr has been testifying before the House Committee where the House Judiciary Chairman, Jerry Nadler, said, 'Your tenure has been marked by a persistent war against the Department's professional care in an attempt to secure favours for the President.' This is as news of the US death rate hits 150,000.

Wednesday 29th July 2020

As DT defends the Texas 'doctor' Stella Immanuel who

claims that pharmaceutical companies are using 'alien DNA' and that the virus is as a result of 'sex with demons,' he also suggests he might ban the Chinese video platform Tik Tok. This is probably because it's a source of youth taunts aimed at the President. Indeed, the President lamented his lack of popularity when compared with Anthony Fauci and others on the virus taskforce. He told a press conference, 'Nobody likes me.'

Thursday 30th July 2020

DT has called for a delay to the 2020 election following the death of one of his key allies, Herman Cain. Very sadly, Mr Cain, a cancer survivor, had belittled mask wearing in the early stages of the virus but later succumbed to it. The President cannot legally do this as it would need to be approved by Congress and that is unlikely to happen. Doctor William Shaffner was equally concerned about the virus but on this occasion specifically about the behaviour of attendees at a Trump rally in Texas where very few of the assembled were wearing masks.

Friday 31st July 2020

The *New York Times* reports that with the fall in the DOW Jones Index to 26,000 since the C-19 outbreak, the virus has in effect wiped out five years of economic growth in the US. With ninety-five days to go until the election, any hope of delaying it to 2021 has been quashed by his own Republican Party who have reminded him that no delay is possible. The Feds have finally been pulled out of Portland but not before getting on everyone's back.

AUGUST 2020

Saturday 1st August 2020

DT has gone ahead with his threat to ban Tik Tok. This is not likely to go down with the US youth vote. The Republican-backed Lincoln Project is gathering momentum in its aim to bring down the Republican President which is frankly weird. Tricky time for DT as the unemployment benefit has now run out.

Sunday 2nd August 2020

As the White House admits it is 'very concerned over the rising C-19 deaths,' a top Democrat Jim Clyburn has likened DT to Mussolini. The President has had a swipe at Anthony Fauci for his comments that the viral increase is as a result of not shutting the country and the economy quickly enough. US deaths 158,000.

Monday 3rd August 2020

A story in the *Independent* newspaper suggests that DT, according to a senior Democrat, may well try to hang onto power by using emergency powers if he loses the election. With Joe Biden well ahead in the most polls, Republican voices are at best muted in their support of the President, as he takes to tweeting attacks on another member of the White House C-19 Taskforce Deborah Birx. He calls her warnings that the virus is extraordinarily widespread 'pathetic.' Mind you Nancy Pelosi has also had a pop at Ms Birx.

Tuesday 4th August 2020

It's likely that what seemed to be an innocuous HBO TV interview conducted by host Australian Jonathan Swan, will be seen by many as a turning point in the 2020 election. When asked for instance about C-19 handling, the President said, 'We're the best in the world.' He said this while waving lots of graphs at the interviewer. The exasperated Mr Swan said, 'But Mr President, 1,000 US citizens are dying every day.' The President responded by saying, 'It's not that many. Read the books. There are those that say we test too much.' 'What books?' asked the clearly confused Mr Swan.

Wednesday 5th August 2020

DT has described Barack Obama's eulogy for John Lewis the Civil Rights Activist which was delivered with such passion at his memorial service, as 'a terrible angry speech.' The President, however, has his own problems as Neil Young the musician, has taken out legal proceedings against his campaign team for using his songs promoting what he says, 'un-American campaign of ignorance and hate.' Yesterday's HBO interview has gone viral with the whole world aghast at the obscure ramblings of the US President.

Thursday 6th August 2020

Both *Facebook* and *Twitter* have come under attack from the White House for what it says is election interference. This all because they suspended temporarily the claims by DT that 'children were virtually immune to C-19.' He also said again that the virus would simply 'go away.' Clearly not quick enough as Mike Dewine has tested positive which is interesting as he's very recently met the President.

Friday 7th August 2020

DT goes onto a monster anti-Biden type attack saying, 'He is anti-God, anti-religion, anti-gun' in a weird rant that even seasoned GOP members thought was a bit off. This despite Joe Biden being the first catholic vice president serving under Barack Obama. It perhaps didn't help his global standing by calling the nation of Thailand using the 'Th' as 'Th' as in 'thigh.' Apparently, China and Iran want DT to lose at the next election while Russia want their man to remain.

Saturday 8th August 2020

The President has signed a number of Executive Orders which are designed to give the failing economy a boost, including eviction delays and welfare cheque supplements. Critics say; however, this will do little to deliver cash any time soon.

Sunday 9th August 2020

DT's latest attempt to try and circumvent Congress has caused a ruckus with Democrats and Republican members. All this to do with the President's attempt to bring in C-virus relief by signing an EO despite objections. The Republican Ben Sasse called it 'an unconstitutional slop.'

Monday 10th August 2020

DT has been accused of stealing from the American people with his use of the Presidential office for 'political campaigning,' with one former government adviser saying that the

President's plan to stage a speech at the White House is 'a form of stealing.' The intimate relationship between China and the US has once again stumbled with the sanctions last week merely provoking the Chinese to mock the President. Death toll in the US from the virus meanwhile is 165,000.

Tuesday 11th August 2020

So, here's a quote from the Leader of the Free World: 'In 1917 the closest thing so they say to the virus today was the Great Pandemic, the Spanish Flu, which was a terrible time where they lost anywhere from 50 to 100 million people. It probably ended the Second World War; all the soldiers were sick.' The fact that the Second World War started twenty-one years later has been pointed out to the President in no uncertain terms. DT also makes a spurious claim that, 'If Biden wins, you'll all need to learn Chinese.'

Wednesday 12th August 2020

So, Joe Biden has finally selected his Vice President and its Senator Kamala Harris, not only female but a woman of colour to boot possibly making history at the next election in eighty-odd days. DT of course spent no time actively thinking and planning what to say, instead going true to form on the Sean Hannity Show by accusing Kamala Harris of being a 'phoney, a liar, nasty' and that 'she wants to support raising taxes, socialising medicine and cutting funds for the Military and stopping fracking.' None of which appears to have any basis in fact.

Thursday 13th August 2020

As we get ever closer to the election, DT seems only to want to vent his spleen at anyone who questions him and anybody in opposition politically. There's little evidence of academic study or intellectualism. He just reels off 'Mad woman', 'Angry person,' 'Condescending', 'Dizzy airhead,' 'Not even a smart person.' There's no attempt at debate. Indeed, many now fear for the sanity of the President. There's nothing new here though; it's merely a stuck xenophobic, sexist record.

Friday 14th August 2020

Tricky start for DT today with the release of excerpts of an upcoming book written by yes, Michael Cohen, a formerly imprisoned former Attorney to the President. Comments such as 'from golden showers in a sex club in Vegas to tax fraud and deals with corrupt Soviet officials, I was an active and eager participant.' In response, the President says that Kamala Harris is a 'mad woman' and bizarrely claims that the Democrats want to 'abolish any kind of animals and tear down the Empire State Building.'

Saturday 15th August 2020

Under Section one, fourteenth Amendment of the Constitution, anyone born in the US is a US citizen yet DT has started his birth of claims yet again regarding Barack Obama. He uses the third person gaslighting sequence, 'I just heard it today. I've no idea whether it's right but that it's very serious.' The Democrats say his comments were abhorrent and pathetic.

Sunday 16th August 2020

Bernie Sanders making the point that the continued attack on the US postal service by DT means that the mail in voting system could have an impact on creating a crisis for US democracy. Robert Trump, DT's younger brother, has sadly died. As yet there's been no reason given for his death.

Monday 17th August 2020

DT has reacted to poll news that the Democrats are twelve points ahead in the polls by saying, 'Biden is shot. We won it last time. We're going to win it again, I think. True.' The United States Postal Service is being supported by the Democrats in that they are launching an emergency effort to thwart the President squeezing the service by removing and reducing funds. They've also demanded that Louis De Joy, the new USPS Postmaster General, testifies to Congress to answer charges that policy changes within the company are deliberately intended to slow voting by mail.

Tuesday 18th August 2020

As we head inexorably to the world title fight that is the US 2020 election, various Republican Senators are sweating on their ability to hang onto their seats. David Schweikert of Arizona is a case in point as he's recently admitted a whole raft of breaches of the House rules, was fired and is now hanging onto a five percent deficit to his rival, Doctor Hiral Tipirneni. This represents a six-point swing to the Democrats and may well be a litmus test for November. Michelle Obama has urged everyone to vote for Joe Biden as DT is, 'way over his head' and warning that 'things will get much worse under his Presidency.'

Wednesday 19th August 2020

'It is what it is.' So said Michelle Obama at the start of the Democratic Congress. These words could be the epitaph of the incumbent Republican President. The previous First Lady's speech again made the point that 'this President is way over his head.' DT responds by saying he wouldn't have been elected in 2016 if the Obama government hadn't been so bad. On a slightly more frightening note, US Hawks are pressing for some sort of conflict with Iran presumably in case it looks like Joe Biden might win in November.

Thursday 20th August 2020

For reasons known only to himself, DT answers a press question about the right-wing Conspiracy Group, QAnon, who've previously said he's fighting deep state paedophiles by saying, 'Well, I don't know much about the movement but I know they like me very much which is great.' When it was pointed out to the President, they thought he was saving the world from cannibals as well, he added, 'I haven't heard that but is that supposed to be a bad or a good thing?' This hasn't gone down too well with some who consider QAnon to be a death cult.

Friday 21st August 2020

The big news today was the arrest and arraignment of Steven Bannon, one of DT's advisers many moons ago and arch Cambridge Analytica engineer. It may be that he's been involved in some Mexico wall skulduggery and other issues which may include the President and UK Prime Minister. As the Postmaster General says he won't return mail sorting machines, the President now says he'll send law enforcement officers to polling locations in November which has been described as an attack on American democracy by a former White House chief.

Saturday 22nd August 2020

With Joe Biden's forceful Democrat acceptance speech hitting points on many fronts, DT is now being pressed to deliver himself. The only Republican response so far to Joe Biden's speech is that 'he managed to read an autocue.' Well, the current incumbent may well look to the moat in his own eye.

Sunday 23rd August 2020

This President is the only one since modern polling was developed never to have achieved fifty percent approval amongst voters. His response to this is to carry on regardless. His sister Maryanne has been recorded saying, 'He has no principles and can't be trusted.'

Monday 24th August 2020

The Republican National Convention got under way and DT was formally renominated by the GOP for the 2020 election. At the same time *Twitter* has said, 'his postal votes tweet was misleading,' with Tik Tok calling his attack on them political. New York Attorney General Democrat Letitia James has filed a petition in the State Court asking to enforce subpoenas in the investigation into whether the President and his businesses inflated assets. All this before he starts going on the campaign trail. US virus deaths now 180,000.

Tuesday 25th August 2020

DT has announced the emergency authorisation of 'convalescent plasma.' This is despite concerns from the FDA that this is a method usually used to treat flu and measles. Ex-FBI Director James Comey has said that Steve Bannon is 'in a world of trouble' following his arrest for cash skimming allegedly off the Mexico wall campaign. How this will affect the President only time will tell. At the Republican National Convention, the President renewed his attack on mail in voting predictions saying, 'This is a road map to a catastrophic disaster pulling in large viewing figures.'

Wednesday 26th August 2020

Following the Republican Convention speeches yesterday, several States have seen a closing of the percentage points between DT and Joe Biden. The problem for viewers, especially images on TV, is compounded by the shooting of yet another black man, this time in Wisconsin. Many have taken to the streets again to show their disgust at the latest violence to a person of colour. Many commentators are saying that we are seeing the end of American democracy and only the 2020 result will show whether this is true or not.

Thursday 27th August 2020

The shooting in the back of Jacob Blake Jr. in Wisconsin has become even worse with the fatal shooting of two protesters by a seventeen-year-old ex-police cadet, Kyle Rittenhouse.

The very sad thing has been the response from the Wisconsin Police, *Fox News* and others who have all made conciliatory sounds regarding the killings. Probably the weirdest thing coming out of the last couple of days has been the demand by DT that he and Joe Biden are drug tested before any debate, TV or otherwise.

Friday 28th August 2020

After the hyperbole, hubris and heavy breathing of the Republican Convention gathering comes the feedback. The use of the White House as a GOP backdrop hasn't gone down well, coupled with the rather odd catwalk appearance of some migrants which was seen by many as just hypocritical. DT's speech was branded flat and too long by *Fox News* who were once his long-time supporters. The fact that the President centred on a) how great he is and b) how wicked Joe Biden is may well impact on the election result.

Saturday 29th August 2020

DT closes the seemingly endless convention with what appears to be either a) a drunken, b) stroke-induced speech where he calls upon everyone to be at peace and praises the 'Uneteded Shates.' All very peculiar and one that stirs some very odd comments on social media.

Sunday 30th August 2020

Polling taken during the Democratic and Republican Conventions suggests that Joe Biden is still showing a six to ten percent lead in most States. This all the while that violence continued, this time in Portland, Oregon, where a local man wearing a 'patriotic prayer' hat was killed, apparently when gunfire broke out.

Monday 31st August 2020

The violence in Portland has been condemned by DT but the Mayor of the City says, 'It's you.' Ted Wheeler went on to say that, 'President Trump, for four years we've had to live with your racist attacks on black people. Do you seriously wonder why we are seeing these levels of violence? It's you who have created the hate and division.' DT responded by name calling saying Ted Wheeler was 'whacky, a fool and a dummy.' Joe Biden has said, 'The President is stoking war on our streets.'

SEPTEMBER 2020

Tuesday 1st September 2020

Eighty-four days to the election. The President responds to a journalist asking about the incident where two protesters were shot dead by Kyle Rittenhouse, an armed seventeen-year-old, saying that '…he was very violently attacked and probably would have been killed if he hadn't shot those two people.' DT, meanwhile, has visited Kenosha where Jacob Blake was shot, despite the mayor saying he wasn't welcome. Jacob Blake Snr, meanwhile, has said, 'I'm not getting into politics' and has refused to meet with the President.

Wednesday 2nd September 2020

At a press conference in Kenosha, Wisconsin, the only black attendees seated with the President were two Pastors, James Ward and Sharon Ward. As a reporter asked the two pastors whether they believed police violence was a systemic issue, DT jumped in and interjected saying, 'I don't believe that. I think the Police do an incredible job.' He also added, 'I think that there are a few bad apples.' Needless to say, the only African-Americans present never got a chance to speak.

Thursday 3rd September 2020

While DT and his team go on a Nancy Pelosi hunt (she allegedly went to get her hair cut during lockdown), the White House election team are trying to backtrack on the President's odd shout-out to voters to, 'Vote twice by mail and in a booth.' This as everyone knows is illegal yet GOP commentators suggest that the President 'was taken out of context.' Joe Biden meanwhile, has been to Kenosha to meet the family of Jacob Blake who's still in hospital with gunshot wounds.

Friday 4th September 2020

US virus deaths are now 190,000. Just as commentators suggest that support for the President from veterans and military leaders is falling, DT has been criticised over comments that he made about visiting a cemetery in Aisne Marne near Paris. He didn't attend in 2018 saying allegedly, 'Why should I go to that cemetery? It's filled with losers.' He made similar comments about marines who'd lost their lives in the First World War. 'Suckers' he apparently called them. 'Who were the good guys in this war?'

Saturday 5th September 2020

When asked about the US's 'rounding the corner' comment regarding the virus made by DT, Anthony Fauci, the Chief Medical Officer on the Covid team responded by saying, 'I'm not sure what he means.' This as other predictions suggest possibly 400,000 people may die in the US.

Sunday 6th September 2020

As Eric Burdon of The Animals rock group says the use of 'House of the Rising Sun' by the President at his rallies is an on-point piece of music and suits him perfectly as 'it's a tale of sin and misery set in a brothel.' Michael Cohen claims the President hired a 'faux-Bama' so he could belittle and fire him whilst being filmed for a home video.

Monday 7th September 2020

DT now concerned that details published in *The Atlantic* re. alleged comments the Presidents had made calling US soldiers killed in wars 'losers and suckers' may actually affect his votes in November. The main impact will be from military veterans who are voicing their disapproval of his words. This as boats parading on a Texas lake in support of the President, caused at least five vessels sink such were the weather conditions.

Tuesday 8th September 2020

The *New York Times* reports that far-right groups in Germany of all places, are using Trump as a rallying cry, presumably because of his past history regarding black Americans, equal rights etc. DT responds to claims that he called dead troops 'suckers' by saying, 'I'm not saying the Military is in love with me but the soldiers are.' He also said, 'John McCain liked wars and Joe Biden sent our youth to fight in these crazy wars.' It is reported his election fund has now dropped from $1.1 billion to $300 million.

Wednesday 9th September 2020

Quite how this happened, and no, this is not a wind-up, DT has been nominated for the Nobel Peace Prize by Tybring-Gjedde a right-wing Norwegian Christian member of Parliament. Apparently, this is specifically for the President brokering a peace agreement between Israel and the United Arab Emirates. Many will raise an eyebrow or two over this. Joe Biden, meanwhile, still leads in six key swing States, and importantly these figures have not changed since the Republican National Convention.

Thursday 10th September 2020

Just as DT quietly celebrates his bizarre Nobel Peace Prize nomination, journalist Bob Woodward is set to release his book 'Rage.' The most dangerous section in this book apparently using the President's own words and clearly recognisable on radio and TV broadcasts, are the statements regarding the virus. 'It's very bad, much worse than the flu. We need to be careful with this.' These comments are all very apt except, as Mr Woodward points out, they were said at the end of February 2020. Shortly after that and throughout March and April, the President was using terms like 'fake' and the virus would 'magically disappear.'

Friday 11th September 2020

The US Treasury Department has placed sanctions on Andrii Derkach on the basis that he had run a campaign against Joe Biden and the department has dubbed him an 'active Russian agent for over a decade.' What's more, Rudy Giuliani has met with him twice since last year and publicised the claims made by the Ukrainian on his podcast. The US death rate has risen to 196,000 on the day that the President has once again indicated to the Press that, 'we have turned a corner.'

Saturday 12th September 2020

Roger Stone whose prison sentence was commuted by DT has said that 'If the President loses the 2020 election, he should seize total power, bringing in martial law and jail the Clintons and Mark Zuckerberg.'

Sunday 13th September 2020

DT says he will negotiate a third term in the White House because, 'I'm entitled to it.' The *CNN* host Jake Tapper lost his patience when interviewing Peter Navarro who wouldn't answer any questions regarding the President's mixed messages about the C-19 virus which apparently veers between deadly one minute and just like the flu the next.

Monday 14th September 2020

DT appears to have discovered a cure for the C-19 virus since he and a very large group of Trump supporters all gathered together in a Nevada arena with few masks and without any worries about the virus itself. This drew accusations that the President might be guilty of 'negligent homicide.' The terrible forest fires still burning in California have claimed the lives of twenty-four people and though the President has decided to visit the beleaguered State, many are saying that he is in complete denial about climate change.

Tuesday 15th September 2020

DT's response to the question 'How will you prepare for the debates Mr President?' is 'If Joe Biden is elected, the market will crash' and 'China sent the virus.' How this will help him prepare is anyone's guess. The President also called Bob Woodward's book 'Rage' boring having apparently read it. The news site 'Politico' reports hearing rumours that Iran wants to assassinate Lana Marks, the US Ambassador to South Africa. DT in response warns of a 'thousand times retaliation.'

Wednesday 16th September 2020

Stats out today suggest that the US President is the least trusted world leader rating at only sixteen percent and few believed he would make the right decision. At an ABC news conference in Philadelphia, DT has claimed he 'didn't downplay the virus. I actually in many ways up-played it in terms of action. My actions were strong.' He also said again that a vaccine would be three or four weeks away, despite scepticism amongst health experts about the timescales. With forty-nine days to go till the election, the US death toll has topped 200,000.

Thursday 17th September 2020

Unlike the ABC performance by DT, Joe Biden appears to have fared quite well in the *CNN* drive-in town hall debate. He took full advantage of the national spotlight to address issues of unity and attack his opponent. There is a conversation going on that is looking at the older vote mainly over sixty-fives, who were crucial in electing the President in 2016. They are now making comments now like 'I've never seen America so divided,' 'Trump isn't a racist, he's from that era,' and 'his tweets are a window into the US soul. Next time I vote Democrat.'

Friday 18th September 2020

DT at a rally in one of the key battleground States of Wisconsin has polls claim he is behind Joe Biden by several points. He announces $13 billion worth of relief which he says will 'benefit the dairy, ginseng and cranberry farms.' The President, again, made spurious and rambling statements that suggested a Biden President would mean 'no guns, no religion, no energy, no oil,' none of which has ever been part of the Democrats' platform.

Saturday 19th September 2020

The death of Supreme Court guru Ruth Bader Ginsburg has thrown up an additional problem now. Does the President make a swift Republican appointment or does the country wait for a new President as per Barack Obama's decision on Merrick Garland in 2016? Meanwhile, the apparent plan to discredit the 2020 vote steams ahead regardless.

Sunday 20th September 2020

The plan by the President to ban the Chinese social media app WeChat is blocked by a US Judge on the grounds that it affected the users' rights to communicate under the first Amendment. DT also threatened to sign an EO that would ban Joe Biden from running for President. Weird.

Monday 21st September 2020

As evidence mounts of a huge slowdown in mail since the DT ally took over the US postal service, the President had dared to Democrats to impeach him again over the issue of the Republicans replacing Ruth Bader Ginsburg. Reporters, meanwhile, are saying that comments by the President re. 'Good genes in Minnesota' are indistinguishable from the Nazi rhetoric about Aryan blood. The President also derided refugees, gloated about a reporter shot with a rubber bullet and praised the Confederacy.

Tuesday 22nd September 2020

It would appear that with Mike Romney's backing, DT says he will appoint his Supreme Court pick on Saturday and this after having met with Ann Coney Barrett, a leading anti-abortionist. The President has also again claimed that the country's death rate was 'amongst the best in the world' and that 'the virus has virtually no effect on young people.' Bernie Sanders has warned that the election is an extremely dangerous moment for the US and that he will push to stop DT from de-legitimising the vote.

Wednesday 23rd September 2020

The *Washington Post* has made the point that it would be unprecedented for a presidential candidate to come back from the position that DT is currently in. The President didn't help his cause by refuting the deathbed wish of Ruth Bader Ginsburg when she apparently said, 'My seat must not be filled until the election is over.' He said the quote 'was a fake.' Most polls have Joe Biden leading by seven percent across the US. However, it remains to be seen what impact *Facebook*, *Twitter* and the US mail situation has.

Thursday 24th September 2020

When asked by a reporter if DT would ensure a peaceful handover of power at the conclusion of the 2020 election, he responded by saying, 'we'll have to wait and see.' The President added that he's 'worried about the ballots, maybe mail votes, and that the Democrats know that too.' As the President and his wife Melania attend the Supreme Court to pay their respects to Ruth Bader Ginsburg, the assembled crowd start to chant 'Vote Him Out!' and 'Honour her wishes!'

Friday 25th September 2020

The President's claim that 'we will wait and see' how the end of his tenure may come about has been somewhat downplayed by the Republicans saying, "The President says crazy stuff.' As DT claims he is being personally targeted by the FDA following their decision to make approval standards more stringent meaning that any virus vaccine won't be available until *after* the election, the White House has attacked the FBI for saying that claims of electoral fraud are non-existent.

Saturday 26th September 2020

The silliness regarding unfounded ballot fraud claims continues apace with Donald Trump Jr calling on supporters of his dad to go out and 'defend your ballot by joining an army made up of able-bodied men and women from an election security team.' Blimey!

Sunday 27th September 2020

The President insists that both he and Joe Biden should take a drug test prior to the live TV debate which was being held on Tuesday. The Biden camp responded by saying, 'If the President can make his best case with urine, he's welcome. We'd expect nothing less.'

Monday 28th September 2020

The *New York Times* runs with what may be an explosive story regarding the elusive tax returns of the President. They report that DT spent $7,000 on his hair but paid just $750 income tax in 2016 and again in '17. They also alleged that DT paid no tax in ten of the preceding fifteen years. The President predictably says that the article was fake news. However, much of the detail must surely be free to view and would surely be libellous if false.

Tuesday 29th September 2020

The revelation on last night's TV news on *Channel 4* in the UK that seemed to suggest that in 2016 the Trump campaign team deliberately targeted millions of black voters to persuade them not to vote, have been dismissed by the White House as fake news. *Channel 4*, however, has said its 'most definitely not fake news.' This as both the President and Joe Biden head to take part in the first televised debate, drug testing permitting one assumes.

Wednesday 30th September 2020

The first debate takes place in Cleveland and most commentators have come to the main conclusion that a) no-one came out on top; b) Joe Biden was diplomatic but passive apart from his comment 'Why don't you shut up man!' to DT and c) the President came across as a shouty bully. *CNN* conducted a poll shortly afterwards which seemed to indicate very little impact so far on the current seven to ten percent lead that the former Democrat Vice President had over the President. The next Presidential debate is on October fifteenth.

OCTOBER 2020

Thursday 1st October 2020

The fall-out from the TV debate continues with both sides claiming a victory but the clear issue is whether a similar debate is going to be useful to either side. Commentators on all sides have said it was lively but embarrassingly damaging to the US. The swing States don't appear to have been overtly affected with current plus/minus percentages unchanged. The Wisconsin governor has called upon the President to cancel rallies as the C-virus data has seen significant rises in many areas.

Friday 2nd October 2020

The only news of today, both the President and the First Lady have tested positive for the C-19 virus. Crucially several other members of the White House election campaign team have also tested positive, including Kellyanne Conway. So how this ultimately affects processes and debates is hard to tell. Late on today it is announced that DT has been admitted to the Walter Reid Medical Centre as a precautionary measure as it appears that the President may have breathing difficulties.

Saturday 3rd October 2020

Nearly every commentator has wished the President a speedy recovery but have noted that the President has by any measure, acted irresponsibly during the pandemic and only as recently as Tuesday was moaning about the masks that Joe Biden had been wearing in the Debate.

Sunday 4th October 2020

Thirty days to go to the election. In a peculiar turn of events, the President has now been released from hospital, driven away in a limo waving at fans. The issue is that no-one who's been diagnosed with C-19 and been held hospitalised has been released shortly afterwards or within forty-eight hours. The messages here are very confusing.

Monday 5th October 2020

Mary Trump, DT's niece, has made the point that the President sees illness as a weakness and an unforgiveable one at that. DT himself says that since he became unwell, he now understands the virus. Many commentators are still furious that the President was well enough to journey in a limo with Secret Service agents. The polls are still indicating that Joe Biden is in front across the US. However, due to the US electoral college voting system, it's still too close to call. All this despite US virus deaths now at 214,000.

Tuesday 6th October 2020

With little else to attack Joe Biden with, the President, who only yesterday was displaying some very poor breathing techniques, has tweeted that his Democratic opponent is in favour of 'executing new-borns.' He adds, 'He's fully in favour of late very term abortions, right up to birth.' There's no justification for these comments save for the messages sent by Joe Biden that he would codify 'Roe versus Wade', the principal action that gave women abortion rights. Doctor Fauci, meanwhile, says that the President's condition 'could worsen.'

Wednesday 7th October 2020

One of the leading immunologists in the US has resigned as a direct result of what he says is due to the Trump Administration ignoring scientific expertise and has chosen to overrule public health guidelines. Doctor Rick Bright had already crossed swords with the President over his claim about hydroxychloroquine. Following his threat to walk out of discussions with Democrats over a second bailout, DT suddenly had a change of heart, sort of, by tweeting that he wanted 'cash to go to our people immediately.' Too little too late maybe.

Thursday 8th October 2020

So, with DT apparently recovering, from the virus and Joe Biden trying to avoid catching it, the suggestion that a second Presidential debate could be held virtually has been roundly kicked into touch by the President. 'I'm not going to waste my time' he said. The President has also claimed that he is cured. He then went on to name call Kamala Harris, calling her 'a monster' and worse as far as US voters are concerned 'a Communist.'

Friday 9th October 2020

As Mitch McConnell steers clear of the White House due to the virus, DT dropped the 'F' bomb on a radio show talking about Iran. 'If you fuck around with us, we'll do things to you that have never been done before.' It has been formally confirmed that the second televised debate between the President and Joe Biden has now been cancelled. The President has also called Joe Biden and Obama to be tried for treason, surreally linking this into the investigation into campaign ties with Russia in 2016.

Saturday 10th October 2020

As the President plans to meet hundreds of people at the White House today, he insists that 'I'm off the meds and feeling really good.' Unfortunately for everyone else attending, it also confirms that the tests on him are still not showing 'negative' which means he may well be a super-spreader.

Sunday 11th October 2020

As the President claims he's now cured and immune from the virus, he speaks to supporters at the White House, urging everyone to 'vote in the most important election in our nation's history.' It is also alleged that some of the attendees at the White House were paid. Lots of hugs on show.

Monday 12th October 2020

I now have twenty-three days left of my self-imposed diary penitence thank goodness. DT goes on the attack this morning by saying 'New York has gone to hell and California will follow suit.' Ann Coney Barrett, meanwhile, is appearing before the Senate Judiciary as the Chamber considers her appointment. Doctor Anthony Fauci has had to defend what appears to be a deliberately misused quote, as his words were used out of context in a political advert. He said, 'In my five years of public service, I've never publicly endorsed any political candidate.'

Tuesday 13th October 2020

Probably one of the oddest things seeing the President of the United States shuffling to the song 'YMCA' at an election rally. As usual DT resorts to more personal language specifically calling Joe Biden 'not very nice' and accusing him of having dementia. The irony is he's already called him that before. Maybe he just forgot. On the campaign trail, the President has tried once again to wow the voters, especially they grey ones in Florida. 'I'm now immune' he claimed, adding 'I can kiss the guys and all the beautiful women.'

Wednesday 14th October 2020

DT tells a virtual audience in a White House speech that 'China will own the US if I lose in November.' He also added that he would hold them accountable for the pandemic. Joe Biden, meanwhile, appears to be increasing his lead in at least three new polls. His leads vary between ten and seventeen percent and this is now very close to the main event, with a steady increase of five percent in September.

Thursday 15th October 2020

Right-wing journalists go on the hunt for Hunter Biden and his Dad less than three weeks before the election proper. DT's repeated attacks on Obamacare may well impact on his vote and even tells loyal Iowans 'For me to be only up to six percent in Iowa, I'm a little bit concerned.' He then follows this up with his usual mocking of his opponent. Reuters show the President having pulled into a statistical tie with Joe Biden in Florida, though this probably means the Democrat has done better than predicted.

Friday 16th October 2020

It appears the 'town hall presentation' plus-points have been wholly captured by Joe Biden as the viewing figures seems to suggest that DT has been 'trounced.' The two men involved in the world's largest demonstration of democracy have both managed to avoid answering key questions during the TV debate 'Meeting the Voter.' DT would not divulge how he would disavow a bizarre online right-wing conspiracy while Joe Biden would not respond to how he would arrange the Supreme Court.

Saturday 17th October 2020

Joe Biden responds to an *NBC* question regarding his son Hunter alleged links with Ukrainian political and financial groups by saying, 'I knew you were going to ask this. You always do and it's fake news.'

Sunday 18th October 2020

DT's attempt to create a new 'Lock Her Up' challenge as he attacks Gretchen Whitmer, the Governor of Michigan. These have been met with dismay by her Director, Tori Saylor, and the Governor herself. 'This rhetoric has put me and my family in danger while we try to save lives of our fellow Americans.'

Monday 19th October 2020

The world meter now places the US virus death rate at 224,000. The President casts aside all pretence that he has a relationship with Anthony Fauci by calling him a 'disaster' during a campaign staff call. Perhaps he was a bit under the weather due to the investigation being undertaken by the Government Accountability Office where he's accused of politically interfering with the CDC and the FDA. *Fox News* it seems has turned down the Rudy Giuliani scoop about 'Hunter Biden and a laptop' apparently due to credibility concerns.

Tuesday 20th October 2020

A historic headline by 'USA Today' saying that the paper, for the first time in its history, has urged its readers to vote for Joe Biden. What impact this may have only time will tell. Melania Trump has now cancelled a rally appearance suffering it is reported with a persistent cough. DT goes all out on his attacks on *CNN*, calling them 'dumb bastards.' Nancy Pelosi says she is optimistic that she may reach a deal with the White House and Treasury Secretary of State Steven Mnuchin for more funds.

Wednesday 21st October 2020

A *Washington Post* study has found no crime increase in cities that adopted sanctuary policies. Not surprisingly, this was in response to a claim by the President that the opposite had happened. Barack Obama has now formally joined the campaign trail and is unsurprisingly stumping for Joe Biden. All this as DT with just thirteen days to go until the election proper walks out of a CBS interview. He then tweeted that he'd left as the interviewer wasn't wearing a mask.

Thursday 22nd October 2020

As a Dutch ethical hacker hacks into the email of the President using what is supposed to be a strong password, 'Maga2020', DT has been called out for lying over the state of the US economy. In response, the President described the interview as a vicious take-down and threatened to release his own edited version of the show. On *NBC* Tonight, both the key protagonists will face each other. However, the debate moderator will be able to mute the microphones of anyone who decides to yell, bully or speak over the other.

Friday 23rd October 2020

Last night's semi-debate doesn't seem to have made much difference to the polling figures which isn't surprising while DT and Joe Biden are back on the campaign trail and it would appear that the President needs to step on the gas. As ex-President Barack Obama gives professional speeches supporting Joe Biden, the current leader is under fire from Alexandra Ocasio Cortez for saying 'she knows nothing about climate.' Alexandra Cortez responds by saying, 'Sisterhood is everything.'

Saturday 24th October 2020

Sort of historic day as the President goes out and votes for himself. Joe Biden is urging everyone to get out and vote, 'The more votes, the more likely a Democrat win' he says. Maybe.

Sunday 25th October 2020

Both Joe Biden and DT make their closing messages for the 2020 messages with both candidates looking to tap into various 'swing' voting groups, e.g., women, the elderly and the young. As we watch the polls at worst, Biden leads by one to two percent, at best his lead is as much as eight and ten percent.

Monday 26th October 2020

This is the last week of my diary I hope as it's been tough. Tougher for the American people though. As Joe Biden tweets 'eight days until the liberation of America', the shocking virus statistics get worse. Hospital admissions are going through the roof, there are no suggestions that death rates are coming down and they may well have been understated. DT, meanwhile, is trying to make capital from the CBS interview with Lesley Stahl where he walked out and he's quick to jump on a TV debate where Joe Biden appears to have mixed the President up with George W Bush. The US death toll is 230,000.

Tuesday 27th October 2020

Joe Biden has revealed his campaign is focusing on so-called expansion states like Iowa, Texas and Wisconsin. Indeed, polls seem to show that his understated approach is paying dividends with his lead up twelve percent and surprisingly appears to be neck and neck in Texas, a historically Republican State. He's also very unhappy about the 'rushed and unprecedented confirmation of Amy Coney Barrett as the Supreme Court pick.' The tension mounts as voters head out to the polling booths in huge numbers again.

Wednesday 28th October 2020

DT not happy with *Fox News* as they broadcast a speech by Barack Obama where he said, 'Donald Trump is jealous of Covid's media coverage.' He's also upset that the Republican official website got hacked with the perpetrator putting the words 'The Word Has Had Enough' right across the front page. Joe Biden has taken a sizeable lead in Wisconsin and Michigan and forty five percent of Texans have now voted while the White House suggests the virus has 'now been beaten,' many still die: death rate now stands at 232,147.

Thursday 29th October 2020

As Nigel Farage attends a DT rally calling him 'the bravest man,' Tucker Carlson who was very keen to shine a light on the Hunter Biden saga on *Fox News* programme, is a bit put out as UPS says it has 'lost the cache of documents' that Mr Carlson had previously said were 'damning.' They might have been but not now. The President, meanwhile, has urged states to shun lockdowns, even as the virus death rate continues to rise and as Joe Biden says, 'The POTUS can't just flip a switch on this virus.'

Friday 30th October 2020

The President said that he's 'way ahead in the polls in Texas' whilst the polls themselves seem to show that the Lone Star State is still a toss-up. Joe Biden and Kamala Harris are focusing the last few days on Texas, Wisconsin and Michigan in order to firm up even further what the polls suggest, a

Democrat victory. None of this is going to simple going on previous rhetoric from the leader of the free world. However, we all live in hope.

Saturday 31st October 2020

A classic DT conspiracy theory comes alive with his announcement that 'doctors earn more cash with the C-19 deaths.' Utter hogwash. This as the virus surges throughout the US killing 1,000 people a day. Armed Republican supporters caused the Democrats to cancel an event due to security reasons.

NOVEMBER 2020

Sunday 1st November 2020

The election is hugely important but of equal value is the possibility of the Republicans losing the Senate which has many GOP members seriously worried. With two days of the voting left, Joe Biden still leads by a reasonably healthy ten percent but many commentators are very much hedging their bets due to the dramatic 2016 result.

Monday 2nd November 2020

This is the last week of the Trump Diaries. US virus deaths today 236,196. Bus ramming incidents by violent GOP fans in Texas notwithstanding, DT defends these actions as 'patriotic' rather than investigate them. 'The FBI should be out looking for terrorists and ANTIFA.' he says. The President also alludes to a scenario where he announces his victory on Tuesday, 'If I feel I've won.' Joe Biden now refers to him as 'America's virus.' As nearly 100 million US citizens have voted already and another 50 million plus are looking to vote tomorrow, the cities are boarding up fearful of the aftermath.

Tuesday 3rd November 2020

Election Day in the US. With fears that the President might not accept defeat if it comes to that, the Democrats have set their hopes on DT's rhetoric actually increasing anti-Republican votes. Either way, today is the last day with the last voting booths closing at 06.00 GMT on the fourth of

November. DT himself has promised a 'White House gathering' until the votes are counted, held behind the erected steel wall. Joe Biden has said again that if he is to win, it's going to be in Pennsylvania. Barack Obama has been to Georgia and Florida to tighten the votes there.

Wednesday 4th November 2020

US Virus deaths now stand at 237,000. All systems go today. DT falls foul at every step. Joe Biden tells Democrats to stay calm. The votes are counted at a phenomenal rate and the conspiracy theorists have gone potty. Nigel Farage allegedly bets $10,000 on a Trump victory while at five o'clock GMT Joe Biden looks set to win Wisconsin, Nevada and Michigan which will probably put him in the White House. As we head into the long dark night, Joe Biden does indeed win the three afore-mentioned States.

Thursday 5th November 2020

It's Guy Fawkes Day today in the UK but it's in the US that the fireworks are going off, not in celebration however just people exploding with rage due to the ongoing propaganda war from the Republicans. As the world waits, four states are in the balance while Arizona probably will go to the Democrats. So which way do they go? As at four o'clock GMT, Biden leads Georgia (Rep) by 18,000 votes, Nevada (Dem) by 8,000 votes, North Carolina (Rep) by 77,000 votes and Pennsylvania (Rep) by 136,000 votes. Very late news – Democrats lead in Georgia by 800 votes and Pennsylvania by a slightly diminishing number.

Friday 6th November 2020

Commentators across the globe are in shock about the President's press conference at the White House last night where he again claimed he'd won despite many votes still to be counted, and that these were 'illegal votes' without any shred of evidence to prove it. As the day progresses, the States of Georgia and Pennsylvania now flip over to the Democrats so they now lead in four of the five swing States, waiting on the final tally but still the debates rage. The Georgia state governor confirms that in his state, there will be a re-count.

Saturday 7th November 2020

Still no formal news but with Joe Biden now in front in four of the five swing States and his lead going up, it's only a matter of time before we hear the words 'The new President of the United States, Joe Biden.' At 16.30 hours *CNN* declares 'Joe Biden is the new US President.' Finally!

Sunday 8th November 2020

So, there it is. Donald J Trump, though still President, is now being replaced by a seemingly better man. Amazingly both candidates achieved 73m and 70m votes respectively (with more to be counted) but ultimately DT's brief and no doubt infamous reign has come to an end. Notwithstanding the next seventy-six days, the US has a new President and a new US begins.

December 2020

After nearly four years of watching and recording the wild antics of the forty fifth president I was very pleased, not to say relieved, for the next POTUS to be announced, that is Joe Biden. I say 'is' since at the formal end of the election the final vote of 156m votes were cast and it was clear that several states had swung significantly towards the Democrats confounding pollsters and critics. This was mainly due to the massive turnout (81.3m Biden – 74.2m Trump) and early postal voting. This has inevitably led to the predictable cries of foul by Donald Trump and a majority of the GOP senators.

Monday 7th December 2020

The build up to the Electoral College vote on the seventh of December was delayed by several states being forced to make recounts and in some, having to counter legal action through the courts. Indeed, the present POTUS pushed the idea of fraudulent voting right up to the Supreme court where, using Texas as it's bulldog and making the assumption that he would be successful, continued to make claims, without any evidence, that the election had been 'stolen.'

Wednesday 9th December 2020

At a Hannukah party DT says he will 'Re-elected if the Supreme Court shows courage.'

Thursday 10th December 2020

Donald Trump speeds up executions. Texas files a request in the Supreme Court to overturn the results in Michigan, Georgia, Pennsylvania and Montana. Donald Trump calls it, 'The big one!.' Joe Biden says 'Trump not conceding is an embarrassment.'

Friday 11th December 2020

The Supreme court dismisses every claim put before it. The court in a brief unsigned order said 'Texas lacked any standing to pursue the case,' saying it:

> 'Has not demonstrated a judicially cognizable interest in the manner in which another state conducts its elections.' Mike Gwin, a spokesperson for the Biden campaign, said the Supreme Court had 'Decisively and speedily rejected the latest of Donald Trump and his allies' attacks on the democratic process. President-elect Biden's clear and commanding victory will be ratified by the Electoral College on Monday (fourteenth December) and he will be sworn in on Jan. 20.'

Throughout this, a 'run off vote' for the Senate had been taking place in Georgia where on the fifth January two Democrats, including the first African American and the youngest senator ever, were both voted into the Senate giving Democrats overall control of both the House of Representatives and the Senate for the first time in six years. It now seems likely that the Georgian vote was heavily influenced by the continual calls from the Trump camp that the POTUS election vote in Georgia had been fake.

Despite this Trump still continues to allude to, or make direct claims that the voting had be 'fake' and that he had '...won the election...' and that it had '...been stolen.' Indeed 'Stop the Steal' became this year's 'lock her up' for the baying Republicans who began to grow increasingly agitated.

Sunday 15th December 2020

Donald Trump Tweets 'Biden has won but I CONCEDE NOTHING!' He still thinks the vote has been stolen.

Saturday 20th December 2020

Donald Trump Jnr tests positive for Covid 19. DT says 'I'll lower drug prices.' He meets Michigan state legislators to try to overturn the election result.

Wednesday 25th December 2020

The current President pardons Mike Flynn. The pardons keep coming...

Monday 30th December 2020

Scott Atlas resigns from the Trump advisory team.

Trump Diary Epilogue - 2021

Immediately after the weekend following the vote (Saturday 8th November 2020) I stopped physically recording *daily* details of the Trump Presidency because a) I thought ahh well, Joe Biden has now won and that was that and b) I really needed a rest from the insanity that was the last four years.

If I'd realised then what we would all see transpire, I would have kept up the daily routine. As it was, I kept making a few notes here and there until the 6th January 2021.

That's when it all went pear-shaped.

JANUARY 2021

Saturday 2nd January 2021
The President uploads a contentious speech that he has recorded onto the internet highlighting his alleged 'voter fraud,' calling it 'maybe the most important speech I've ever made.'

Monday 4th January 2021
The President holds a rally in Georgia supporting Republican senators David Perdue and Kelly Loeffler in the run-off elections.

Tuesday 5th January 2021
In the Georgia run off voting, US District Judge Mark Cohen denies an emergency injunction of the Georgia election result calling the request 'Beyond unprecedented.'

Wednesday January 6th 2021
Today being the day of the formal declaration of the newly appointed President, Donald Trump gave a speech to followers at the White House where he spoke for a long time using 11,000 words. This is a summary, with the words taken directly from the transcript of that speech. In front of a large crowd of supporters he said:

> *'You know, I say, sometimes jokingly, but there's no joke about it: I've been in two elections. I won them both and the second one, I won much bigger than the first. OK. Almost 75*

million people voted for our campaign, the most of any incumbent president by far in the history of our country, 12 million more people than four years ago. And I was told by the real pollsters – we do have real pollsters – they know that we were going to do well and we were going to win. What I was told, if I went from 63 million, which we had four years ago, to 66 million, there was no chance of losing. Well, we didn't go to 66, we went to 75 million, and they say we lost. We didn't lose. You will have an illegitimate president. That's what you'll have. And we can't let that happen These are the facts that you won't hear from the fake news media. It's all part of the suppression effort. They don't want to talk about it. I think one of our great achievements will be election security. Because nobody until I came along had any idea how corrupt our elections were. And again, most people would stand there at 9 o'clock in the evening and say I want to thank you very much, and they go off to some other life. But I said something's wrong here, something is really wrong, can have happened. And we fight. We fight like hell. And if you don't fight like hell, you're not going to have a country anymore.

Our exciting adventures and boldest endeavours have not yet begun. My fellow Americans, for our movement, for our children, and for our beloved country. And I say this despite all that's happened. The best is yet to come. So, we're going to, we're going to walk down Pennsylvania Avenue. I love Pennsylvania Avenue. And we're going to the Capitol, and we're going to try and give.'

On the back of this, the sixth of January 2021 has now entered the history books as the infamous day that a riotous mob invaded a sparsely defended Washington Capitol building. Screaming and shouting the very words and phrases made so infamous by Trump. The crowd later described as 'seditionists' by Joe Biden, forced senators and staff to hide in fear for their lives, assaulting security offices and defacing offices. One member of the crowd – a women – was shot and killed during the initial melee while one staff member was attacked and killed with three demonstrators dying during the riot.

It took several hours for the crowd to be disbursed and while the Capitol building was being cleaned up after the vandalism and damage caused by the rioters, the Vice President Mike Pence and other senators gathered again to work through the night to again formally decide on the new president. At 03.45 on the morning of the seventh January 2021, Joe Biden and Kamala Harris were duly pronounced POTUS and VP.

Saturday January 9th 2021

Several social media groups including *Instagram*, *Twitter*, *Facebook* and YouTube announced that they were barring Donald Trump from their platforms as he was deemed 'dangerous and inflammatory.'

Wednesday January 13th 2021

A vote in the House of Representatives was decisively carried out to impeach the president and once again the name of Donald Trump has been historically recorded, this time as the first US president to be impeached twice. The inevitable trial is based on the formal charge that the president directly 'incited insurrection' which ended in the riot.

Thursday January 14th 2021

Washington has seen the largest number of security and military personnel seen on any US street, in any US city ever to head off the violence that is threatened to take place before and during the inauguration on January twenty first. Much of the information being investigated by the FBI appears to be coming from the dark web with far-right groups like QAnon ramping up the rhetoric.

Wednesday January 20th 2021

As we approach the day, military chiefs reveal that at least two active serving members of the security forces have been removed from those in Washington because of their links with far-right groups. The POTUS meanwhile is spending his last day (Tuesday twentieth) holed up in the Whitehouse and, unable to communicate with anyone through social media, apparently quietly contemplating issuing Presidential Pardons to between sixty and hundred US citizens. Rumours that he would also pardon himself seem to be unfounded: so far. Melania Trump issues an impassioned farewell speech online saying she would remember the many '...people she had taken away in her heart.'

It went without saying that Mr and Mrs Trump have cancelled or ignored many of the 147-year-old traditional handover rituals such as tea at the Whitehouse with the incoming President, a tour of the Whitehouse by the incumbent First

Lady with the incoming one: one of only four Presidents to have done so. Donald Trump has also confirmed that he will forego attending the inauguration and instead be holding his own 'Send-off event' at a military airfield in Maryland and has issued invitations in which he has asked attendees to arrive between 06.00 and 7.45. It remains unclear whether a twenty-one-gun salute will be fired. Latest reports suggest however he will not be afforded a big military send off and will simply be boarding the Air Force One jumbo jet for Mar a Lago.

Attendees have been warned not to bring any firearms, ammunition, explosives, laser pointers or toy guns. His stay at the Mar a Lago resort will be short lived however as twenty-four hours later he will need to leave the resort having become an ordinary citizen.

The senate meanwhile are making plans to meet as soon as Joe Biden has been sworn into office in order to commence the second impeachment trial of the outgoing president with many GOP members indicating that will be voting in favour of a guilty verdict on the charge of 'incitement of insurrection.' If this happens Mr Trump will never again be allowed to hold a political office.

Thursday January 21st 2021 8.00

And so, to the day that changes everything. The POTUS and his first lady leave the Whitehouse by helicopter for the last time and head to Joint Base Andrews to deliver what will be last ever Presidential address. He makes reference to how '...horrified he was at the assault on the Capitol...', '...my fellow Americans...,' all his '...great achievement's...' and closes by suggesting 'we will be back...'

The President refrains from mentioning Joe Biden by name.

8.45

The POTUS and his first lady board Airforce One for the last time and head to Mar-e-Lago beach resort.

11.00

Joe Biden, Kamala Harris and their families and dignitaries including past-presidents (bar one) arrive at the Capitol building to meet and greet and are then taken to their seats. In front of the podium and stretching for many metres the central grid and watercourse right up to the Washington Monument is packed with thousands of flags representing the many people who could not attend this important day.

11.15

The inauguration ceremony begins with an invocation from Father Leo J. O'Donovan, a former Georgetown University president. A firefighter from Georgia named Andrea Hall leads the Pledge of Allegiance, and Amanda Gorman, who made history in 2017 by being named the first-ever National Youth Poet Laureate, reads a poem. Lady Gaga opens by singing the national anthem while the ceremony also features musical performances from Jennifer Lopez and Garth Brooks.

11.55

Kamala Harris is sworn in as the forty ninth vice president of the United States by Supreme Court Justice Sonia Sotomayor shortly before noon on a Bible that once belonged to first the African American to serve on the Supreme Court, Thurgood Marshall. Historically, Kamala Harris is the first women of colour to attain this political position.

12.00

Joe Biden is sworn in as the forty sixth president of the United States at noon, in accordance with the twentieth Amendment of the Constitution. *Donald Trump's term ends and he is now officially a 'civilian.'* The newly sworn in president gives his inaugural address and speaks for twenty minutes without referring to notes and without error. His speech focuses on 'Our Determined Democracy: Forging a More Perfect Union' and is well received by the attendees and the limited numbers of invitees. The Rev. Silvester Beaman, a pastor from Delaware who was a friend of Biden's late son Beau Biden, will conclude the inauguration by giving the benediction.

14.25

The new President Biden, his VP Kamala Harris and former Presidents Barack Obama, George W. Bush and Bill Clinton, along with their spouses, participate in a wreath-laying ceremony at the Tomb of the Unknown Soldier at Arlington National Cemetery. Despite his nationalist rhetoric this is a ceremony now ex-POTUS Mr Trump chooses not to attend.

15.15

The new president and vice president then proceed to the

White House, receiving a Presidential Escort, with each branch of the military represented. Instead of the traditional parade down Pennsylvania Avenue, there is a virtual 'Parade Across America' with performances from all fifty states and several territories. TV presenter Jon Stewart makes an appearance and Earth Wind & Fire is among the musical acts.

17.15

Joe Biden enters the Oval Office for the first time as president. He immediately signs more than a dozen executive actions reversing some of Trump's signature policy initiatives and setting a new tone; future-proofing for his administration. He issues an immediate national mask-wearing 'challenge,' stops the construction of the southern border wall, revokes the so-called Muslim ban and re-joins both the World Health Organization and the Paris climate agreement, among many other things. Leadership.

17.45

Joe Biden then swears in Day One presidential appointees in a virtual ceremony.

19.00

White House press secretary Jen Psaki gives her first briefing from the historic Brady Press Briefing Room with reporters.

Donald Trump - President of the United States of America 2017 to 2021; his legacy...

- First POTUS to shake hands with a leader of North Korea across no man's land
- Split a nation in half along race lines
- Threatened democracy by continually crying fake news and fraud
- First POTUS in modern history not to attain a popularity vote above 50 percent
- Highest turnover of staff at a staggering 92 percent over his 4-year tenure
- May still face investigation over the attack on the Capitol building
- Impeached twice
- 408,832 dead through Covid 19 on his watch

Now, the beginning of hope.

Acknowledgments

Collating data on a day to basis would have been impossible without the print/TV/radio media, on-line search engines and reference sites like Google and Wikipedia. I would like to especially acknowledge the following publications and TV stations:

New York Times, The *Washington Post*, *Vanity Fair*, The *Guardian*, The *Independent*, The *Daily Mail*, *Fox News*, *Fox and Friends*, *BBC*, *Channel 4*, *ITV*, *National Enquirer*, *Christianity Today*, *MSNBC*, *Twitter*, *Time Magazine*, *Drudge Report*, *Boston Globe*, *Wall Street Journal*, the *Observer*, *The Late Show*, *The Atlantic*, *Saturday Night Live*.

Jim G. Sitch is an artist, poet and sometime diarist living in London England. He is married and has a son. Jim has been creating artwork since the early 1980's and has exhibited his work at several prestigious shows including the Henley Summer Festival, Chelsea Art College, The Riverside Studios Hammersmith and in Lalin, Galicia, Northern Spain.

Jim has released four poetry booklets and his poems have been published in a number of journals including the Paris-based 'Upstairs at Duroc,' 'Salopoet,' 'Dial 174,' 'The Frogmore Papers,' and the United Press Anthology – 'Poems with Meaning.' This diary compilation is Jim's first and he says, 'If this experience is anything to go by, probably the last.'